W9-AOM-324

Welcome to

McGraw-Hill's

Conquering LSAT Logic Games

Congratulations! You've chosen the LSAT games guide from America's leading educational publisher. You probably know us from many of the textbooks you used in school and college. Now we're ready to help you take the next step — and get into the law school of your choice.

Most LSAT test-takers find the Logic Games section to be the most difficult section of the test. This book gives you everything you need to succeed on that section. You'll get in-depth instruction and review of every game type tested, tips and strategies for every question type, and plenty of practice games to boost your test-taking confidence.

In addition, in the following pages you'll find:

- **How to Use This Book:** Step-by-step instructions to help you get the most out of your test-prep program.
- **Your LSAT Logic Games Action Plan:** Learn how to make the best use of your preparation time.
- **Game-Solving Strategies at a Glance:** Have a quick strategy review for every game type right at your fingertips.

ABOUT McGRAW-HILL EDUCATION

This book has been created by a unit of McGraw-Hill Education, a division of The McGraw-Hill Companies. McGraw-Hill Education is a leading global provider of instructional, assessment, and reference materials in both print and digital form. McGraw-Hill Education has offices in 33 countries and publishes in more than 65 languages. With a broad range of products and services — from traditional textbooks to the latest in online and multimedia learning — we engage, stimulate, and empower students and professionals of all ages, helping them meet the increasing challenges of the 21st century knowledge economy.

Learn more. Mc Graw Hill **Do more.**

How to Use This Book

This book provides all the material you need to score well on the LSAT Logic Games section. It will teach you the knowledge that is required for this difficult section, including information about each type of game and question the test includes. It also provides ample practice for you to refine the skills you are learning and then test yourself with two full-length practice sections. You can follow the straightforward five-step program below to work your way through this book or develop your own personalized LSAT Logic Games action plan (see the next page).

1 Learn about the LSAT

Before you dive into the detailed study of LSAT Games, you should make sure that you are familiar with the LSAT in general. Read Appendix A at the end of this book to learn about the structure of the test, including the different test sections, the number of questions in each section, and the section time limits. You'll also find valuable test-taking strategies and important information about how the test is scored and how to register.

2 Learn the basics of Logic Games

LSAT Logic Games do not "come naturally" to most people. They require a certain way of analytical thinking that you will need to learn and practice. Formal logic also comes with its own vocabulary and set of ideas. Start by reading the Introduction and the first part of Chapter 1, through page 9. This will introduce you to the basics of LSAT logic.

3 Learn the different types of Logic Games

Chapters 1–8 provide detailed directions for how to do each of the various types of Logic Games. Each chapter contains sample fact patterns to help you recognize the game type, strategies for working that game type, and several games that are fully explained so that you can learn the methods for solving them. In addition, each chapter contains several practice games for you to do on your own to refine your knowledge. You should probably work through the chapters in order. Focus on one game type at a time until you have mastered it.

4 Take the Practice Tests

Get ready for the actual exam by taking the Logic Games practice sections in Chapter 9. When you take each section, try to simulate actual testing conditions. Use a timer and use the answer sheet provided. You'll gain experience with the test format, and you'll learn to pace yourself so that you can earn your highest score in the time allowed.

5 Final preparation for the real LSAT

If you work hard and follow your study plan, you should be prepared for LSAT Logic Games. Appendix B provides you with information about how to spend the week before the real LSAT and some strategies to use during the test to maximize your score.

Your LSAT Logic Games Action Plan

To make the best use of your preparation time, you'll need a personalized action plan that's based on your needs and the time you have available. Before you start studying this book, maximize the effectiveness of your preparation time by spending a few minutes to develop a realistic action plan that provides the discipline you need to pace yourself and achieve your goals.

Your 4-Step Preparation Strategy

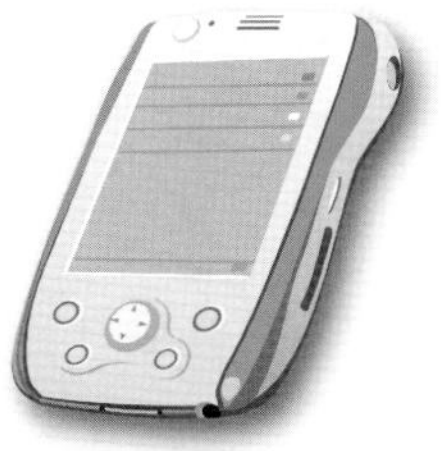

The following four steps comprise an effective preparation strategy for LSAT Logic Games. You should make sure they're part of your action plan.

Step 1: Make a Study Plan

You should make an LSAT study plan that you can stick to. For example, it is a good idea to take a practice test each weekend on a Saturday morning in order to simulate actual LSAT testing conditions (McGraw-Hill's *LSAT* includes several full-length LSAT practice exams). You should also map out consistent times each week when you will be able to work through at least part of each Logic Games lesson. Two sample study plans are included on the next few pages, but feel free to modify them to create a personalized study plan for yourself.

Step 2: Work Hard

The LSAT is a test that can be mastered if you are dedicated to improving your skills and getting a good score. Passively reading through lessons is not going to do much good. Instead, be sure to work through the problems in this book when you are wide awake and can give them your full attention. If you do this consistently, your score will improve steadily. Stick to your study plan. Do not procrastinate. Cramming at the last minute is not effective for the LSAT.

Step 3: Work Slowly

Take your time as you are working though the lessons in this book. Don't skim through the basics of Logic Games. Spend some time learning LSAT logic. It is the basis for all the games you will do. Then focus on learning the characteristics of each game type and the strategies to use. Do not worry about how quickly or how slowly you are answering the questions. You will work on improving your test-taking speed when you take the practice sections at the end of the book.

Step 4: Identify Your Weaknesses

As you are working though this book, pay extra attention to the parts you find difficult. Be sure to do every practice question in those lessons. When you take a practice Logic Games section or a practice LSAT, make sure to go back and study the questions that you got wrong. These simple steps can make all the difference in your LSAT preparation program. They will enable you to identify your weaknesses and focus your study so that you will not make the same mistakes in the future.

Sample LSAT Logic Games Action Plans

The one thing that limits you is time. Your LSAT Logic Games preparation strategy will depend on how much time you have to prepare. The more time and energy you devote to preparation, the better your odds are of achieving your goals. Below are two sample action plans—one if you have a month to prepare and one if you have only two weeks. You can use one of these as a basis for your own plan or develop your own plan from scratch. The important thing is to have a well thought-out plan of attack.

Sample Action Plan 1 — If You Have One Month to Prepare

One month is an adequate time for most people to prepare for the LSAT Logic Games section, but the time you'll need depends on how busy you are with school, work, or personal commitments and on how much of an effort you'll need to reach your target score.

Week 1

- Read through the front section of this book, the Introduction, and the first part of Chapter One (to page 9) to learn the basics of Logic Games.
- Take one of the two Practice Tests in Chapter 9 of this book. It is best to do this on a Saturday morning and take the entire test in one sitting. Evaluate how you did on the different game types. Identify three key areas to work on first. Since you have a month to prepare, you can probably focus on each game type in depth, but you should start with simpler game types and then work up to harder ones. This book is basically structured from easiest to hardest, so start with whichever of your three key areas comes first in the book.
- Work through the chapter that deals with your first key area. Read and work through the example game carefully. Do all the practice problems in the chapter.

Week 2

- Schedule time over this week to work on the chapters in this book that correspond to your other two key areas. Be sure you read and review each whole chapter, in addition to working the drills at the end of the chapter. For best retention, read the chapter and work half of the practice problems in one study session, then review the chapter and work the remainder of the practice problems in the next study session.

Week 3

- On Saturday, take the other Practice Test in Chapter 9. Review the explanations not only for the questions you missed, but also for the questions you got right but found difficult.
- Complete the chapters you have not worked on yet. For chapters that cover material with which you are already proficient, start with the practice questions at the end of the chapter. Do half of them and check your accuracy. If you've made any mistakes, review the explanations and use the chapter to brush up on your knowledge and skills. Then complete the rest of the end-of-chapter questions.

The Day Before the Test

- Make sure you're not in for any surprises on test day. For example, it's a good idea to actually go to the test center location so you know exactly how to get there, how long it might take, and where you will park (if you are driving).
- Try to schedule some relaxing activity so that you keep the stress level low. A brisk walk or other physical activity is great for relieving stress. The goal is to keep the stress from building so that you get a good night's sleep.
- Don't cram and don't stay up late. Eat healthy foods and don't do anything to dehydrate yourself. Obviously, drinking a lot of alcohol is not advisable even if it might help to reduce stress.

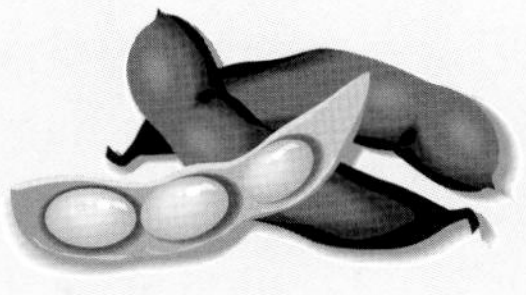

Sample Action Plan 2—If You Have Two Weeks to Prepare

If you plan to master the Logic Games section in only two weeks, you'll have to prioritize; focus on your weaknesses and take at least two practice tests. The more time and energy you can carve out for preparation, the better.

Week 1

- Read through the front section of this book, the Introduction, and the first part of Chapter One (to page 9) to learn the basics of Logic Games.
- Take one of the two Practice Tests in Chapter 9 of this book. It is best to do this on a Saturday morning and take the entire test in one sitting. Evaluate how you did on the different game types. Identify three key areas to work on first. You should start with simpler game types and then work up to the harder ones. This book is basically structured from easiest to hardest, so start with whichever of your three key areas comes first in the book.
- Read and review each of those three chapters. For best retention, read the chapter and work half of the practice problems in one study session, then review the chapter and work the remainder of the practice problems in the next study session.

Week 2

- Work through the chapters you have not done yet. Quickly skim chapters that cover material with which you are already proficient. For the others, start with the practice questions at the end of the chapter. Do half of them and check your accuracy. If you've made any mistakes, review the explanations and use the chapter to brush up on your knowledge and skills. Then complete the rest of the end-of-chapter questions.
- At the end of the week, work on your pacing. Take the other Practice Test in Chapter 9. Review the answers and explanations.
- Don't get stressed out. Visualize yourself succeeding and try to relax.

The Day Before the Test

- Make sure you're not in for any surprises on test day. For example, it's a good idea to actually go to the test center location so you know exactly how to get there, how long it might take, and where you will park (if you are driving).
- Try to schedule some relaxing activity so that you keep the stress level low. A brisk walk or other physical activity is great for relieving stress too. The goal is to keep the stress from building so that you get a good night's sleep.
- Don't cram and don't stay up late. Eat healthy foods and don't do anything to dehydrate yourself. Obviously, drinking a lot of alcohol is not advisable even if it might help to reduce stress.

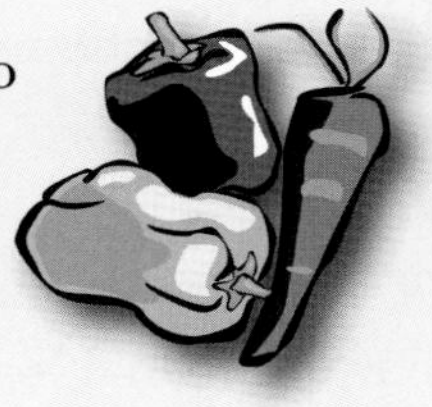

Game-Solving Strategies at a Glance

Game Type: Formal Logic

Typical Fact Pattern: Formal Logic Games consist mostly of sufficient-necessary statements that can be constructed into contrapositives and logic chains.

Example:

Six lightbulbs on a board are either on or off according to the following conditions:

When light 1 is on, light 4 is off.
When light 2 is off, light 1 is on.
When light 5 is on, light 6 is on.

Strategy:

1. Diagram the sufficient-necessary statements.
2. Form the contrapositive of each sufficient-necessary statement.
3. Form logic chains: focus on the left side of the sufficient-necessary statement or the contrapositive.
4. Form the final logic map.
5. Determine the implications of the logic map: are there any vacancies or occupancies you can put in your diagram? Any double or triple possibilities? Diagram as much as possible.

Game Type: Sequencing

Typical Fact Pattern: Sequencing Games require you to put the variables in a certain order, relative to each other.

Example:

Seven runners finished a race in the following order:

Isabella finished before Marisa.
Osea finished before Lori.
Lori finished after Jack.
Noah finished before Kathy and Jack.
Kathy finished after Lori.

Strategy:

1. Diagram each of the constraints. Use either > or < to denote sequence, but do not use both symbols.
2. Form logic chains, if possible. For example, if A > B and B > C, you can construct the chain A > B > C.
3. Fill in vacancies and occupancies. Put any direct placements into your diagram. Note any double or triple occupancies.
4. Form the final logic map. These games allow you to form one large, relatively simple logic map.
5. Determine the implications of the logic map. These games may have only two or three options.

Game Type: Linear (and Complex Linear)

Typical Fact Pattern: Linear Games are similar to Sequencing Games, in that all the variables are arranged along a linear continuum. The constraints, however, may include sufficient-necessary statements, direct placements, box rules, and sequencing constraints.

Example:

Mrs. Webster is giving a piano lesson to each of six students on Tuesday, from 8:00 AM to 1:00 PM. The order of the lessons is subject to the following conditions:

Amee has her lesson before Britt has his.
Felix cannot be scheduled at 11:00 AM.
David has his lesson immediately after Eli.
Carolyn has her lesson two hours after Felix has his.

Strategy:

1. Create a diagram with the correct number of spaces to accommodate all your variables.
2. Diagram each of the constraints. Note any burdensome constraints, such as direct placements or box rules.
3. Form logic chains, if possible.
4. Fill in vacancies and occupancies. Put any direct placements into your diagram. Note any double or triple occupancies. Note a vacancy by crossing out the variable.
5. Make deductions.
6. Form the final logic map.

Game Type: Grouping

Typical Fact Pattern: Grouping Games require you to separate the variables into groups. Depending on the difficulty of the game, you may or may not know the number of variables in each group. Variables might be used more than once or not at all. Often, a question will supply additional constraints specific to that question.

Example:

There are three ponies at the fair. Each can hold up to three children. Eight children will ride the ponies according to the following conditions:

Philip cannot ride with his sister Sue.
Randy and Taylor must ride together.
If Vernon rides on the first pony, Wendy will ride on the second.

Strategy:

1. Create a diagram with the correct number of groups and spaces within each group (if known).
2. Diagram each of the constraints. Note any burdensome constraints, such as direct placements or box rules.
3. Fill in vacancies and occupancies. Put any direct placements into your diagram. Note any double or triple occupancies. Note a vacancy by crossing out the variable.
4. Make deductions.
5. Form the final logic map.

Game Type: Mapping

Typical Fact Pattern: Mapping Games require you to create or use a given map based on the constraints. This game type is less common than others.

Example:

The rectangular park in the middle of Bellville has a restroom at each corner. Some are open and some are closed for cleaning according to the following conditions:

If the northwest restroom is closed, then the southwest one is open.
At least one restroom on the northside must be open.
The southeast restroom is closed whenever the southwest one is open.

Strategy:

1. Diagram the constraints.
2. If you are not given a diagram, create one. Use the constraints to help you decide what form the diagram should take (traditional map, Venn diagram, etc.)
3. Make a hierarchy of consolidated constraints.
4. Make deductions.
5. Form the final logic map.

Game Type: Pattern

Typical Fact Pattern: Pattern Games may resemble complex linear or grouping games, but they take place in two or more rounds. They tend to be much more difficult than other game types, but they are rare.

Example:

The law firm of Bell and Slade has 2 partners, 5 associates, and 7 junior associates this year. The firm gives promotions based on the following conditions:

Each year, one associate will be made partner.
Each year, the firm will hire 3 new junior associates.
Each year, 4 junior associates will be promoted to associate.

Strategy:

1. Create a diagram with the appropriate number of rounds. If the number is not known, draw spaces for 5 or 6 rounds. That is usually sufficient.
2. Diagram the constraints.
3. Make a hierarchy of consolidated constraints.
4. Make deductions.
5. Form the final logic map.

McGRAW-HILL's

CONQUERING LSAT LOGIC GAMES

McGRAW-HILL's

CONQUERING LSAT LOGIC GAMES

Third Edition

CURVEBREAKERS®

New York / Chicago / San Francisco / Lisbon / London / Madrid / Mexico City
Milan / New Delhi / San Juan / Seoul / Singapore / Sydney / Toronto

The McGraw·Hill Companies

Copyright © 2010, 2008, 2006 by McGraw-Hill. All rights reserved. Printed in the United States of America. Except as permitted under the United States Copyright Act of 1976, no part of this publication may be reproduced or distributed in any form or by any means, or stored in a database or retrieval system, without the prior written permission of the publisher.

9 10 11 12 13 14 QVS/QVS 20 19 18 17 16

ISBN 978-0-07-171788-5
MHID 0-07-171788-9

This publication is designed to provide accurate and authoritative information in regard to the subject matter covered. It is sold with the understanding that neither the author nor the publisher is engaged in rendering legal, accounting, or other professional services. If legal advice or other expert assistance is required, the services of a competent professional person should be sought.

—From a Declaration of Principles jointly adopted by a Committee of the American Bar Association and a Committee of Publishers.

McGraw-Hill books are available at special quantity discounts to use as premiums and sales promotions, or for use in corporate training programs. To contact a representative please e-mail us at bulksales@mcgraw-hill.com.

LSAT® is a registered trademark of the Law School Admission Council, which was not involved in the production of, and does not endorse, this product.

Curvebreakers is not affiliated with Harvard University.

Curvebreakers® is a registered trademark. Maximized Variables Games™, Minimized Variables Games™, Complex Linear Games™, Advantage Course™, Double Possibilities™, Triple Possibilities™, Direct Placement™, Vacancy-Occupancy Rules™, and Logic Chain Addition™ are all the exclusive service-marked property of Curvebreakers. Any use of these terms without the express written consent of Curvebreakers is prohibited.

Library of Congress Cataloging-in-Publication Data

McGraw-Hill's conquering LSAT logic games / Curvebreakers. — 3rd ed.
p. cm.
ISBN-13: 978-0-07-171788-5
ISBN-10: 0-07-171788-9
1. Law School Admission Test—Study guides. 2. Law schools—United States—Entrance examinations—Study guides. I. Curvebreakers. II. Title: Conquering LSAT logic games.
KF285.Z9M39 2010
340.076—dc22

2010010356

CONTENTS AT A GLANCE

CONTENTS

CHAPTER 2 Sequencing Games 29

CHAPTER 3 Linear Games 47

CHAPTER 4 Complex Linear Games 65

Editor

Chris Keenum

Special Thanks

Nick Degani
Josh Salzman
Matt Ott
Evan Magers

ABOUT CURVEBREAKERS

Curvebreakers is an LSAT preparation program created by Harvard Law students. Our program dissects the LSAT at a depth unparalleled by other programs currently available and at a price that is a small fraction of what competing programs charge. We watch each year as numerous aspiring law students pay exorbitant amounts for LSAT courses that do not adequately subdivide the LSAT into manageable and learnable portions. Many of these students pay over a thousand dollars and still end up missing out on the education and scores that they deserve. Curvebreakers provides the answer to this problem by offering superior educational materials at reasonable prices—a rare combination in today's test prep market.

We believe, and know personally, that the only way to achieve on the LSAT is through the dedicated study of materials that effectively separate the different types of LSAT questions into their logical components. Our system introduces and analyzes complicated logical components in a step-by-step fashion that allows students to assimilate the information easily and quickly. We elucidate the simpler concepts first in order to develop a secure base for students, allowing them to progress to mastery of the more difficult concepts at later stages. When students combine our methodological programs with a good work ethic, they maximize their potential to receive an excellent LSAT score.

McGRAW-HILL's

CONQUERING LSAT LOGIC GAMES

INTRODUCTION

The analytical reasoning section is one of the most difficult LSAT sections for novice test-takers. However, test-takers who are willing to work at it can greatly improve their analytical reasoning score. Many analytical reasoning questions can be simplified and solved with very basic diagramming techniques that people would not use intuitively. Even the most complicated logic games can be solved using advanced techniques derived from these basic techniques, which is why it helps to learn and consistently adhere to a single solving system for this question type.

The Curvebreakers logic games solving system helped us to master the logic games section on the LSAT and to gain admittance to top-notch law schools across the country. We are confident that the system can do the same for you. After learning the Curvebreakers system, you will be able to

1. *Recall* all facets of the fact pattern.
2. Organize the fact pattern into *manageable parts*.
3. Solve logic game questions *quickly*.
4. Solve logic game questions *accurately*.

LSAT Logic Games

Structure

The LSAT logic games section always contains exactly four different logic games. Each game consists of a fact pattern that contains a couple of sentences describing the general and universal constraints of the game. Based on the constraints set by the fact pattern, five to seven questions are asked about the configuration of the variables in the game. Sometimes the questions repeal certain constraints set in the fact pattern, and sometimes they add to the constraints. Regardless, any constraint set within a specific question ends immediately after you answer that specific question; it does not apply to subsequent or preceding questions. Only the constraints in the fact pattern have universal influence on the entire game. Here is an example of a logic game:

Fact Pattern	Seven passengers, named Anna, Bill, Chris, Dave, Emily, Fanny, and Gina are traveling by train from Atlanta to Boston. No two passengers sit in the same car, and there is a total of seven cars on the train, numbered 1 through 7. The placement of the passengers in the cars is governed by the following constraints:
Constraints	Anna sits in a higher-numbered car than Chris. Chris sits in a higher-numbered car than Emily and Fanny. Gina and Dave do not sit in cars that are consecutively numbered.
Questions	1. If Chris sits in car 3, then who could sit in car 2? (A) Anna (B) Bill (C) Dave (D) Fanny (E) Gina

The correct answer here is (D), Fanny, since she and Emily are required to sit in cars with lower numbers than the car that Chris sits in. Note that the question imposed a constraint on the game: "Chris sits in car 3." Remember that this constraint will not apply to question 2; in that question, Chris could be sitting anywhere. However, Fanny and Emily will always be required to sit in cars with lower numbers than the car that Chris sits in.

Logic Game Types

There are a number of different types of logic games, and to solve each type you need different diagrams, problem-solving heuristics, and logic tools. You'll want to learn to identify each game type just by looking at the fact pattern. Knowing the game type is useful because it will alert you to look for the specific tricks the test-makers commonly use for that game type in order to trip you up. You'll also be able to choose the diagrams, heuristics, and logic tools that will help you solve that game in the quickest and most accurate way possible.

In Chapters 1 through 7, we examine each game type in turn, and we teach you what diagrams and logic tools to use to solve each type. In Chapter 8, we discuss the different game types with minimized and maximized variables.

The Seven Major Types of LSAT Logic Games

1. Formal Logic
2. Sequencing
3. Linear
4. Complex Linear
5. Grouping
6. Mapping
7. Pattern

Variable Types

Beyond the game types, there are also alternative ways that the variables in each game can be presented. The variables in the fact pattern can be mostly determined either by the constraints in the fact pattern or by the constraints in the questions. The former type we call **minimized-variable**, the latter we call **maximized-variable**. Of the two, maximized-variable games are the more difficult and time-consuming. The characteristics of minimized- and maximized-variable games follow:

1. **Minimized-Variable Games**
   a. *Difficulty Level:* Moderate
   b. *Diagramming:* You should spend a lot of time on the fact pattern.
   c. *Questions:* They are easy and can be solved extremely quickly when you use the diagram that you made based on the fact pattern.
2. **Maximized-Variable Games**
   a. *Difficulty Level:* Hard
   b. *Diagramming:* You can spend only a little time diagramming the fact pattern, because the constraints are not very constraining.
   c. *Questions:* At times, you are required to diagram each question separately based on the overall diagram of the fact pattern.

Telling the difference between minimized- and maximized-variable games is very important, since it will help you determine how much time to spend diagramming the fact pattern initially and how much time you should save for diagramming the individual questions. We will cover both of these variable types in depth in Chapter 8.

The Solution Process

The following statement might seem obvious, but it bears repeating: there are good methods for solving games, and there are very poor ones. Bumbling through the fact pattern by just reading it and then moving on to the questions is *never* a good idea unless you are a genius. Fact patterns contain a lot of useless information that must be weeded out. The information that is important must be organized and consolidated into useful parts. You need to process this information using a consistent system for summarizing it in writing. Our system for doing this is called "fact pattern organization heuristics."

Fact Pattern Organization Heuristics

Our fact pattern organization heuristics can help you efficiently organize and process the information presented in the fact pattern. The heuristics differ depending on the game type and even on the specific game, but if you learn what we teach in the following lessons, you will be able to successfully apply heuristics to every game that you encounter on the LSAT. Here is an example of a fact pattern organization heuristic used for linear logic games:

1. Transcribe the constraints.
2. Draw the scenarios of a burdensome constraint.
3. Write out the vacancy-occupancy rules.
4. Make deductions and draw in double possibilities.

In the following lessons, you will learn the heuristics that apply to each of the seven game types. You will learn how to organize the information in the fact pattern through the use of "logic tools." Logic tools allow you to construct a diagram that concentrates all of the pertinent information from the fact pattern into an easily readable and accessible unit of information. By becoming adept at using these tools and assembling these units of information, you can answer logic games questions more quickly and accurately.

Logic Tools

The logic tools listed below will each be explained fully in the chapters that follow. You will learn how to use each one to solve logic games questions.

1. **Sufficient-Necessary Conditions**
   Used for all types of games.
2. **Logic Chain Addition**
   Used for Formal Logic, Sequencing, Linear, and Grouping games.
3. **Sequencing Chains**
   Used for Sequencing and Linear games.
4. **Direct Placement**
   Used for almost all types of games.
5. **Box Rules**
   Used for Linear, Complex Linear, Minimized-Variable, and Grouping games.
6. **Vacancy-Occupancy Rules**
   Used for Linear, Complex Linear, Minimized-Variable, and Grouping games.
7. **Double Possibilities**
   Used for Linear, Complex Linear, Minimized-Variable, and Grouping games.

Diagramming

Very often a good method for diagramming one type of game is a very poor method for diagramming another type of game. Logic games test your ability to utilize a number of different organizational methods and different logical structures effectively. One type of diagram cannot cover all the possible variations. Therefore, you will need to learn different diagrams for each type of game. The following chapters will teach you about all of the different diagramming types and show you how to apply them correctly to each type of game.

General LSAT Preparation Tips

Before you begin studying all of the different types of logic games, we'd like to offer you the following general LSAT preparation tips.

Work Hard

Your LSAT score is the most important number on your law school application. People may tell you differently in order to comfort you and prevent you from stressing out about the test, but truth be told, in admissions offices across the country, the LSAT is referred to as "the great equalizer." It is the one number that objectively and directly compares you to the rest of the applicant pool in a standardized fashion. Because of the stark and simple comparisons that LSAT scores provide, admissions officials tend to overrely on them when making admissions decisions.

It is disheartening that so many important personal qualities of applicants are overshadowed by three digits on a piece of paper, but it is a fact, and students would be wise to accept it and find ways to deal with it instead of wasting time lamenting it. Curvebreakers offers you the most effective available system for beating the LSAT. However, our efforts to deconstruct the test mean nothing unless you apply yourself and strive to learn our system. We will give you the tools for success, but it is up to you to learn how to use them.

Take the Time to Make Sure You Master Each Problem-Solving Technique

During the test, time is definitely an important factor. For now, however, don't worry about how quickly you can solve logic games questions. As you work your way through the lessons in this book, you'll need to spend a large amount of time on each lesson just to master the logical tricks that correspond to each type of game. Nevertheless, by the time you have finished all of the lessons in the book, you will need to start improving your speed. The goal is eventually to average about 8 minutes and 30 seconds per game.

One main purpose of this book is to teach you the importance of dissecting the fact pattern and constraints before you even get to the questions. That way, when you arrive at the questions, you will virtually fly through them with near-perfect accuracy. So be prepared to spend a large amount of time interpreting logic games' fact patterns. Keeps these time guidelines in mind:

1. Go through the logic games in the lessons *very slowly*.
2. Spend the majority of your time on the fact patterns, not the questions.

Make a Schedule

Hard work is easier when you approach it in a systematic fashion. To avoid feeling overwhelmed by the task of LSAT preparation, create a schedule for yourself and stick to it. Start your preparation at least two months ahead of your chosen test date. That should give you plenty of time to learn all facets of the LSAT and to obtain an excellent score.

Make Sure Your Preparation Is Effective

There are several factors you can control that will determine the effectiveness of your preparation program. You should do your best to ensure that all the following factors are working in your favor:

1. **Quality of Your Preparation Materials**
2. **Total Length of Study Program**
   Curvebreakers recommends starting to study at least two months before the date of the LSAT.
3. **Amount of Daily Study Time**
   Taking four test sections five days a week is about the right amount of study time to prepare for the test.
4. **Quality of Study Time**
   a. Bad factors
      i. Are you **distracted**?
      ii. Are you **tired**?
      iii. Are you **sleepy**?
      iv. Are you approaching the study materials **haphazardly**?
   b. Good factors
      i. Read Critically
      As you read, learn to pay close attention to every word. If you get into the habit of doing this, then you will just get better and better at it as your mind gets stronger and habituates itself to the exercise.
      ii. Do Not Worry about Pacing During the Lessons
      Learning time is qualitatively different from testing time. If you rush through the lessons in this book, you will never learn the system well in the first place. While you are learning the material, give yourself as much time as you need, because you will soon speed up naturally and because there is plenty of material to practice with to gain speed once you have learned the basic concepts.
      iii. Identify Your Weaknesses
      Whenever you finish a lesson, the first thing you should do is review the questions that you missed. Even though this is a tiresome exercise, it will help you by alerting you to your weaknesses. Some people have a harder time with certain game types, with certain question types, or with certain logic tools. Recognizing your weaknesses helps you to eliminate them.

Conclusion

This book will teach you how to approach and efficiently solve each logic game that you encounter on the LSAT. Start at the first lesson and do not skip around, because each lesson builds on the previous lesson. Answer keys and explanations are provided for every game. Take as much time as you need with each lesson so that you learn the basic tenets of our problem-solving system. It may take you a little while to master the system, but once you do, you will be able to solve LSAT logic games far more quickly and accurately than you ever could without it. Chapter 1 introduces you to formal logic games and the sufficient-necessary logic tool that is required to solve them.

CHAPTER 1

FORMAL LOGIC GAMES

Formal logic games are games that are composed of **if-then statements.** The more statements there are, the more complicated the game becomes. It becomes even more complicated when statements are linked together. But for now, it is sufficient to know that every if-then statement must take one of the following four forms:

1. If an act A occurs → act B occurs.
2. If an act A does **not** occur → act B occurs.
3. If an act A occurs → act B does **not** occur.
4. If an act A does **not** occur → act B does **not** occur.

Statements in these forms should always be noted and **transcribed** in the following four ways:

1. $A \rightarrow B$
2. $\not{A} \rightarrow B$
3. $A \rightarrow \not{B}$
4. $\not{A} \rightarrow \not{B}$

Typical Fact Pattern

Six shoppers, named Anna, Ben, Chris, Dana, Evan, and Fanny, decide to go to the grocery store this weekend on either Saturday or Sunday. Each shopper's choice of day is dependent on another shopper's choice. Their choices are determined by the following constraints:

> If Anna goes to the store on Saturday, then Chris will go to the store on Saturday.
> If Ben does not go to the store on Saturday, then Dana will go to the store on Saturday.
> If Evan goes to the store on Saturday, then Fanny will not go to the store on Saturday.
> If Anna does not go to the store on Saturday, then Evan will not go to the store on Saturday.

The constraints in this game are transcribed below. Each transcription uses only the first letter of each actor's name, since the first letters of the names of the actors are always different. Notice that aside from the letters used, these transcriptions are exactly the same as the ones shown previously.

1. $A \rightarrow C$
2. $\not{B} \rightarrow D$
3. $E \rightarrow \not{F}$
4. $\not{A} \rightarrow \not{E}$

Logic Tools

From the preceding known conditions, we can deduce all of the following information from the game:

1. $E \rightarrow A \rightarrow C$ = If Evan goes to the store on Saturday, then Anna and Chris will also go.
2. $\not{C} \rightarrow \not{A} \rightarrow \not{E}$ = If Chris does not go to the store on Saturday, then neither Anna nor Evan will go.
3. $\not{D} \rightarrow B$ = If Dana does not go to the store on Saturday, then Ben will go.
4. $F \rightarrow \not{E}$ = If Fanny goes to the store on Saturday, then Evan will not go.

This information is partly intuitive, but many test-takers have a hard time gleaning it quickly in a time-pressured situation. How did we deduce it in this game? We did so through the use of logic tools: **sufficient-necessary conditions**, the **contrapositive**, and **logic chain addition.**

Sufficient-Necessary Conditions

Every if-then statement is also a sufficient-necessary condition. However, sufficient-necessary conditions are also formulated when the existence of one condition necessitates or hinges upon the existence or absence of another. To understand this idea, take a look at a different kind of LSAT question, the kind called a logical reasoning question:

> Originally, life on moons developed only on those moons which had water. Through 200,000 B.C., the moons of Neptune were of moderate temperatures, but none of them had water. By that period, Jupiter's moons all did have water. The water on Jupiter's moons was mostly frozen on some days, and it boiled mainly at the bottoms of oceans.
>
> If all of the statements in the passage are true, then which one of the following must also be true?
>
> (A) In 200,000 B.C., Jupiter's moons were the only moons with water.
> (B) There was life present on some of Jupiter's moons in 200,000 B.C.
> (C) In 200,000 B.C., life existed on Earth's moon because it did have water.
> (D) After 200,000 B.C., Neptune's moons had water and life on them.
> (E) The moons of Neptune in 200,000 B.C. did not have life.

If you transcribe the information within the question, you can make a series of deductions.

The first sentence of the question states the following sufficient-necessary condition:

Life on moons ("L") *developed only on those moons which had water* ("W").

To correctly transcribe the information in this sentence, you must understand which condition (**sufficient**) requires the presence of another condition (**necessary**). Here it is clear that "water" was necessary for there to be "life." These conditions are transcribed as follows:

Sufficient condition → Necessary condition

Therefore: 1.a. L → W (Life → Water)

This "logic chain" denotes, in a simple, easy-to-remember manner, that the **existence** of *life* **required** the presence of *water*.

THE CONTRAPOSITIVE

From the information given in any and all sufficient-necessary chains, we can deduce an additional piece of information. This information is called the **contrapositive**.

In this specific example, since L → W, we also know that:

Without water ("W"), *a moon could not have had life* ("L").

1.b. ~~W~~ → ~~L~~ (~~Water~~ → ~~Life~~)

This fact is not stated explicitly in the question, but it is true based on the truth of statement 1.a., which was held to be true in the question. The contrapositive of every true statement is also true, and you can deduce contrapositives from every true statement using a logical reversal that will be explained in full later in this chapter. Don't worry right now about how exactly to form the contrapositive. Just try to see how the contrapositive fits into the **big picture** in making the complete logic map. For every sufficient-necessary condition, you can also transcribe the contrapositive of that statement. Your logic map for this question now looks like this:

1.a. L → W 1.b. ~~W~~ → ~~L~~

Now let's look at the second sentence of the question.

Through 200,000 B.C., the moons of Neptune ("NM") *were of moderate temperatures, but none of them had water* ("W").

Look for the sufficient condition and the necessary condition in this statement while weeding out the irrelevant information. This statement differs somewhat from previous sufficient-necessary conditions, because it is more a statement of fact than an if-then statement, but you should still be able to recognize the conditions.

2.a. NM → ~~W~~ (Neptune Moon → ~~Water~~)

The second logical fact that you can derive from this statement is equivalent to the statement's contrapositive. Think for a moment what that would be. It corresponds to the following:

If a moon had water ("W"), *then it was not a moon of Neptune* ("NM").

2.b. W → ~~NM~~ (Neptune Moon → ~~Water~~)

So as soon as you read the sufficient-necessary statement in the second sentence of the question, you should have immediately written down both pieces of information: the sufficient-necessary condition and its contrapositive.

2.a. NM → ~~W~~ 2.b. W → ~~NM~~

Now let's look at the third sentence of the question:

By that period, Jupiter's moons ("JM") *all did have water* ("W").

This statement should be automatically transcribed in the following manner:

3.a. JM → W   3.b. W̸ → ~~JM~~

The fourth sentence in this question is largely irrelevant, because it doesn't really tell you anything for sure. It merely describes things that happen "sometimes" and "mostly." It is not a true statement that you can transcribe and make deductions from. Therefore, this statement and others like it that you will see later are completely irrelevant and should be disregarded as useless fluff meant to confuse you. Now, let's take a look at your complete logic map of the sentences in the question:

1. a. L → W   b. W̸ → L̸
2. a. NM → W̸   b. W → ~~NM~~
3. a. JM → W   b. W̸ → ~~JM~~

Logic Chain Addition

Notice how some chains end with the same variable that begins another chain. When chains have variables in common in this way, they can and should be consolidated through a technique called **logic chain addition**:

4.a. 1.a. + 2.b. = L → W → ~~NM~~ or (L → ~~NM~~)

This statement reads literally as follows:

"If there was life on the moon, then the moon was not a moon of Neptune."

Such a statement also has its contrapositive:

4.b. 2.a. + 1.b. = NM → W̸ → L̸ or (NM → L̸)

This statement reads literally as follows:

"If it was a moon of Neptune, then it did not have life."

This deduction will answer the question for you. First, though, let's look at the **complete** and **consolidated** logic diagram:

3. a. JM → W   b. W̸ → ~~JM~~
4. a. L → W → ~~NM~~   b. NM → W̸ → L̸

Notice that 4.a. and 4.b. are contrapositives of each other and that they completely encompass 1 and 2. Let's review the answer choices in light of your new and improved logic diagram:

If all of the statements in the passage are true, then which one of the following must also be true?

(A) In 200,000 B.C., Jupiter's moons were the only moons with water.
(B) There was life present on Jupiter's moons with water in 200,000 B.C.
(C) In 200,000 B.C., life existed on Earth's moon because it did have water.
(D) After 200,000 B.C., Neptune's moons had water and life on them.
(E) The moons of Neptune in 200,000 B.C. did not have life.

(A) You do not have enough information to support this answer choice.
(B) This answer choice feels as if it should be correct. However, when you map it out, you see that it states the following: W → L. You do not know this for sure. You only know that L → W and W̸ → L̸. Therefore, you cannot support this answer choice.
(C) You do not have enough information to support this answer choice.
(D) You do not know what happened to Neptune's moons after the time frame described by the question stem, so you cannot support this answer choice.
(E) This is the correct answer, as shown by your final deduction in 4.b. (NM → W̸ → L̸).

Forming the Contrapositive

Let's look again at the four ways that if-then statements can appear. Each statement yields a contrapositive:

1.	A → B	B̸ → A̸
2.	A̸ → B	B̸ → A
3.	A → B̸	B → A̸
4.	A̸ → B̸	B → A

You do not have to memorize each of these four formulations. Instead, notice that for each one the **transition** from the sufficient-necessary to the contrapositive is consistent. The contrapositive is formed by switching the necessary condition in the original statement with the sufficient condition in the contrapositive while also switching the sign (i.e., the presence or absence of the strikethrough) of each variable.

Look at the first statement above:

Sufficient-Necessary:

A → B

To get to the contrapositive, you must

1. Switch the **positions** of the variables: B → A
2. Switch the **signs** of the variables: ~~B~~ → ~~A~~

Contrapositive:

~~B~~ → ~~A~~

Look at the third statement above:

Sufficient-Necessary:

A → ~~B~~

To get to the contrapositive, you must

1. Switch the **position** of the variables: ~~B~~ → A
2. Switch the **signs** of the variables: B → ~~A~~

Contrapositive:

B → ~~A~~

Remember that switching just the positions or just the signs is not enough—you must do both! Test-makers commonly test to see if you have switched only one by designing answer choices to trap students making this mistake.

Let's make sure that you get the hang of this by practicing the initial transcription of sufficient-necessary statements and the subsequent formation of the contrapositive.

First Sufficient-Necessary Statement:

Turtles (T) are not mammals (M).

Sufficient-Necessary:

T → ~~M~~

Contrapositive:

M → ~~T~~

The contrapositive literally reads: "Mammals are not turtles" or, "If the animal is a mammal, then it is not a turtle."

Second Sufficient-Necessary Statement:

All turtles (T) are reptiles (R).

Sufficient-Necessary:

T → R

Contrapositive:

~~R~~ → ~~T~~

The contrapositive literally reads: "If the animal is not a reptile, then it is not a turtle."

Third Sufficient-Necessary Statement:

If the cat does not eat tuna (CT ~ Cat Tuna), then the kitten will not drink milk (KM ~ Kitten Milk).

Sufficient-Necessary:

~~CT~~ → ~~KM~~

Contrapositive:

KM → CT

The contrapositive literally reads: "If the kitten drinks milk, then the cat will eat tuna." Think about this for a second and ask yourself why it is true.

Fourth Sufficient-Necessary Statement:

If the environment is not clean (EC ~ Environment Clean), then factories emitted smoke for a number of years (FES ~ Factories Emitted Smoke).

Sufficient-Necessary:

~~EC~~ → FES

Contrapositive:

~~FES~~ → EC

The contrapositive literally reads: "If factories did not emit smoke for a number of years, then the environment is clean." Notice how intuitively this statement does not seem true because, based on your outside knowledge, you know that many factors besides factories can pollute the environment. However, during the LSAT you must put aside all outside knowledge and operate solely on the information provided by the test.

It's easy to make mistakes when transcribing sufficient-necessary conditions and formulating their contrapositives, and the test-makers load answer choices with incorrect formulations, hoping to trick students. That is why it is so important to be able to tell which conditions are sufficient and which ones are necessary and how to translate them correctly into their contrapositives.

Fact Pattern Organization Heuristics

For every type of game, there is a step-by-step procedure that you should undertake before trying to solve the game. We call this procedure "using fact pattern organization heuristics." Although there are some differences, the steps are similar for most game types, so, with practice, you should find this procedure easy to remember and apply. For formal logic games, the procedure is the following:

1. **Transcribe** the constraints in the fact pattern.
2. Use **logic chain addition** to consolidate the constraints.
   a. Combine similar sufficient constraints from sufficient-necessary and contrapositive columns.
   b. Focus on the left side of the sufficient-necessary chains.
   c. Focus on the left side of the contrapositive chains.
   d. Form the final logic map.
3. Determine the **implications** of your logic map.

If you follow this procedure whenever you encounter a formal logic game, you should be able to answer the questions quickly and accurately.

Review

In this section, you have learned all of the following:

1. How to diagram *sufficient-necessary statements*
2. How to create *contrapositives* from these statements
3. How to consolidate logic chains through the process of *logic chain addition*
4. The appropriate *fact pattern organization heuristic* for formal logic games

Now you are ready to try your hand at solving some real formal logic games. Look to see where you can apply the preceding concepts in each game. Do not worry if the games take you some time, because, once you get better at using this method, your speed and accuracy will increase dramatically.

FORMAL LOGIC GAME 1

There is a string of seven lights encircling a billboard outside of a theater on opening night. The lights are connected to a circuit so that certain lights are on while other lights are off. The conditions under which certain lights are on while others are off are governed by the following constraints:

Light 1 is on when light 2 is off.
Light 3 is on when light 4 is on.
If light 5 is on, then light 1 is on and light 4 is on.
If light 6 is off, then light 2 is off.
If light 7 is on, then light 6 is off.

1. When light 7 is on, which of the following must be true?

   (A) Light 2 is off.
   (B) Light 6 is on.
   (C) Light 4 is off.
   (D) Light 5 is on.
   (E) Light 3 is on.

2. When light 5 is on, which of the following must NOT be true?

   (A) Light 4 is on.
   (B) Light 1 is on.
   (C) Light 6 is off.
   (D) Light 3 is off.
   (E) Light 7 is on.

3. If light 1 is off, then which of the following could be true?

   (A) Light 5 is on.
   (B) Light 2 is off.
   (C) Light 3 is off.
   (D) Light 7 is on.
   (E) Light 6 is off.

4. When light 5 is off, which of the following could NOT be true?

   (A) Lights 1 and 2 are on.
   (B) Lights 3 and 7 are off.
   (C) Lights 4 and 6 are on.
   (D) Lights 2 and 4 are off.
   (E) Lights 7 and 2 are on.

5. When light 3 is off, which of the following must be true?

   (A) Lights 1 and 6 are on.
   (B) Lights 4 and 5 are off.
   (C) Lights 7 and 1 are on.
   (D) Lights 6 and 5 are off.
   (E) Lights 2 and 4 are on.

6. If light 1 is turned off, then the configuration of how many other lights is influenced?

   (A) one
   (B) two
   (C) three
   (D) four
   (E) five

SOLUTION STEPS

Start your analysis of this game by applying the fact pattern organization heuristic for formal logic games:

1. Transcribe the Constraints. When transcribing the constraints, determine which conditions are sufficient and which ones are necessary by asking yourself which condition is dependent on which other condition. For example, the first constraint is diagrammed as follows: $\not{2} \rightarrow 1$. Many students will mistakenly assume that the correct diagram is $1 \rightarrow \not{2}$ merely because that is how the sentence is organized. Don't fall into that trap! The following is a correct list of transcribed constraints along with their contrapositives:

1. a. $\not{2} \rightarrow 1$; b. $\not{1} \rightarrow 2$
2. a. $4 \rightarrow 3$; b. $\not{3} \rightarrow \not{4}$
3. a. $5 \rightarrow 1$; b. $\not{1} \rightarrow \not{5}$
4. a. $5 \rightarrow 4$; b. $\not{4} \rightarrow \not{5}$
5. a. $\not{6} \rightarrow \not{2}$; b. $2 \rightarrow 6$
6. a. $7 \rightarrow \not{6}$; b. $6 \rightarrow \not{7}$

2. Add Logic Chains Together. These logic chains can be consolidated through logic chain addition. This step is complicated, so it will be broken up into sub-steps here.

Focus on the left side of the sufficient-necessary chains. Look at the left side of each sufficient-necessary chain in turn. Chain 1.a. begins with 2̸, so ask yourself, "Does any other sufficient-necessary chain start or end with the variable 2̸?" The answer is yes—5.a. ends with 2̸—so add these two logic chains to obtain 6̸ → 2̸ → 1. Move to the next variable on that side in the row. "Does any chain start or end with the variable 4̸?" The answer is yes, so more addition is possible. Keep going down the row. The variable 5 has no matches and therefore no additions. The variable 6̸ does have matches, so addition is possible. The variable 7 has no matches.

Make the chain additions:

A.	5.a. + 1.a.	=	6̸ → 2̸ → 1
B.	4.a. + 2.a.	=	5 → 4 → 3
C.	6.a. + 5.a.	=	7 → 6̸ → 2̸

Notice that A and C can be consolidated further:

D. 7 → 6̸ → 2̸ → 1

Focus on the left side of the contrapositive chains. After you finish this process on the left side of the sufficient-necessary chains, move to the left side of the contrapositive chains. Starting with 1.b., ask yourself, "Does any chain end with the variable 1̸?" No. "Does any chain end with the variable 3̸?" No. "Does any chain end with the variable 4̸?" Yes. Does any chain end with the variable 2?" Yes. "Does any chain end with the variable 6?" Yes.

Now add these chains together:

E.	2.b. + 4.b.	=	3̸ → 4̸ → 5̸
F.	1.b. + 5.b.	=	1̸ → 2 → 6
G.	5.b. + 6.b.	=	2 → 6 → 7̸

Notice that F and G can be consolidated:

H. 1̸ → 2 → 6 → 7̸

Notice that many of the chains formed in this step are actually contrapositives of the chains formed in the previous step. This will be true in general, but, unlike this game, other games will require you to form chains that are not merely contrapositives of previously formed chains.

Form the final logic map. Now cross out all of the original chains that were added together to make larger chains. Retain any original chains that were not added to others. Next, make a logic map of all of the consolidated chains and remaining original chains in the game.

3.a. 5 → 1	; 3.b. 1̸ → 5̸
B. 5 → 4 → 3	; E. 3̸ → 4̸ → 5̸
D. 7 → 6̸ → 2̸ → 1	; H. 1̸ → 2 → 6 → 7̸

This map essentially represents the causative linkages between the variables. But you can still make one more round of consolidations. If you find two *sufficient variables* that are the same, consolidate them. This should be done with 5 and 1̸ in the map. Notice that this **cannot** be done with 5̸ or 1 (common *necessary conditions*) because knowing the status of these variables does not allow you to deduce anything else about the game. However, knowing the status of common sufficient variables does allow you to make deductions. Your final map should look as follows:

D. 7 → 6̸ → 2̸ → 1

E. 3̸ → 4̸ → 5̸

I. ↗ 1
5 → 4 → 3

J. ↗ 5̸
4̸ → 2 → 6 → 7̸

Now that you have completed the map, you can move on to step 3 of the fact pattern organization heuristic.

3. Determine the Implications of the Logic Map. This step requires you to think about which variables are not included in the constraints. It also encourages you to interpret the meaning of the logic map so that you can use it accurately when answering questions. For instance, if light 5 is on, then you know that lights 1, 4, and 3 will also be on. However, if light 5 is off, then you actually know nothing about the variables in the rest of the game. You are now ready to answer the questions in the game.

Answering the Questions

Question 1: When light 7 is on, which of the following must be true?

When light 7 is on, as in constraint D, you know that lights 6 and 2 are off and light 1 is on. Therefore, choice **A** must be true.

Question 2: When light 5 is on, which of the following must NOT be true?

When light 5 is on, as in chains 3.a. and B, you know that lights 1, 4, and 3 are on. Therefore, it must not be true that light 3 is off, as in choice **D**.

Question 3: If light 1 is off, then which of the following could be true?

When light 1 is off, as in constraints 3.b. and H, you know that lights 2 and 6 are on and lights 7 and 5 are off. Therefore, choice **C** is correct, since light 3 could be off.

Question 4: When light 5 is off, which of the following could NOT be true?

When light 5 is off, you know absolutely nothing about the rest of the game. Therefore, you must look for contradictions inherent in the answer choices to find a scenario that could not occur. Choice **E** has a scenario in which lights 7 and 2 are on concurrently; due to constraints **D** and **H**, we know that this is impossible.

Question 5: When light 3 is off, then which of the following must be true?

When light 3 is off, you know that lights 4 and 5 must also be off, which corresponds to answer choice **B**.

Question 6: If light 1 is turned off, then the configuration of how many other lights is influenced?

If light 1 is off, then lights 2 and 6 must be on and lights 5 and 7 must be off. This is a tricky question since constraints 3.b and H are separate in our logic map. However, you will learn how to consolidate these further in the future into more complicated but more helpful logic chains. The answer is four lights (choice **D**).

FORMAL LOGIC GAME 2

At the camp pool a number of youngsters are all vying to get into the water. The camp counselors know that certain kids cannot be in the pool at the same time if any semblance of order is to be maintained. The youngsters Anna, Ben, Chris, Dana, Evan, Frank, and Garry all want to get into the pool, but whether or not they are admitted is determined by the following:

> Anna gets into the pool only if Chris gets into the pool.
> If Ben gets into the pool, then Chris also gets into the pool.
> Anna gets into the pool if Dana gets in.
> Garry gets into the pool only if Chris and Evan get into the pool.
> Ben gets into the pool if Garry gets into the pool.
> If Garry is out of the pool, then Dana is out of the pool.

1. Which of the following could be a group of all of the youngsters in the pool at the same time?
   (A) Dana, Evan, Chris, Ben
   (B) Garry, Evan, Ben, Chris
   (C) Ben, Garry, Evan, Dana
   (D) Dana, Chris, Anna, Garry
   (E) None of the above

2. If Dana is in the pool, then how many people, including Dana, must be in the pool?
   (A) three
   (B) four
   (C) five
   (D) six
   (E) seven

3. If Frank is in the pool, then what is the fewest number of people, including Frank, who could be in the pool?
   (A) one
   (B) two
   (C) three
   (D) four
   (E) five

4. If Chris is not in the pool, then who could be in the pool?
   (A) Anna
   (B) Evan
   (C) Garry
   (D) Dana
   (E) None of the above

5. If exactly two children are out of the pool, then who must be out of the pool?
   (A) Anna
   (B) Ben
   (C) Chris
   (D) Dana
   (E) Evan

6. If Evan is out of the pool, then which of the following must be true?
   (A) Anna is out of the pool.
   (B) Dana is in the pool.
   (C) Garry is in the pool.
   (D) Ben is out of the pool.
   (E) Dana is out of the pool.

SOLUTION STEPS

1. Transcribe the Constraints. The constraints in this game should be transcribed in the following way:

1.a. $A \rightarrow C$	b. $\not{C} \rightarrow \not{A}$
2.a. $B \rightarrow C$	b. $\not{C} \rightarrow \not{B}$
3.a. $D \rightarrow A$	b. $\not{A} \rightarrow \not{D}$
4.a. $G \rightarrow C$	b. $\not{C} \rightarrow \not{G}$
5.a. $G \rightarrow E$	b. $\not{E} \rightarrow \not{G}$
6.a. $G \rightarrow B$	b. $\not{B} \rightarrow \not{G}$
7.a. $\not{G} \rightarrow \not{D}$	b. $D \rightarrow G$

2. Add Logic Chains Together. *Focus on the left side of the sufficient-necessary chains.* Going down the chains, you can see that 1.a., 2.a., 4.a., 5.a., 6.a., and 7.a. can all be added to some part of another chain:

A. 3.a. + 1.a. = $D \rightarrow A \rightarrow C$
B. 6.a. + 2.a. = $G \rightarrow B \rightarrow C$
C. 7.b. + 4.a. = $D \rightarrow G \rightarrow C$
D. 7.b. + 5.a. = $D \rightarrow G \rightarrow E$
E. 7.b. + 6.a. = $D \rightarrow G \rightarrow B$
F. 4.b. + 5.b. + 6.b. + 7.a. = $\not{C}$ ↘
$\not{E} \rightarrow \not{G} \rightarrow \not{D}$
$\not{B}$ ↗

You will have to consolidate the sufficient variables in order to form the final logic map, so go ahead now and consolidate all the chains that start with the variable D:

G.
↗ $A \rightarrow C$
D
↘ G

Next, you see that you can also consolidate chains around the variable G. G is consolidated in two ways. First, you notice that if G is in the pool, then so are B, E, and C. However, you also know that if B is in the pool, then C is in the pool. Therefore, you do not directly connect G to C, since G is already directly connected to B. Your diagram of B, C, E, and G should look like this:

H.

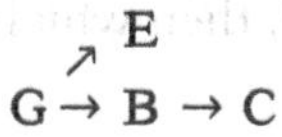

Think about other ways that you could draw this diagram and realize why this way is the most efficient.

Finally, note that you can combine meta-diagrams **G** and **H**.

I.

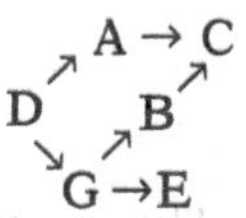

Focus on the left side of the contrapositive chains. Of these chains, you can add together the ones that end and begin with $\not{A}$ (1.b. and 3.b.) and the ones that end and begin with $\not{B}$ (2.b. and 6.b.).

$$1.b. + 3.b. = \not{C} \rightarrow \not{A} \rightarrow \not{D}$$

$$2.b. + 6.b. = \not{C} \rightarrow \not{B} \rightarrow \not{G}$$

These chains can then be further combined to form:

J.

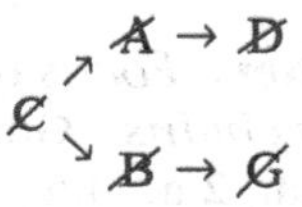

Form the final logic map. 1. After crossing out all information that you used to form your meta-logic chains, you are left with the following:

I.

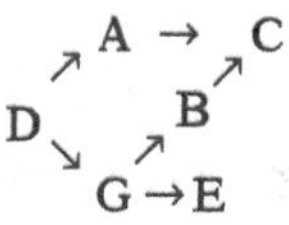

J.

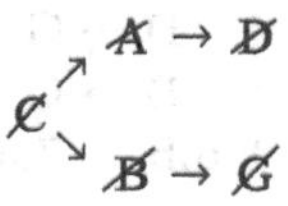

F.

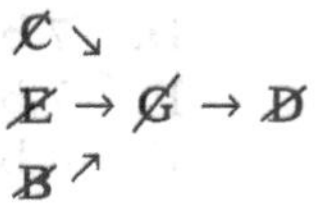

You can integrate the F and J chains further, since there are useless linkages in F. For example, you know that $\not{C} \rightarrow \not{G}$, because $\not{C} \rightarrow \not{B} \rightarrow \not{G}$. So eliminate the linkages in diagram F that are already included in diagram J.

First, from J, you know that $\not{C} \rightarrow \not{G}$ and $\not{B} \rightarrow \not{G}$, so you can cross out these repetitive linkages, making:

$$\not{E} \rightarrow \not{G} \rightarrow \not{D}$$

You do not know that $\not{E} \rightarrow \not{G}$ or that $\not{G} \rightarrow \not{D}$, so let's include these two pieces in the diagram of J.

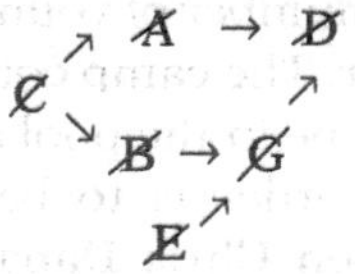

So your complete final logic map is:

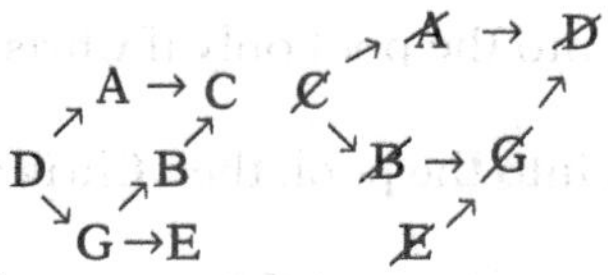

3. Determine the Implications of the Logic Map. There are not many further implications of this map once you arrive at the final version. But let's go back over how you got there:

1. You drew out the constraints.
2. You added together the sufficient conditions of the sufficient-necessary chains.
   a. You crossed out the information you added together.
3. You added together the sufficient conditions of the contrapositive chains.
   a. You crossed out the information you added together.
4. You looked at the meta-constraints.
   a. You weeded out repetitive information from the meta-constraints.
   b. You combined the information in the meta-constraints wherever possible. From there, you arrived at a logic map that will completely explain the game.

A word of solace for those who are having trouble with this: you will get much better at these skills and will be able to use them more efficiently as long as you take time to pin the basics down now. These types of logical transitions will be the foundation for your study of logic games, and we will continue to build upon these concepts in later lessons. This does not take away from the fact that these are difficult concepts. However, if you have started two months ahead of time, as we recommend, you will have plenty of opportunities to practice and master these skills before the LSAT arrives. If you get discouraged, ask yourself whether your peers have taken the opportunity to learn the games to this depth. The answer is no, and, on test day, it will show very highly in your favor.

ANSWERING THE QUESTIONS

Question 1: Which of the following could be a group of all of the youngsters in the pool at the same time?

(B) You know from diagram I that Garry, Ben, Evan, and Chris could all be in the pool at the same time.

Question 2: If Dana is in the pool, then how many people including Dana must be in the pool?

(D) If Dana is in the pool, then from diagram I you know that Garry, Ben, Evan, Chris, Anna, and Dana must be in the pool. This makes six people.

Question 3: If Frank is in the pool, then what is the fewest number of people, including Frank, who could be in the pool?

(A) Frank's presence in the pool is not connected to anyone else's presence. Additionally, no one has to be in the pool when another person is out of the pool. Therefore, the answer is one, Frank.

Question 4: If Chris is not in the pool, then who could be in the pool?

(B) If Chris is not in the pool, then Anna, Ben, Garry, and Dana cannot be in the pool. Therefore, Frank or Evan can be the only person in the pool.

Question 5: If exactly two children are out of the pool, then who must be out of the pool?

(D) Dana and Frank must be out of the pool, because if any other person is out of the pool, then the constraints require more than two people to be out of the pool.

Question 6: If Evan is out of the pool, then which of the following must be true?

(E) If Evan is out of the pool, then Garry and Dana must also be out of the pool.

FORMAL LOGIC GAME 3

A number of fighting fish named Anna, Ben, Chris, Dana, Evan, Frank, and Garry are placed into an aquarium. Their owner knows that some of these fish dislike each other, so she places certain fish in the aquarium only along with certain other fish. Additionally, some fish are not placed in the aquarium when other fish are present. These arrangements are determined by the following constraints:

If Anna is in, then Frank is out.
If Chris is out, then Anna is in and Ben is in.
If Evan is out, then Chris is out.
If Dana is in, then Evan is out.

1. Which of the following could be a group of fish that are placed into the aquarium?
   (A) Evan, Frank, Anna, Ben
   (B) Garry, Chris, Evan, Frank
   (C) Dana, Ben, Evan, Chris
   (D) Chris, Frank, Dana
   (E) None of the above

2. Which fish could be present in the aquarium regardless of the presence of any other fish?
   (A) Anna
   (B) Chris
   (C) Dana
   (D) Frank
   (E) Garry

3. What is the maximum number of fish that could be present in the aquarium?
   (A) three
   (B) four
   (C) five
   (D) six
   (E) seven

4. If Ben is in the aquarium, then which fish must be out of the aquarium?
   (A) Chris
   (B) Frank
   (C) Evan
   (D) Anna
   (E) None of the above

5. If Chris is out of the aquarium, then which of the following must be true?
   (A) Anna is in the aquarium and Evan is out.
   (B) Frank is out of the aquarium.
   (C) Evan is in the aquarium.
   (D) Dana is out of the aquarium and Ben is in.
   (E) None of the above.

6. If Frank is in the aquarium, then which of the following must NOT be true?
   (A) Evan is in the aquarium.
   (B) Garry is in the aquarium.
   (C) Chris is out of the aquarium.
   (D) Ben is out of the aquarium.
   (E) None of the above.

SOLUTION STEPS

1. Transcribe the Constraints

1. a. $A \rightarrow \not{F}$; b. $F \rightarrow \not{A}$
2. a. $\not{C} \rightarrow A$; b. $\not{A} \rightarrow C$
3. a. $\not{C} \rightarrow B$; b. $\not{B} \rightarrow C$
4. a. $\not{E} \rightarrow \not{C}$; b. $C \rightarrow E$
5. a. $D \rightarrow \not{E}$; b. $E \rightarrow \not{D}$

2. Add Logic Chains. *Combine all similar sufficient conditions.* Since you have now had plenty of practice combining logic chains in the previous two games, we are ready to introduce this step in order to simplify the addition process. This step requires you to look at the sufficient-necessary and contrapositive sides of the chains and consolidate all sufficient conditions that are similar. You will get the following chain:

A. $\not{C} \nearrow B$, $\not{C} \searrow A$

Focus on the left side of the sufficient-necessary chains. Now add what you can from the sufficient conditions of the sufficient-necessary chains.

5.a. + 4.a. = $D \rightarrow \not{E} \rightarrow \not{C}$

A. + 1.a. = $\not{C} \nearrow B$, $\not{C} \searrow A \rightarrow \not{F}$

These two chains can be added to make the following chain:

B. $D \rightarrow \not{E} \rightarrow \not{C} \nearrow B$, $\searrow A \rightarrow \not{F}$

Focus on the left side of the contrapositive chains.

$1.b. + 2.b. = F \rightarrow \not{A} \rightarrow C$
$4.b. + 5.b. = C \rightarrow E \rightarrow \not{D}$

These chains can be added to form:

$F \rightarrow \not{A} \rightarrow C \rightarrow E \rightarrow \not{D}$

After you cross out all the initial chains you wrote down that you did not combine, you see that you have only one remaining: 3.b.: $\not{B} \rightarrow C$. This can be added to the preceding chain:

C.
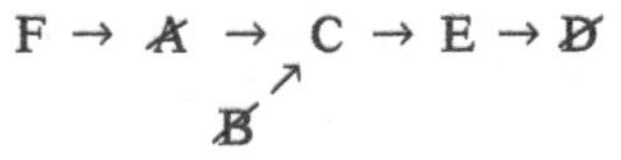

Form the final logic map. You now have two meta-chains that can be used to solve the game:

B.
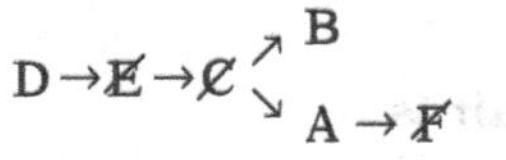

C.
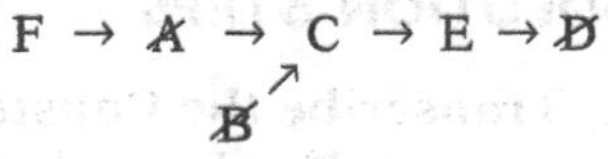

It is also important to notice that these chains are each other's contrapositives.

3. Determine the Implications of the Logic Map. Each logic map has its tricks that you should alert yourself to before solving the questions. In this one, for instance, in diagram C, you should realize that if Frank is in, that does not mean that Ben is out just because Ben resides to the right of Frank in the chain. Ben and Frank are not causally connected in any way, and it is important for you to realize this.

Answering the Questions

Question 1: Which of the following could be a group of fish that are placed into the aquarium?

(B) Garry, Chris, Evan, and Frank all could be in the tank together.

Question 2: Which fish could be present in the aquarium regardless of the presence of any other fish?

(E) The only fish that is not connected by a constraint is Garry.

Question 3: What is the maximum number of fish that can be present in the aquarium?

(C) In diagram C, you can have four fish in the aquarium. Also, diagram B shows that fish Ben can be in the aquarium and not affect the rest of the variables. When you add Garry to these fish, you get five fish in total.

Question 4: If Ben is in the aquarium, then which fish must be out of the aquarium?

(E) The answer is "none of the above," since Ben, when in the aquarium, does not affect the rest of the variables (see diagram B).

Question 5: If Chris is out of the aquarium, then which of the following must be true?

(B) According to diagram B, if Chris is out of the aquarium, then Anna and Ben must be in and Frank must be out.

Question 6: If Frank is in the aquarium, then which of the following must NOT be true?

(C) Frank's being in the aquarium means Anna and Dana must be out and requires that Chris and Evan be in. Therefore, Chris cannot be out of the aquarium.

FORMAL LOGIC GAME 4

A group of singers is chosen from a group of applicants. However, in order to accentuate the attributes of the future singing group, some applicants must be selected along with other applicants. The following constraints apply to the singers who are chosen from the group of applicants named Anna, Ben, Chris, Dana, Evan, Frank, Garry, and Hillary:

If Hillary is not chosen, then Evan is chosen.
If Dana is chosen, then Frank, Chris, and Anna are chosen.
If Garry is chosen, then Evan is not chosen.
If Anna is chosen, then Ben, Frank, and Garry are chosen.

1. Which of the following could be a complete list of the singers who are chosen?

(A) Anna, Frank, Garry, Hillary
(B) Garry, Evan, Hillary
(C) Dana, Frank, Anna, Ben, Garry, Hillary
(D) Evan, Anna, Hillary, Frank
(E) Ben, Frank, Garry, Hillary

2. If Garry is not chosen, then which of the following could be true?

(A) Ben and Anna are chosen.
(B) Chris and Frank are chosen.
(C) Dana and Ben are chosen.
(D) Dana and Hillary are chosen.
(E) Evan is not chosen and neither is Hillary.

3. If Evan is selected, then which of the following is the complete group who must NOT be chosen?

(A) Anna, Garry, Dana
(B) Dana, Chris, Anna, Garry
(C) Frank, Ben, Anna, Garry, Dana
(D) Frank, Ben, Anna, Garry, Dana, Chris
(E) Hillary, Frank, Ben, Anna, Garry, Dana, Chris

4. How many people at most could be chosen for the singing group?

(A) four
(B) five
(C) six
(D) seven
(E) eight

5. If Frank is selected, then which of the following could NOT be true?

(A) Anna is chosen.
(B) Anna is not chosen.
(C) Dana is selected and Hillary is not chosen.
(D) Chris is selected and Evan is chosen.
(E) Ben is selected and Garry is not chosen.

6. If Evan is selected, then who could NOT be chosen?

(A) Hillary
(B) Chris
(C) Dana
(D) Frank
(E) Ben

SOLUTION STEPS

1. Transcribe the Constraints

1.	a. $\not{H} \rightarrow E$	b. $\not{E} \rightarrow H$
2.	a. $D \rightarrow F$	b. $\not{F} \rightarrow \not{D}$
3.	a. $D \rightarrow C$	b. $\not{C} \rightarrow \not{D}$
4.	a. $D \rightarrow A$	b. $\not{A} \rightarrow \not{D}$
5.	a. $G \rightarrow \not{E}$	b. $E \rightarrow \not{G}$
6.	a. $A \rightarrow B$	b. $\not{B} \rightarrow \not{A}$
7.	a. $A \rightarrow F$	b. $\not{F} \rightarrow \not{A}$
8.	a. $A \rightarrow G$	b. $\not{G} \rightarrow \not{A}$

2. Add Logic Chains Together. *Combine all similar sufficient conditions.* If you combine all sufficient conditions in both the sufficient-necessary and the contrapositive chains, then you will get these chains:

A.
```
   ↗ C
D → F
   ↘ A
```

B.
```
   ↗ G
A → B
   ↘ F
```

C.
```
   ↗ A̸
F̸ → D̸
```

The question arises: "Why not just combine the constraints seen in 2.a., 3.a., and 4.a. (logic chain A) before even transcribing them?" The answer is that if you do this, you can easily forget to make their contrapositives in 2.b., 3.b., and 4.b., which could be vitally important in other parts of the chain that are yet to be visualized or constructed.

Notice that chains A and B can be added:

D.
```
   ↗ C
D → F
  ↘    ↗ G
     A → B
       ↘ F
```

You should eliminate repetitive constraints, since D → F and D → A → F:

```
D.      ↗ C
     D
      ↘  ↗ G
        A → B
          ↘ F
```

Focus on the left side of the sufficient-necessary chains.

5.a. + 1.b. = G → E̸ → H

Notice that this can be added to your previous logic chain:

```
D.      ↗ C
     D
      ↘  ↗ G → E̸ → H
        A → B
          ↘ F
```

Focus on the left side of the contrapositive chains.

1.a. + 5.b. + 8.b. + 4.b. = H̸ → E → G̸ → A̸ → D̸
4.b. + C = F̸ → A̸ → D̸*

*It is important to learn this type of transition. You were told that F̸ → D̸, F̸ → A̸, and A̸ → D̸. F̸ → D̸ is an unnecessary piece of information that you should weed out of your drawing, since you know that F̸ → A̸ and A̸ → D̸, or F̸ → A̸ → D̸.

Nothing else can be added together as far as sufficient conditions go. So you could either just remember your extra contrapositives or add them. Many times it is good to just add them even though there are often no direct causal links between all variables in the diagram. Your second diagram should look as follows:

```
E.             B̸
                ↘
   H̸ → E → G̸ → A̸ → D̸
              ↗     ↗
            F̸     C̸
```

Form the final logic map.

The final diagram is equivalent to your two main diagrams that have been consolidated with all the variable chains:

```
D.      ↗ C
     D
      ↘  ↗ G → E̸ → H
        A → B
          ↘ F

E.             B̸
                ↘
   H̸ → E → G̸ → A̸ → D̸
              ↗     ↗
            F̸     C̸
```

3. Determine the Implications of the Logic Map. Sit back for a second to take a look at both diagrams and try to assimilate exactly what they mean. In diagram E, realize that if Frank is out, then Anna and Dana are also out but that we know nothing about Chris. In the same vein, if you know that Garry is out, then you know nothing about Ben, Frank, or Chris, but you do know the configurations of Anna and Dana.

Answering the Questions

Question 1: Which of the following could be a complete list of the singers who are chosen?

(E) In diagram D, you see that Ben, Frank, Garry, and Hillary could all be chosen.

Question 2: If Garry is not chosen, then which of the following could be true?

(B) In diagram E, you see that if Garry is not chosen, then Anna and Dana are also not chosen. You know nothing about Chris, Frank, and Ben. You know that either Hillary or Evan or both must be chosen. All other answer choices have contradictions in them.

Question 3: If Evan is chosen, then which of the following is the complete group who must NOT be chosen?

(A) If Evan is chosen, then you know that Anna, Garry, and Dana are not chosen.

Question 4: How many people at most could be chosen for the singing group?

(D) In diagram D, you see that seven people could be chosen. If you did not accurately eliminate the excess constraints in your diagram or if you have several representations of the same variable in your diagram, then questions like this one can be a problem.

Question 5: If Frank is chosen, then which of the following could NOT be true?

(C) Frank's being chosen tells you nothing about the rest of the game. Therefore, you must look for a contradiction in one of the answer choices to provide the correct answer. You see from diagram D that if Dana is chosen, then Hillary must also be chosen.

Question 6: If Evan is chosen, then who could NOT be chosen?

(C) If Evan is chosen, then diagram E tells us that Garry, Anna, and Dana all cannot be chosen.

On Your Own

Now work through these games on your own in order to practice and put to use the principles you were introduced to earlier in this chapter.

FORMAL LOGIC GAME 5

A number of bandits need to hole up in their hideout. The problem is that, as with many criminal groups, there are a number of personality conflicts that disallow certain members of the bandit group from being in the hideout at the same time as certain other members. The personality issues of the bandits Anna, Ben, Chris, Dana, Evan, Frank, Garry, and Hillary are illuminated by the following constraints:

If Dana is in the hideout, then Evan is in the hideout.
If Evan is not in the hideout, then Anna is in the hideout.
If Ben is not in the hideout, then Chris is not in the hideout.
If Frank is in the hideout, then Hillary is not in the hideout.
If Anna is not in the hideout, then Ben is in the hideout.

1. Which of the following could be a complete list of the bandits in the hideout?
   (A) Anna, Evan, Frank, Hillary
   (B) Frank, Dana, Chris, Ben
   (C) Evan, Hillary, Dana, Anna
   (D) Hillary, Ben, Evan, Chris, Frank
   (E) None of the above

2. Who could be the only person in the hideout?
   (A) Anna
   (B) Ben
   (C) Evan
   (D) Hillary
   (E) Garry

3. If there are seven people in the hideout, then who could potentially be outside of the hideout?
   (A) Garry
   (B) Frank
   (C) Anna
   (D) Dana
   (E) Chris

4. If Anna is not in the hideout, then which of the following must be true?
   (A) Dana is not in the hideout.
   (B) Evan is not in the hideout.
   (C) Ben must be in the hideout.
   (D) Chris is not in the hideout.
   (E) None of the above.

5. If Dana and Chris are in the hideout, then who could be outside of the hideout?
   (A) Anna and Evan
   (B) Ben and Garry
   (C) Evan and Ben
   (D) Hillary and Frank
   (E) None of the above

6. If Frank must be in the hideout when Anna or Ben is in the hideout, then which of the following must be true?
   (A) Chris is never outside of the hideout.
   (B) Chris and Ben are always in the hideout.
   (C) Hillary is never in the hideout.
   (D) Dana and Evan are always in the hideout.
   (E) None of the above.

FORMAL LOGIC GAME 6

Eight fighter pilots flying over the Amazon notice some hostile activity taking place on a sugar plantation. To peaceably resolve the conflict, they land their planes and decide that it would be best to send those pilots who would best complement each other as negotiators to talk to the warring parties. The pilots Anna, Ben, Chris, Dana, Evan, Frank, Garry, and Hillary are chosen as negotiators according to the following conditions:

Anna is chosen if Ben is chosen.
If Garry is not chosen, then Anna and Frank are chosen.
Ben and Hillary are chosen if Anna is chosen.
If Frank is not chosen, then Garry is chosen.
If Hillary is not chosen, then Evan is chosen.
If Chris is not chosen, then Dana is not chosen, and if Dana is not chosen, then Chris is not chosen.

1. Which of the following could be a complete group of the negotiators?
   (A) Frank, Anna, Hillary, Ben
   (B) Garry, Dana, Chris
   (C) Evan, Anna, Hillary, Frank
   (D) Anna, Ben, Frank, Garry
   (E) None of the above

2. Who could be sent to negotiate alone?
   (A) Garry
   (B) Anna
   (C) Chris
   (D) Dana
   (E) None of the above

3. What is the greatest number of pilots that could be sent to negotiate?
   (A) four
   (B) five
   (C) six
   (D) seven
   (E) eight

4. If Garry is not sent to negotiate, then which of the following is a complete and accurate list of pilots who must be sent to negotiate?
   (A) Frank, Anna, Evan, Hillary, Ben
   (B) Anna, Ben, Hillary, Frank
   (C) Hillary, Ben, Anna, Chris, Dana
   (D) Hillary, Chris, Dana, Ben, Anna, Frank
   (E) None of the above

5. If Hillary is not sent to negotiate, then which of the following must NOT be true?
   (A) Frank is sent to negotiate.
   (B) Evan is sent to negotiate.
   (C) Ben is sent to negotiate.
   (D) Garry is sent to negotiate.
   (E) None of the above.

6. Which pair of pilots cannot be sent to negotiate if Ben does not negotiate?
   (A) Anna and Hillary
   (B) Garry and Frank
   (C) Evan and Hillary
   (D) Garry and Evan
   (E) None of the above

FORMAL LOGIC GAME 7

At a conference about corporate governance in data technology companies, a series of speakers is selected from the group of Anna, Ben, Chris, Dana, Evan, Frank, and Garry in order to start engaging discussions that would interest the crowd. The speakers who are selected are determined by the following constraints:

If Evan speaks, then Dana does not speak.
If Frank does not speak, then Dana speaks.
If Chris does not speak, then Ben does not speak.
If Frank speaks, then Anna speaks.
If Dana speaks, then Ben speaks.

1. Which of the following could be a complete series of speakers?

(A) Evan, Frank, Anna
(B) Dana, Chris, Evan
(C) Anna, Frank, Ben, Dana
(D) Frank, Anna, Ben
(E) Frank, Ben, Chris, Evan

2. What is the greatest number of speakers that could speak at the conference?

(A) four
(B) five
(C) six
(D) seven
(E) eight

3. If Evan speaks, then which of the following could be true?

(A) Frank and Dana speak.
(B) Ben and Chris speak.
(C) Garry and Dana speak.
(D) Neither Anna nor Garry speaks.
(E) Neither Chris nor Frank speaks.

4. If Frank does not speak, then which of the following could NOT be true?

(A) Ben speaks with Anna.
(B) Garry speaks with Anna.
(C) Evan speaks with Chris.
(D) Ben speaks with Dana.
(E) Dana speaks and Garry does not speak.

5. Which of the following people could be the only two speakers at the conference?

(A) Garry and Frank
(B) Ben and Chris
(C) Evan and Anna
(D) Garry and Chris
(E) Anna and Frank

6. If Ben does not speak, then which of the following must be true?

(A) Garry speaks with Anna.
(B) Frank does not speak, but Evan does speak.
(C) Anna speaks, but Dana does not speak.
(D) Garry and Evan both speak.
(E) Dana and Frank both speak.

FORMAL LOGIC GAME 8

Eight pilots want to be in the group chosen to go and monitor the latest hurricane crossing over Florida. The Florida politicians realize that it is dangerous to let pilots fly so near to storms, but they would like the information about the storms that the pilots would be able to recover. Pilots Anna, Ben, Chris, Dana, Evan, Frank, Garry, and Hillary are brave enough to volunteer for the job. Whether or not they are chosen depends on the following constraints:

Dana is chosen if Chris is chosen.
If Garry is chosen, then Hillary is not chosen.
Frank is not chosen if Anna is not chosen.
If Ben is not chosen, then Evan is chosen.
Garry is chosen if Evan is chosen.
If Dana is chosen, then Anna is not chosen.

1. Which of the following could be a list of the pilots chosen for the job?

(A) Frank, Anna, Chris, Dana
(B) Evan, Garry, Anna, Chris
(C) Ben, Frank, Hillary, Dana
(D) Hillary, Ben, Evan, Garry
(E) Ben, Garry, Dana, Chris

2. If Ben is not chosen, then which of the following must be true?

(A) Frank and Anna are chosen.
(B) Dana and Chris are chosen.
(C) Garry and Anna are chosen.
(D) Evan and Garry are chosen.
(E) Hillary and Anna are chosen.

3. At least how many pilots must fly to check on the storm?

(A) one
(B) two
(C) three
(D) four
(E) five

4. If Hillary goes and checks on the storm, then who else could go to check on the storm with her?

(A) Dana, Chris, Evan
(B) Garry, Frank, Evan
(C) Frank, Anna, Ben
(D) Anna, Chris, Ben
(E) Dana, Garry, Ben

5. What is the greatest number of pilots that could go and check on the storm?

(A) four
(B) five
(C) six
(D) seven
(E) eight

6. If Anna does not go to check on the storm, then which of the following must NOT be true?

(A) Evan and Hillary go to check on the storm.
(B) Chris and Dana go to check on the storm.
(C) Ben and Hillary go to check on the storm.
(D) Neither Chris nor Dana goes to check on the storm.
(E) Neither Evan nor Garry goes to check on the storm.

Game 5

Initial Setup:

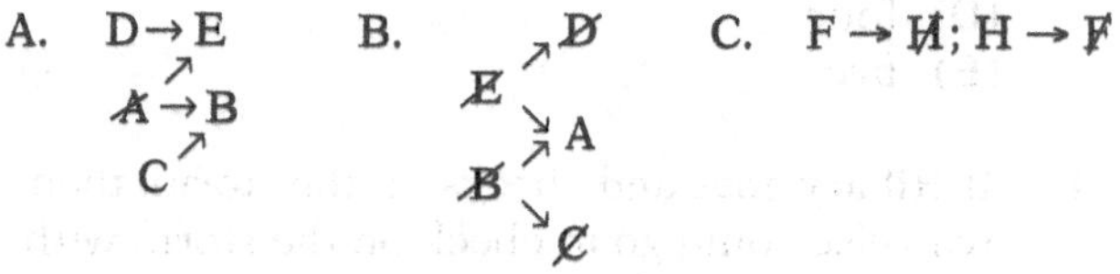

Question 1: Which of the following could be a complete list of the bandits in the hideout?

(C) Dana, Evan, Hillary, and Anna could all be in the hideout at the same time.

(A) Frank and Hillary cannot be in the hideout at the same time.

(B) If Dana is in, then Evan also has to be in.

(D) Frank and Hillary cannot be in the hideout at the same time.

(E) **C** is the correct answer.

Question 2: Who could be the only person in the hideout?

(A) Anna could be the only person in the hideout, as shown in diagram B. While Frank and Hillary cannot be in the hideout at the same time, they can be out at the same time.

(B) If Evan is out, then Anna is in.

(C) If Ben is out, then Anna is in.

(D, E) If Evan or Ben is out, then Anna must be in. This means that Anna must accompany Hillary or Garry so long as either Evan or Ben is out. Therefore, we know **A** must be the correct answer.

Question 3: If there are seven people in the hideout, then who could potentially be outside of the hideout?

(B) The answer to this is Frank or Hillary. They cannot be in the hideout together, and there are only eight people in the game, so one of these two must be out.

Question 4: If Anna is not in the hideout, then which of the following must be true?

(C) If Anna is not in the hideout, then according to diagram A, Evan and Ben must be in the hideout.

Question 5: If Dana and Chris are in the hideout, then who could be outside of the hideout?

(D) According to diagram A, Evan and Ben must be in the hideout. Therefore, Anna, Garry, Frank, or Hillary could be out.

(A) Evan must be in.
(B) Ben must be in.
(C) Evan and Ben must be in.
(E) **D** is the correct answer.

Question 6: If Frank must be in the hideout when Anna or Ben is in the hideout, then which of the following must be true?

(C) This question adds a constraint to the game, and you should add marks to your diagrams to represent this additional constraint. It is generally not wise to add marks directly to your diagram from individual questions, since these question-constraints will not influence the game aside from that one question. Many people still mark the question-constraint in pencil and then erase it after the question is over. Here is what your diagram would look like:

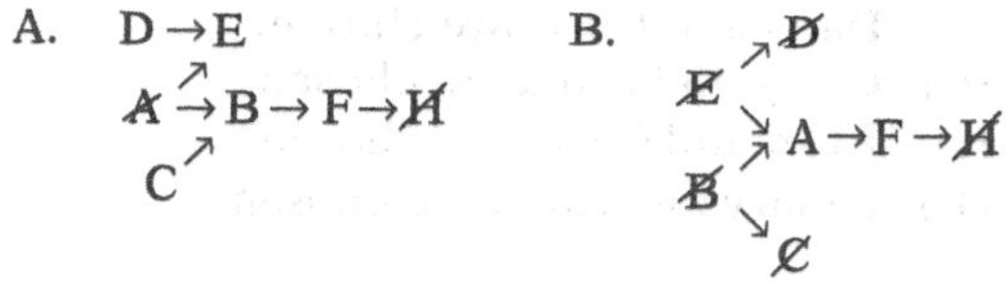

You see in both scenarios that Frank must be in the hideout and Hillary must be out of the hideout.

(A) Negation possible in diagram B.
(B) Negation possible in diagram B.
(D) Negation possible in diagram B.
(E) **C** is the correct answer.

Game 6

Initial Setup:

This game introduces the idea of **reciprocal causation**. For example, the constraint that says "If A, then B, and if B, then A" should be transcribed in one of the following two ways, based on the configurations of the other variables in the diagram:

1. B⟷A 2. A⟷B

You will run into reciprocal causation in the final constraint of this logic game.

Here are the final diagrams that you should create:

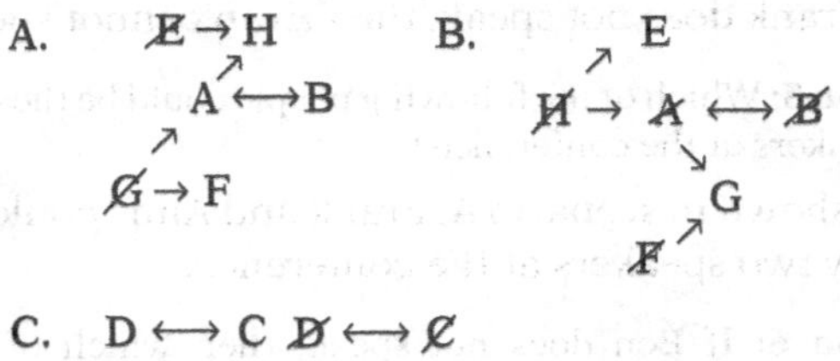

Notice how the reciprocal causation constraints are diagrammed. Be aware of the implications of these constraints. For instance, if Ben is not sent (diagram B), then Anna cannot be sent and Garry must be sent. In diagram A, if Ben is sent, then Anna and Hillary are sent.

Question 1: Which of the following could be a complete group of the negotiators?

(A) Frank, Anna, Hillary, and Ben could all be sent.

(B) If Hillary is not sent, then Evan must be sent.
(C) If Anna is sent, then Ben must be sent.
(D) If Anna is sent, then Hillary must be sent.
(E) **A** is the correct answer.

Question 2: Who could be sent to negotiate alone?

(E) None of the other choices is correct.

(A) If Hillary is not sent, Evan must be sent, which means that Garry cannot be sent alone.
(B) If Anna is sent, Ben must also be sent.
(C) If Chris is sent, Dana must also be sent.
(D) If Dana is sent, Chris must also be sent.

Question 3: What is the greatest number of pilots that could be sent to negotiate?

(E) It is possible, using diagrams A and C, to see that all eight plots could be sent to negotiate.

Question 4: If Garry is not sent to negotiate, then which of the following is a complete and accurate list of pilots who must be sent to negotiate?

(B) If Garry is not sent, then diagram A demonstrates that Hillary, Anna, Frank, and Ben must be sent to negotiate.

Question 5: If Hillary is not sent to negotiate, then which of the following must NOT be true?

(C) If Hillary is not sent, then Evan and Garry must be sent, but Anna and Ben must not be sent. You know nothing about whether or not Frank is sent.

(A) You know nothing about what Frank must do.
(B) This must be true.
(D) This must be true.
(E) **C** is the correct answer.

Question 6: Which pair of pilots could not be sent to negotiate if Ben does not negotiate?

(A) If Ben is not sent then diagram B shows that Anna also must not be sent. Clearly, then, Anna and Hillary cannot be sent together.

(B) Garry and Frank can be sent together.
(C) Evan and Hillary can be sent together.
(D) Garry and Evan can be sent together.
(E) **A** is the correct answer.

Game 7

Initial Setup:

Your logic maps should correspond to the following:

A.

E ↘

~~C~~ → ~~B~~ → ~~D~~ → F → A

B.

↗ ~~E~~

~~A~~ → ~~F~~ → D → B → C

Question 1: Which of the following could be the complete group of speakers?

(A) As shown in diagram A, Evan, Frank, and Anna could be the complete group of speakers.

(B) Ben has to speak if Dana does.
(C) Chris has to speak if Ben does.
(D) Chris has to speak if Ben does.
(E) Anna has to speak if Frank speaks.

Question 2: What is the greatest number of speakers that could speak at the conference?

(C) In both scenarios, at least one person cannot speak each time. Therefore, when you add Garry, a total of six people can speak at the conference.

Question 3: If Evan speaks, then which of the following could be true?

(B) If Evan speaks, then Dana does not speak and Frank and Anna do speak. However, Ben and Chris could also speak, since they are to the left in the logic chain.

(A) Dana cannot speak if Evan speaks.
(C) Dana cannot speak if Evan speaks.
(D) Anna must speak if Evan speaks.
(E) Frank speaks if Evan speaks.

Question 4: If Frank does not speak, then which of the following could NOT be true?

(C) If Frank does not speak, then Evan cannot speak.

Question 5: Which of the following people could be the only two speakers at the conference?

(E) As shown in scenario A, Frank and Anna could be the only two speakers at the conference.

Question 6: If Ben does not speak, then which of the following must be true?

(C) If Ben does not speak, then Dana does not speak but Frank and Anna do.

Game 8

Initial Setup:

Your logic map should resemble the following:

1. a. $C \rightarrow D \rightarrow \not{A} \rightarrow \not{F}$ b. $F \rightarrow A \rightarrow \not{D} \rightarrow \not{C}$
2. a. $\not{B} \rightarrow E \rightarrow G \rightarrow \not{H}$ b. $H \rightarrow \not{G} \rightarrow \not{E} \rightarrow B$

Question 1: Which of the following could be a list of the pilots chosen for the job?

(E) See diagrams 2.b. and 1.a.

(A) If Anna is chosen, then neither Dana nor Chris can be chosen.
(B) If Anna is chosen, then Chris cannot be chosen.
(C) If Dana is chosen, then Frank cannot be chosen.
(D) If Hillary is chosen, then neither Garry nor Evan can be chosen.

Question 2: If Ben is not chosen, then which of the following must be true?

(D) Diagram 2.a. demonstrates that if Ben is not chosen, then Evan and Garry must be chosen and Hillary must not be chosen.

Question 3: At least how many pilots must fly to check on the storm?

(A) None of the pilots from the Chris, Dana, Anna, or Frank logic chain has to go. However, either Ben or both Evan and Garry have to go from the other chain.

Question 4: If Hillary goes and checks on the storm, then who else could go to check on the storm with her?

(C) Based on diagrams 1.b. and 2.b., if Hillary goes out into the storm, then neither Garry nor Evan could go with her.

(A) Evan cannot go if Hillary goes.
(B) Neither Garry nor Evan can go if Hillary goes.
(D) Anna cannot go if Chris goes.
(E) Garry cannot go if Hillary goes.

Question 5: What is the greatest number of pilots who could go and check on the storm?

(B) Chris and Dana or Frank and Anna can go from diagrams 1.a. and 1.b. In diagram 2.a., Ben, Evan, and Garry could go. This makes five people.

Question 6: If Anna does not go to check on the storm, then which of the following must NOT be true?

If Anna does not check on the storm, then Frank cannot check on the storm. This is not much information, so you will have to look for a contradiction in the constraints for the answer to this question.

(A) Evan and Hillary can never go to check on the storm together.

CHAPTER 2

SEQUENCING GAMES

Sequencing logic games should be relatively simple now that you have learned the ins and outs of diagramming sufficient-necessary constraints. Sequencing games require you to answer questions about the order in which the variables in the fact pattern will occur based on a series of constraints.

Typical Fact Pattern

> Six teenagers named Anna, Ben, Chris, Dana, Evan, and Frank are in line for the movies on Sunday night. They wait one behind another in line to get into the show, and their order is determined by the following:
>
> Anna is third in line.
> Ben is in line before Anna.
> Evan is in line after Dana and before Frank.
> Frank is in line after Chris.

This question stem introduces the idea of *direct placement*. In this kind of constraint, the game tells you exactly where Anna will always be, so you can note this by writing A = 3. The rest of the constraints should be transcribed in the same way you described them for the formal logic games. However, you should be sure to take two additional precautions with sequencing games:

1. Write either *all* "greater than" signs or *all* "less than" signs. Do not write both types of signs when transcribing, since that would inevitably confuse you.
2. Make sure that you get the *overall direction* of the variables correct. Otherwise, you will answer questions with the wrong directional reference and get almost all of them wrong.

The constraints above should be transcribed in the following fashion:

1. A = 3
2. B < A
3. D < E
4. E < F
5. C < F

Logic Tools

Sequencing Constraints

Sequencing constraints are similar to sufficient-necessary constraints in that they read in a definite direction, but they are much easier to work with, since you do not have to form contrapositives when interpreting them. When diagramming sequencing constraints, make it a habit to draw the constraints in one consistent way. We recommend using all "less than" symbols (<) and writing the variables before and after the "less than" symbols immediately after you read the constraint. This way you will draw diagrams with a certain number of consistencies that you can rely on, including the direction of the variables and the overall direction of the game.

Logic Chain Addition

In sequencing games, you can add logic chains just as you added them with sufficient-necessary constraints. Here is how this works for the constraints transcribed above:

A. 1. + 2. = B < A = 3
B. 3. + 4. = D < E < F
C. B + 5. = D < E < F
                    C ↗

These three diagrams will help you solve any questions that refer to this fact pattern. The left side of the diagram represents those people who are positioned in line *before* those referred to on the right side. If you had inconsistent symbols ("greater than" mixed with "less than" symbols), then making any assumptions on the basis of the overall diagram would be very difficult. It is important to note the limitations of this diagram: C is in line before F, but you do not know if D or E is in line before C. C could be first in line, for all you know.

Fact Pattern Organization Heuristics

Sequencing logic games have a heuristic that is very similar to that of formal logic games but much less complicated.

1. **Transcribe** the constraints in the fact pattern.
   a. Make sure to use all "less than" signs.
   b. Reconcile the direction of your diagrams with the direction of the fact pattern and questions.
2. Use **logic chain addition** to consolidate the constraints.
   a. Combine similar variables.
   b. Form the final logic map.
3. Determine the **implications** of your logic map.

Review

In this section, you have learned all of the following:

1. How to transcribe sequencing constraints.
2. How to ensure that the direction of your diagram is consistent and corresponds with the direction of the fact pattern.
3. How to add sequencing variables into logic chains.
4. The appropriate fact pattern organization heuristic for sequencing games.

Using this knowledge and what you learned about diagramming from the formal logic chapter, you will now practice solving four sequencing games. Take your time initially; you will speed up naturally as you gain mastery of these techniques.

Sequencing Games Explained

SEQUENCING GAME I

Eight people—Anna, Ben, Chris, Dana, Evan, Frank, Garry, and Hillary—are standing in line for the Ferris wheel at a local fair. Standing before someone in line denotes being closer to the beginning of the line, or earlier in line, than the other person. The order of the people in line can fluctuate, but only according to the following constraints:

> Hillary stands before Anna but after Dana.
> Garry stands after Dana.
> Evan stands after Anna.
> Chris stands before Dana and Frank.
> Ben stands before Anna.

1. Which of the following could be the order of the line?
   - (A) Ben, Chris, Dana, Hillary, Anna, Evan, Garry, Frank.
   - (B) Chris, Hillary, Dana, Anna, Evan, Ben, Garry, Frank.
   - (C) Chris, Frank, Dana, Hillary, Garry, Anna, Ben, Evan.
   - (D) Ben, Chris, Dana, Garry, Hillary, Evan, Frank, Anna.
   - (E) None of the above.

2. How many people could be third in line?
   - (A) three
   - (B) four
   - (C) five
   - (D) six
   - (E) seven

3. Which of the following is the earliest position that Anna could hold in the line?
   - (A) third
   - (B) fourth
   - (C) fifth
   - (D) sixth
   - (E) seventh

4. Which people could stand consecutively in line before *or* after Hillary?
   - (A) Chris, Anna
   - (B) Ben, Chris
   - (C) Evan, Dana
   - (D) Frank, Garry
   - (E) None of the above

5. If Garry is third in line, then which of the following must be true?
   - (A) Frank is fourth.
   - (B) Ben is fifth.
   - (C) Hillary is fifth.
   - (D) Evan is last.
   - (E) None of the above.

6. If Frank, Ben, and Garry are in line consecutively (Frank, Ben, Garry—Garry, Frank, Ben—Frank, Garry, Ben—Garry, Ben, Frank—etc.) then which of the following must be true?
   - (A) Ben stands consecutively with Frank or Anna.
   - (B) Garry stands after Anna and Dana.
   - (C) Hillary stands consecutively with Dana or Anna.
   - (D) Hillary stands sixth in line or fourth in line.
   - (E) None of the above.

SOLUTION STEPS

1. Transcribe the Constraints. *Use only "less than" signs.* When transcribing sufficient-necessary constraints, you would break up compound constraints such as "Chris stands before Dana and Frank" so that you could diagram the contrapositives of both individual statements. However, this is not necessary in sequencing games.

1. D < H < A
2. D < G
3. A < E
4.
```
     F
  C <
  C <
     D
```
5. B < A

Reconcile the direction of the diagram.

Earlier in line < Later in line

2. Add Logic Chains Together. These chains can be added to form one large, relatively simple logic map that encompasses the entire game:

```
  F   G
 <   <
C < D < H < A < E
           B<
```

3. Determine the Implications of the Logic Map. This logic map describes the constraints governing the placement of eight people waiting in line. As you solve the problem, it may help to keep in mind the following diagram as well:

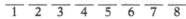

1	2	3	4	5	6	7	8

In order to get a feel for the game, ask yourself: Who must be first in line? (Chris or Ben) Who must be last? (Frank, Garry, or Evan)

Answering the Questions

Question 1: Which of the following could be the order of the line?

(A) This could be the order of the line.

(B) Dana must go before Hillary.
(C) Ben must go before Anna.
(D) Anna must go before Evan.
(E) A is the answer.

Question 2: How many people could be third in line?

(C) There are a number of people who could be third in line, so it might be better to start by asking yourself, "Who could not be third?" Anna and Evan cannot be third because at least three people have to be before them in the line. Chris cannot be third because everyone but Ben has to be after him in the line. It appears that anyone else could be third, out of the five people who have not been eliminated.

Question 3: Which of the following is the earliest position that Anna could hold in the line?

(C) Looking at your diagram, it is clear that Chris, Dana, Hillary, and Ben all must precede Anna in the line. Therefore, her earliest position is fifth.

Question 4: Which people could stand consecutively in line with Hillary?

(D) It is clear that Dana and Anna could stand consecutively with her. However, you should also realize that Frank, Garry, and Ben could also stand next to her.

Question 5: If Garry is third in the line, then which of the following must be true?

This is where you should use your linear diagram:

C D G _ _ _ _ _

(E) You know nothing about the game except for the first three places.

Question 6: If Frank, Ben, and Garry are in line consecutively, then which of the following must be true?

There are two scenarios in which this could occur:

A.

C	D				H	A	E
1	2	3	4	5	6	7	8

B.

C	D	H				A	E
1	2	3	4	5	6	7	8

In both scenarios, Chris and Dana are first and second and Anna and Evan are seventh and eighth, respectively. Ben, Garry, and Frank can be in any order in the middle of the diagram.

(C) Hillary in both diagrams stands consecutively with Anna or Dana.

SEQUENCING GAME 2

Eight astronauts—Anna, Ben, Chris, Dana, Evan, Frank, Garry, and Hillary—are all vying for positions to be on the next mission to the moon. The head of NASA has analyzed the attributes of each individual astronaut and has made a list of the order of people to whom he will offer the mission. The order of the list is determined by the following constraints:

Garry is after Anna.
Chris is after Dana.
Ben is before Hillary.
Frank is before Anna and Dana.
Ben is after Garry and Chris.
Evan is before Frank.

1. Which of the following could be a list of the astronauts from first to last?

(A) Anna, Evan, Frank, Garry, Dana, Chris, Ben, Hillary.
(B) Evan, Dana, Frank, Chris, Anna, Garry, Ben, Hillary.
(C) Hillary, Ben, Chris, Dana, Garry, Anna, Frank, Evan.
(D) Evan, Frank, Dana, Anna, Garry, Chris, Ben, Hillary.
(E) Anna, Garry, Evan, Frank, Dana, Chris, Ben, Hillary.

2. If Garry is fourth on the list, then which of the following must be true?

(A) Frank is third.
(B) Dana is fifth.
(C) Anna is second.
(D) Ben is sixth.
(E) Chris is fifth.

3. If Dana is fourth on the list, then which of the following must be true?

(A) Garry is fifth.
(B) Anna is third.
(C) Chris is sixth.
(D) Ben is eighth.
(E) Frank is third.

4. We know the exact positions of how many astronauts on the list?

(A) two
(B) four
(C) six
(D) eight
(E) None of the above

5. Which of the following pairs of astronauts could be sixth?

(A) Chris or Anna
(B) Dana or Garry
(C) Chris or Ben
(D) Ben or Hillary
(E) Chris or Garry

6. If Dana is not consecutive on the list with Frank or Garry, then which of the following must be true?

(A) Chris is fifth.
(B) Garry is fourth.
(C) Anna is fourth.
(D) Ben is fifth.
(E) Frank is third.

SOLUTION STEPS

1. Transcribe the Constraints. *Use only "less than" signs.* The two combination constraints should be added together initially, but you should realize that often they will be broken apart because they offer repetitive information. For instance, Garry and Chris are before Ben, but you do not need to write out all of this with "less than" symbols if you know that Garry is before Chris. Think about why this is the case and how you should be vigilant to eliminate repetitive information that would confuse your diagram.

1. A < G
2. D < C
3. B < H
4. 

5. 

6. E < F

Reconcile the direction of the diagram.

Chosen earlier < Chosen later

2. Add Logic Chains Together

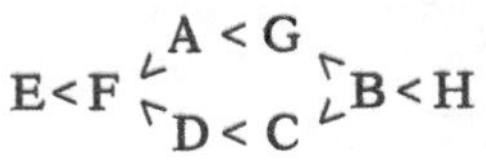

3. Determine the Implications of the Logic Map. The background of this map is once again a numbered line:

1	2	3	4	5	6	7	8

Notice that Evan must always be first and Hillary must always be last. Frank must be second and Ben must be seventh:

E	F					B	H
1	2	3	4	5	6	7	8

ANSWERING THE QUESTIONS

Question 1: Which of the following could be a list of the astronauts from first to last?

(D) This is the correct order.

(A) Evan must be first.
(B) Frank must be second.
(C) Evan must be first.
(E) Evan must be first.

Question 2: If Garry is fourth on the list, then which of the following must be true?

(B) If Garry is fourth, then the following diagram maps the placement of the variables—showing that Dana must be fifth.

E	F	A	G	D	C	B	H
1	2	3	4	5	6	7	8

Question 3: If Dana is fourth on the list, then which of the following must be true?

(B) If Dana is fourth, then Anna must be third.

E	F	A	D			B	H
1	2	3	4	5	6	7	8

Question 4: We know the exact positions of how many astronauts on the list?

(B) As shown by your initial linear diagram, you know four people's positions.

Question 5: Which of the following pairs of astronauts could be sixth?

(E) Only Chris or Garry could be sixth.

Question 6: If Dana is not consecutive on the list with Frank or Garry, then which of the following must be true?

(A) That means that Dana cannot be third, because then she would be consecutive with Frank; therefore, she must be fourth. This makes Anna third. In order not to be consecutive with Garry, Dana must be consecutive with Chris, making Chris fifth.

SEQUENCING GAME 3

Eight penguins named Anna, Ben, Chris, Dana, Evan, Frank, Garry, and Hillary, all waddle down the fake ice at the San Diego zoo. After waddling to the edge of the ice, they all dive into the pool to play a game of underwater chase. The chasing game forms a big underwater line that stays constant for the duration of the game. The order of penguins in the chasing line is governed by the following rules:

Anna is before Dana.
Hillary is after Garry and Ben.
Chris is after Garry.
Dana is before Frank and Evan.
Evan is before Garry and Ben.

1. Which of the following could be the order of the penguins in the chasing line?
   (A) Ben, Anna, Dana, Frank, Evan, Garry, Chris, Hillary.
   (B) Frank, Anna, Dana, Evan, Garry, Ben, Hillary, Chris.
   (C) Anna, Dana, Evan, Frank, Garry, Ben, Hillary, Chris.
   (D) Garry, Evan, Dana, Frank, Anna, Ben, Hillary, Chris.
   (E) Chris, Anna, Dana, Evan, Frank, Garry, Ben, Hillary.

2. How many penguins could be fourth in the line?
   (A) two
   (B) three
   (C) four
   (D) five
   (E) six

3. If Frank goes fifth, then which of the following could NOT be true?
   (A) Ben goes fourth.
   (B) Garry goes sixth.
   (C) Ben goes seventh.
   (D) Garry goes seventh.
   (E) Chris goes seventh.

4. If Chris goes seventh, then which of the following must be true?
   (A) Hillary goes eighth.
   (B) Evan goes third.
   (C) Garry goes sixth.
   (D) Ben goes fourth.
   (E) Dana goes second.

5. If Ben goes after Chris, then which of the following must be true?
   (A) Ben goes seventh.
   (B) Hillary goes eighth.
   (C) Chris goes fifth or sixth.
   (D) Frank goes third or fourth.
   (E) Evan goes fourth or fifth.

6. If Chris is after Frank, then which of the following is the last position that Frank could be in?
   (A) fourth
   (B) fifth
   (C) sixth
   (D) seventh
   (E) eighth

SOLUTION STEPS

1. Transcribe the Constraints. *Use only "less than" signs.*

1. A < D
2. 
3. G < C
4. 
5. 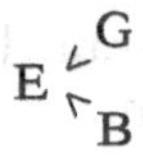

Reconcile the direction of the diagram.

Beginning of line < End of line

2. Add Logic Chains Together

3. Determine the Implications of the Logic Map. The background of this map is once again a numbered line:

___ ___ ___ ___ ___ ___ ___ ___
1 2 3 4 5 6 7 8

Notice that Anna must always be first and Dana must always be second, but Frank, Chris, or Hillary could be last.

Answering the Questions

Question 1: Which of the following could be the order of the penguins in the chasing line?

(C) Anna must be first.

Question 2: How many penguins could be fourth in the line?

(C) Frank, Garry, Ben, or Evan could be fourth in the line.

Question 3: If Frank goes fifth, then which of the following must NOT be true?

The following diagram corresponds to this situation. Notice the introduction of the double possibilities, which we will discuss more in depth in the next chapter:

A	D	E	G	F	C	B	H
1	2	3	4	5	6	7	8

A	D	E	G	F	B	C/H	H/C
1	2	3	4	5	6	7	8

A	D	E	B	F	G	C/H	H/C
1	2	3	4	5	6	7	8

The H/C denotes that either Hillary or Chris could go in that spot. This is called a *double possibility.* If Chris goes there, then Hillary must go in the other spot where the double possibility is in the game.

(D) Garry cannot go seventh in any diagram, because both Hillary and Chris must go after him.

(A) This can happen in the third diagram.
(B) This can happen in the third diagram.
(C) This can happen in the first diagram.
(E) This can happen in either the second or the third diagram.

Question 4: If Chris goes seventh, then which of the following must be true?

(E) If Chris goes seventh, then either Frank or Hillary could go eighth. Hillary, Frank, Garry, or Ben could go sixth. You already know that Anna must go first and Dana must go second.

Question 5: If Ben goes after Chris, then which of the following must be true?

This is a very open-ended question, because it tells you the relative order of several variables but not exactly where they go in the game. The process of elimination is the best method for finding the right answer choice in this situation.

(C) You know that Chris must go fifth or sixth.

(A) Ben could go seventh, but he could also go earlier in the line.
(B) Frank could also go eighth.
(D) Frank could really go anywhere after Dana in the game.
(E) Evan could go third.

Question 6: If Chris is after Frank, then which of the following is the last position that Frank could be in?

(D) The final order could be Hillary, Frank, and then Chris, so Frank could go as far back as seventh in this scenario. Chris is the *only* penguin that has to go after Frank.

SEQUENCING GAME 4

Nine engineers are working on new ideas for nuclear fusion for a power company. Each engineer is well respected in the fusion field, but the power company has only enough money to experiment with a certain number of ideas. Therefore, an executive of the company ranks the tenability of the ideas in order to decide which ones should receive funding. Lower rankings correspond to higher levels of tenability. Therefore, lower rankings are more likely to receive funding. The ideas of the engineers Anna, Ben, Chris, Dana, Evan, Frank, Garry, Hillary, and Iris are ranked according to the following conditions:

Frank's idea is after Garry's and Dana's.
Hillary's idea is after Ben's.
Anna's idea is after Chris's and before Hillary's.
Evan's idea is before Ben's and after Chris's.
Dana's idea is after Ben's.

1. Which of the following could be a ranking of the engineers from those whose ideas are most likely to those whose ideas are least likely to receive funding?
   - (A) Chris, Iris, Evan, Ben, Hillary, Anna, Dana, Garry, Frank.
   - (B) Garry, Chris, Anna, Evan, Iris, Hillary, Dana, Frank, Ben.
   - (C) Iris, Garry, Chris, Anna, Evan, Ben, Hillary, Dana, Frank.
   - (D) Chris, Evan, Ben, Anna, Hillary, Iris, Garry, Frank, Dana.
   - (E) None of the above.

2. If Dana's idea is ranked fourth, then which of the following must be true?
   - (A) Anna's is fifth.
   - (B) Ben's is third.
   - (C) Frank's is ninth.
   - (D) Hillary's is fifth.
   - (E) None of the above.

3. If Garry's idea is ranked second, then which of the following must be true?
   - (A) Frank's is ninth.
   - (B) Chris's is first.
   - (C) Evan's is fourth.
   - (D) Hillary's is sixth.
   - (E) None of the above.

4. If Iris, Dana, Anna, and Garry have their ideas ranked consecutively, then which of the following must be true?
   - (A) Anna's is ranked fourth, fifth, or sixth.
   - (B) Dana's is ranked sixth or seventh.
   - (C) Ben's is ranked second or fourth.
   - (D) Hillary's is ranked eighth or ninth.
   - (E) None of the above.

5. How many people's ideas could be ranked fifth?
   - (A) five
   - (B) six
   - (C) seven
   - (D) eight
   - (E) nine

6. Of the following, which person's idea has the potential to be ranked in the most positions?
   - (A) Frank
   - (B) Chris
   - (C) Dana
   - (D) Garry
   - (E) Evan

SOLUTION STEPS

1. Transcribe the Constraints. *Use only "less than" signs.*

1. G < F, D < F
2. B < H
3. C < A < H
4. C < E < B
5. B < D

Reconcile the direction of the diagram.

More likely to get funding < Less likely to get funding

2. Add Logic Chains Together

```
   A  <  H
  ↙     ↙
C < E < B < D < F
               ↙
              G
```

3. Determine the Implications of the Logic Map. Notice that there are no constraints on Iris. She could literally be anywhere on the following line:

__ __ __ __ __ __ __ __ __
1 2 3 4 5 6 7 8 9

Answering the Questions

Question 1: Which of the following could be a ranking of the engineers from those whose ideas are most likely to those whose ideas are least likely to receive funding?

(C) This is a possible order.

(A) Anna's must be before Hillary's.
(B) Hillary's must be after Ben's.
(D) Dana's must be before Frank's.
(E) **C** is the answer.

Question 2: If Dana's idea is ranked fourth, then which of the following must be true?

(B) If Dana's idea is ranked fourth, then Chris's must be first, Evan's must be second, and Ben's must be third. Because of the presence of Iris, we cannot really tell about the configuration of the rest of the game, only that her idea is excluded from the first four positions.

Question 3: If Garry's idea is ranked second, then which of the following must be true?

(E) If Garry's idea is second, then Iris's or Chris's must be first and Frank's, Hillary's, or Iris's must be last. We can tell very little about the rest of the game, though.

Question 4: If Iris, Dana, Anna, and Garry have their ideas ranked consecutively, then which of the following must be true?

(D) In this scenario, Frank and Hillary would have to have their ideas ranked eighth and ninth (not necessarily in that order).

Question 5: How many people's ideas could be ranked fifth?

(C) Chris and Frank are the only two people whose ideas could not be ranked fifth. This means that seven people's ideas could be fifth.

Question 6: Of the following, which person's idea has the potential to be ranked in the most positions?

(D) Garry could be in any position except ninth, so he could be in as many or more positions than everyone besides Iris.

(A) Frank could go sixth, seventh, eighth, or ninth.
(B) Chris could go first, second, or third.
(C) Dana could not go in the first, second, third, or ninth position.
(E) Evan could not go in the seventh, eighth, ninth, or first position.

On Your Own

SEQUENCING GAME 5

A scout ant finds a crumb on the floor in a house. She reports back to the anthill and recruits eight worker ants, Anna, Ben, Chris, Dana, Evan, Frank, Garry, and Hillary, to go and retrieve the food. The worker ants walk in a line following the scent of the scout to go retrieve the food. The order of the worker ants is determined by the following constraints:

Chris follows Anna and Hillary.
Anna follows Frank.
Evan, Frank, and Garry follow Dana.
Ben follows Evan.
Hillary follows Garry.

1. Which of the following could be an order of the worker ants from first to last?
   (A) Dana, Frank, Anna, Garry, Evan, Hillary, Chris, Ben.
   (B) Dana, Evan, Ben, Frank, Anna, Garry, Chris, Hillary.
   (C) Chris, Ben, Anna, Hillary, Frank, Evan, Garry, Dana.
   (D) Evan, Ben, Dana, Frank, Garry, Anna, Hillary, Chris.
   (E) Dana, Evan, Ben, Garry, Frank, Hillary, Chris, Anna.

2. How many different ants could be second in line?
   (A) one
   (B) two
   (C) three
   (D) four
   (E) five

3. How many different ants could be third in line?
   (A) four
   (B) five
   (C) six
   (D) seven
   (E) eight

4. What is the earliest position in the line that Chris could hold?
   (A) fourth
   (B) fifth
   (C) sixth
   (D) seventh
   (E) eighth

5. If Frank goes fifth, then which of the following could NOT be true?
   (A) Anna goes seventh and Chris goes eighth.
   (B) Ben goes fourth and Garry goes third.
   (C) Garry goes second and Hillary goes third.
   (D) Evan goes third and Garry goes second.
   (E) Hillary goes sixth and Ben goes seventh.

6. If Garry goes after Ben and Anna, then which of the following must be true?
   (A) Evan goes second.
   (B) Hillary goes seventh.
   (C) Anna goes third.
   (D) Ben goes fifth.
   (E) Frank goes fourth.

SEQUENCING GAME 6

Nine snake charmers named Anna, Ben, Chris, Dana, Evan, Frank, Garry, Hillary, and Iris wait to perform for the king. The king's attendant makes them stand in a line based on their relative charming skills. The charmers with greater skills will go toward the end of the performance. The skills of the charmers and therefore the order that they perform in is determined by the following constraints:

Evan's skills are greater than Garry's, Anna's, and Dana's skills.
Chris's skills are less than Hillary's and Ben's.
Ben's skills are less than Anna's and Dana's.
Hillary's skills are less than Garry's.

1. Which of the following could be the order in which the snake charmers perform?
   (A) Iris, Chris, Hillary, Garry, Ben, Anna, Dana, Evan, Frank.
   (B) Frank, Iris, Chris, Hillary, Garry, Anna, Ben, Dana, Evan.
   (C) Chris, Ben, Iris, Dana, Anna, Evan, Hillary, Garry, Frank.
   (D) Chris, Ben, Anna, Dana, Garry, Hillary, Frank, Iris, Evan.
   (E) None of the above.

2. If Ben performs sixth, then which of the following must be true?
   (A) Dana performs seventh.
   (B) Chris performs first.
   (C) Evan performs ninth.
   (D) Garry performs fifth.
   (E) None of the above.

3. If Frank, Iris, Anna, and Evan perform consecutively, then which of the following must be true?
   (A) Anna performs sixth.
   (B) Evan performs ninth.
   (C) Hillary performs second.
   (D) Garry performs fifth.
   (E) None of the above.

4. How many charmers could potentially perform third?
   (A) four
   (B) five
   (C) fix
   (D) seven
   (E) eight

5. If Garry performs fifth and Ben performs fourth, then which of the following could NOT be true?
   (A) Frank performs seventh and Iris performs sixth.
   (B) Chris performs first and Iris performs third.
   (C) Evan performs eighth and Anna performs sixth.
   (D) Hillary performs second and Dana performs sixth.
   (E) None of the above.

6. If six people perform between Chris's performance and Anna's performance, then which of the following could be true?
   (A) Ben performs seventh.
   (B) Garry performs second.
   (C) Iris performs ninth.
   (D) Hillary performs fifth.
   (E) None of the above.

SEQUENCING GAME 7

Nine caterpillars form a line to crawl up to the leaves in a tree. The caterpillars' names are Anna, Ben, Chris, Dana, Evan, Frank, Garry, Hillary, and Iris. The order of the caterpillars is determined by the brightness of their green fur. Duller-colored caterpillars always travel nearer to the front than brighter-colored caterpillars. The fur color of the caterpillars can be described by the following constraints:

Chris's fur is brighter than Iris's fur.
Evan's fur is brighter than Garry's and Hillary's fur.
Frank's fur is brighter than Ben's fur.
Dana's fur is duller than Ben's fur.
Anna's fur is brighter than Frank's and Chris's fur.
Ben's fur is duller than Garry's fur.

1. Which of the following could be the order of the caterpillars climbing up the tree, from first to last?

   (A) Dana, Ben, Frank, Anna, Iris, Chris, Garry, Hillary, Evan.
   (B) Hillary, Iris, Dana, Ben, Frank, Chris, Anna, Evan, Garry.
   (C) Hillary, Dana, Ben, Frank, Iris, Anna, Chris, Garry, Evan.
   (D) Dana, Ben, Iris, Chris, Frank, Garry, Evan, Hillary, Anna.
   (E) Iris, Chris, Dana, Hillary, Ben, Frank, Anna, Garry, Evan.

2. Which of the following is a pair of caterpillars that could go first and second, in that order?

   (A) Dana, Chris
   (B) Hillary, Iris
   (C) Ben, Frank
   (D) Iris, Ben
   (E) Anna, Evan

3. Which of the following caterpillars could be in any position in the line except for last?

   (A) Chris
   (B) Dana
   (C) Hillary
   (D) Evan
   (E) Iris

4. How many caterpillars could go second in line?

   (A) four
   (B) five
   (C) six
   (D) seven
   (E) eight

5. Which pair of caterpillars could never travel in the line consecutively?

   (A) Iris, Frank
   (B) Hillary, Chris
   (C) Anna, Garry
   (D) Frank, Hillary
   (E) Ben, Evan

6. Which of the following is a complete list of the caterpillars that could go first in the line?

   (A) Dana
   (B) Iris, Hillary
   (C) Hillary, Dana, Iris
   (D) Garry, Dana, Hillary
   (E) Ben, Dana, Iris

SEQUENCING GAME 8

In a political motorcade, the order of the cars is very important, because the more famous people receive the most attention. More attention is given to cars toward the front of the motorcade. Nine famous people, named Anna, Ben, Chris, Dana, Evan, Frank, Garry, Hillary, and Iris, are in the motorcade. The order of the cars of these famous people is determined by the following:

Anna's car is before Dana's and Garry's cars.
Evan's car is after Chris's and Ben's cars.
Evan's car is before Anna's car.

1. Which of the following is a possible order of the cars in the motorcade?
   (A) Chris, Evan, Ben, Frank, Anna, Dana, Hillary, Iris, Garry.
   (B) Garry, Dana, Iris, Frank, Anna, Evan, Hillary, Chris, Ben.
   (C) Hillary, Chris, Ben, Iris, Evan, Anna, Dana, Garry, Frank.
   (D) Ben, Chris, Evan, Frank, Garry, Iris, Hillary, Anna, Dana.
   (E) None of the above.

2. If Evan's car goes third in the motorcade, then which of the following must be true?
   (A) Chris's car goes first.
   (B) Ben's car goes first.
   (C) Anna's car goes fourth.
   (D) Garry's car goes ninth.
   (E) None of the above.

3. If Anna's car goes sixth and Evan's car goes fourth, then which of the following could be true?
   (A) Dana's car goes third.
   (B) Ben's car goes sixth.
   (C) Hillary's car goes fifth.
   (D) Iris's car goes fourth.
   (E) None of the above.

4. How many cars could go eighth in the motorcade?
   (A) four
   (B) five
   (C) six
   (D) seven
   (E) eight

5. If Anna goes sixth, then which of the following must be true?
   (A) Dana goes before Garry.
   (B) Hillary goes before Iris.
   (C) Anna goes after Frank.
   (D) Ben goes before Garry.
   (E) None of the above.

6. If Frank, Hillary, and Iris go consecutively, then which of the following must NOT be true?
   (A) Ben and Hillary go consecutively.
   (B) Dana and Garry do not go consecutively.
   (C) Evan and Dana go consecutively.
   (D) Chris and Ben do not go consecutively.
   (E) None of the above.

ANSWERS AND EXPLANATIONS

Game 5

Initial Setup:

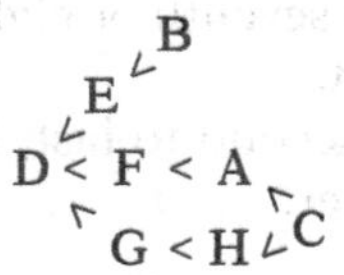

Question 1: Which of the following could be an order of the worker ants from first to last?

(A) This is a possible order of the ants.
(B) Chris or Ben must be last.
(C) Dana must be first.
(D) Dana must be first.
(E) Chris or Ben must be last.

Question 2: How many different ants could be second in line?

(C) Evan, Frank, and Garry could all be second in line.

Question 3: How many different ants could be third in line?

(C) Evan, Frank, Garry, Anna, Hillary, and Ben could all go third.

Question 4: What is the earliest position in the line that Chris could hold?

(C) Dana, Frank, Anna, Garry, and Hillary all have to precede Chris, so the earliest that Chris could go is sixth.

Question 5: If Frank goes fifth, then which of the following could NOT be true?

(E) You know that Anna and Chris must go after Frank. But if Frank is fifth, and Hillary and Ben are sixth and seventh, then there is no room for both Anna and Chris to go after Frank.

Question 6: If Garry goes after Ben and Anna, then which of the following must be true?

(B) In this scenario, by looking at the diagram we know that Garry must go sixth, Hillary must go seventh, and Chris must go eighth.

Game 6

Initial Setup:

You do not know where Frank or Iris is in this list.

Question 1: Which of the following could be the order in which the snake charmers perform?

(A) This is a possible order.

(B) Ben must go before Anna.
(C) Hillary must go before Evan.
(D) Hillary must go before Garry.
(E) Choice A is the correct answer.

Question 2: If Ben performs sixth, then which of the following must be true?

(C) If Ben is sixth, then that means that every person who can precede him must do so. Therefore, the only people after him in the performance can be Anna, Ben, and Evan, and Evan must perform last.

(A) We do not know the order of Anna's and Dana's performances.
(B) Iris or Frank could go first.
(D) You do not know whether this is true.
(E) Choice C is the correct answer.

Question 3: If Frank, Iris, Anna, and Evan perform consecutively, then which of the following must be true?

(E) While initially it might seem that this question's temporary constraint would tell you a lot about the game, it really tells you only the order of four of the variables while revealing nothing about their specific positions.

Question 4: How many charmers could potentially perform third?

(E) Frank, Iris, Chris, Hillary, Garry, Ben, Anna, and Dana could perform third. This is everyone but Evan—eight people.

Question 5: If Garry performs fifth and Ben performs fourth, then which of the following could NOT be true?

(A) If this is the case, then you know that Chris and Hillary must occupy two of the first three positions. There is an extra position before Ben that must be occupied either by Iris or Frank, but not both, because it cannot be occupied by any of the other snake charmers.

Question 6: If six people perform between Chris's performance and Anna's performance, then which of the following could be true?

(D) This question stem would force Chris to be first, Anna to be eighth, and Evan to be ninth. This would allow Hillary to perform fifth.

(A) Ben could not perform seventh because there would be no space for Dana and Evan after him in the performance.
(B) Garry could not perform second because then there would be no room for Hillary to precede him in the performance.
(C) Evan must perform ninth to ensure that there are enough performers in between Chris and Anna.
(E) **D** is the correct answer.

Game 7

Initial Setup:

Question 1: Which of the following could be the order of the caterpillars climbing up the tree, from first to last?

(E) This is a possible order of the variables.

(A) Iris and Chris must precede Anna.
(B) Garry must precede Evan.
(C) Chris must precede Anna.
(D) Hillary must precede Evan.

Question 2: Which of the following is a pair of caterpillars that could go first and second, in that order?

(B) Hillary and Iris could go first and second.

(A) Iris must precede Chris.
(C) Dana must precede Ben.
(D) Dana must precede Ben.
(E) Neither Anna nor Evan could go near the beginning of the line.

Question 3: Which of the following caterpillars could be in any position in the line except for last?

(C) Hillary is the only caterpillar for which this is possible.

(A) Chris cannot go first.
(B) Dana cannot go seventh or eighth.
(D) Evan can go last.
(E) Iris cannot go second to last, because Chris and Anna must follow her.

Question 4: How many caterpillars could go second in line?

(B) Iris, Dana, Chris, Ben, and Hillary could all go second.

Question 5: Which pair of caterpillars could never travel in the line consecutively?

(E) Garry must always travel in between Ben and Evan.

Question 6: Which of the following is a complete list of the caterpillars that could go first in the line?

(C) Iris, Dana, and Hillary could all go first in line.

Game 8

Initial Setup:

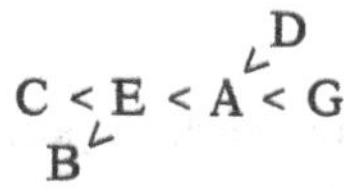

Remember that you do not know the positions of Frank, Hillary, and Iris! They could go anywhere in the motorcade.

Question 1: Which of the following is a possible order of the cars in the motorcade?

(C) This is a possible order for the variables.

(A) Ben must precede Evan.
(B) Garry cannot precede Chris. This answer choice was designed for those who mixed up the order of the game.
(D) Garry cannot precede Anna.
(E) **C** is the correct answer.

Question 2: If Evan's car goes third in the motorcade, then which of the following must be true?

(E) This question's temporary constraint means that Chris's and Ben's cars must go first and second, but *not necessarily in that order.* Chris's car could go first and Ben's second, or vice versa. You just do not know. It also means that Frank's, Hillary's, and Iris's cars must follow Evan's car somewhere in the line, which could affect the positions of Anna's and Garry's cars.

Question 3: If Anna's car goes sixth and Evan's car goes fourth, then which of the following could be true?

(C) This question's temporary constraint means that Hillary, Iris, or Frank must go between Evan and Anna's car.

(A) Dana must follow Anna.
(B) The constraint tells us that Anna's car goes sixth.
(D) The constraint tells us that Evan's car goes fourth.
(E) **C** is the correct answer.

Question 4: How many cars could go eighth in the motorcade?

(B) Dana, Garry, Frank, Hillary, or Iris could all go eighth in the motorcade.

Question 5: If Anna goes sixth, then which of the following must be true?

If Anna goes sixth, then only one from the group of Frank, Hillary, and Iris could follow her.

(D) You know that this fact must be true, even if the constraint added by the question did not exist.

Question 6: If Frank, Hillary, and Iris go consecutively, then which of the following could NOT be true?

(C) This does not tell you much about the exact position of the rest of the variables, but it does tell you that they must also all go consecutively, because the Frank, Hillary, and Iris variables are not present to split them up. There is no time in the game when Evan and Dana could go consecutively.

CHAPTER 3

LINEAR GAMES

Linear games are similar to sequencing games in that all the variables are arranged along a linear continuum. Linear games mix things up a little bit, because when ordering the variables, you must be able to interpret sequencing, sufficient-necessary, and direct placement constraints. Additionally, you are required to utilize box rules to identify certain scenarios in which the variables are able to exist.

Typical Fact Pattern

> Their coach has placed seven basketball players in line so that they can each take a practice shot before the game. The players' names are Anna, Ben, Chris, Dana, Evan, Frank, and Garry. The order of the players in line is determined by the following:
>
> Garry is fourth in line.
> Evan is not last and not second.
> Ben is not in line consecutively with Garry.
> Dana is farther back in the line than Frank and Evan.
> Anna is sixth or third.
> Chris is sixth or third.

Logic Tools

VACANCY-OCCUPANCY RULES

The fact pattern above brings up the use of vacancy-occupancy diagramming tools. These tools assume two forms, the first being **vacancy** rules and the second corresponding to a *direct placement* of the variables through a **double** or **triple possibility.**

Vacancy rules should be noted directly underneath the linear continuum that is used to diagram a linear game. Note them as soon as you read the constraint.

Constraint 2: Evan is not last and not second.

			G			
1	2	3	4	5	6	7
	~~E~~					~~E~~

Constraint 3: Ben is not in line consecutively with Garry.

			G			
1	2	3	4	5	6	7
	~~E~~	~~B~~		~~B~~		~~E~~

This constraint informs you that Ben cannot be third or fifth, since Garry is fourth.

Constraint 4: Dana is farther back in the line than Frank and Evan.

			G			
1	2	3	4	5	6	7
~~D~~	~~E~~	~~B~~		~~B~~		~~E~~
	~~D~~					

This constraint informs you that Dana needs at least two variables (F and E) in front of her in line. Therefore, she could not go first or second.

After filling out all of the vacancy rules, you should draw in the occupancy rules over the diagram. The double possibility between Anna and Chris is shown:

		A/C	G		C/A	
1	2	3	4	5	6	7
~~D~~	~~E~~	~~B~~		~~B~~		~~E~~
	~~D~~					

Notice that after learning that Chris and Anna could only go third or sixth, you could have drawn vacancy rules for C and A underneath every single position except 6 and 3. However, doing this would only put repetitive information in your diagram. Whenever a more complex rule is added that includes information that previously existed only in a vacancy rule, you should cross out the vacancy rule to conserve space. That way, you will be more likely to remember the vacancy rules whose information is not included elsewhere in the game. Based on this idea, you should delete the vacancy rule for B underneath 3, because it gives repetitive information. You now know that, based on the double possibility, B could not go in 3.

Box Rules

Box rules are some of the most helpful organization tactics in linear and complex linear games. You should use them whenever possible to organize your constraints and then to visualize them along the linear continuum.

The following fact pattern demonstrates the utility of box rules:

> The variables A, B, C, D, E, and F are in line. Their order is determined by the following:
>
> A is third.
> B is in line immediately before C.
> One person separates D and E in line.

The first constraint is a direct placement, so that is easy to deal with. The second constraint invokes a box rule:

[B C]

The third constraint also invokes a box rule:

[D __ E]

Since A is third, it is clear that the D and E box can go in one of only two places in the game. You should draw these two scenarios and see what else you can deduce about each scenario. Based on where the D and E box goes, it is clear where the rest of the variables in the game must also go.

F	D/E	A	E/D	B	C
1	2	3	4	5	6

B	C	A	D/E	F	E/D
1	2	3	4	5	6

The following is a list of the different types of box rules and their names. Each one is shown with the constraint or constraints that typically invoke them.

1. **Typical Constraint:**
   A is immediately before B.

Box Rule
Write on your paper:

[A B]

2. **Typical Constraints:**
   A is not immediately before B.
   B is not immediately after A.

No-Box Rule
Write on your paper:

[A/B]

3. **Typical Constraint:**
   A is not next to B.

Switching No-Box Rule
Write on your paper:

[A/B] (with arc)

4. **Typical Constraint:**
   A is immediately next to B.

Switching Box Rule
Write on your paper:

[A B] (with arc)

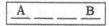

Note that when you diagram switching box rules along a linear continuum, their variables should always be mapped with double possibilities. The previous box would correspond to the following diagram:

A/B	B/A
1	2

5. **Typical Constraints:**
   Ben is seen three days after Anna is seen.
   A is less than B, and two people are in between A and B.

Expanded-Box Rule
Write on your paper:

[A __ __ B]

6. **Typical Constraint:**
   Two people are in between A and B.

Switching Expanded Box Rule
Write on your paper:

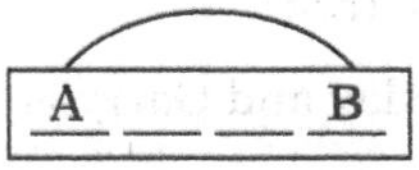

Note that since this is a switching box rule, when it is diagrammed along a linear continuum, it will have double possibilities:

A/B ___ ___ B/A
1 2 3 4

7. **Typical Constraint:**
   Exactly two people do not separate A and B.

Switching Expanded No-Box Rule
Write on your paper:

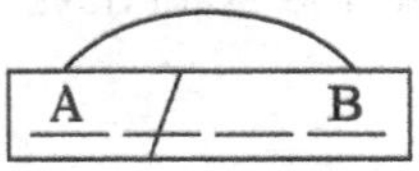

Fact Pattern Organization Heuristics

The heuristic for linear logic games is the following:

1. **Transcribe** the constraints.
2. Draw the **linear scenarios.**
   a. Is there a burdensome constraint?
3. Write out the **vacancy-occupancy rules.**
   a. Draw in vacancy rules.
   b. Draw in double possibilities and other occupancy rules.
   c. Eliminate repetitive rules.
4. Make **deductions** from the diagram.

Review

In this section you have learned:

1. How to use vacancy-occupancy rules.
2. How to use box rules to organize information from the fact pattern.
3. How to diagram information represented by box rules.
4. The fact pattern organization heuristic for linear logic games.

These ideas will help you to solve linear games in an expeditious fashion. Go through the following four games slowly, making sure that you grasp the major concepts, because these concepts will be built on in the next chapter, on complex linear games—linear games that are in two dimensions.

LINEAR GAME I

Preschoolers Anna, Ben, Chris, Dana, Evan, Frank, and Garry all require tetherball lessons this week. The tetherball teacher can see one student per day from Monday through Sunday. The order in which the students are seen is determined by the following constraints:

Ben is seen on the day after Anna.
Dana is seen later in the week than Garry and Anna.
Garry is seen later in the week than Anna.
Evan is seen two days after Ben is seen.

1. Which of the following could be an order in which the students are seen from Monday to Sunday?
   (A) Anna, Ben, Dana, Evan, Frank, Garry, Chris.
   (B) Frank, Chris, Anna, Ben, Garry, Dana, Evan.
   (C) Chris, Anna, Ben, Garry, Evan, Frank, Dana.
   (D) Anna, Frank, Chris, Ben, Garry, Evan, Dana.
   (E) Ben, Anna, Garry, Evan, Dana, Chris, Frank.

2. If Ben is seen on Wednesday, then which of the following must be true?
   (A) Frank is seen on Monday.
   (B) Chris is seen on Thursday.
   (C) Garry is seen on Saturday.
   (D) Evan is seen on Friday.
   (E) Ben is seen on Tuesday.

3. If Evan is seen on Saturday, then which of the following must be true?
   (A) Frank is seen on Monday.
   (B) Dana is seen on Sunday.
   (C) Ben is seen on Wednesday.
   (D) Chris is seen on Monday.
   (E) Garry is seen on Tuesday.

4. Which is the latest day in the week that Anna can be seen?
   (A) Tuesday
   (B) Wednesday
   (C) Thursday
   (D) Friday
   (E) Saturday

5. If Ben is seen on Wednesday, then which of the following must NOT be true?
   (A) Dana is seen on Saturday and Garry is seen on Thursday.
   (B) Frank is seen on Saturday and Chris is seen on Sunday.
   (C) Anna is seen on Tuesday and Evan is seen on Friday.
   (D) Chris is seen later in the week than Evan.
   (E) Evan is seen on a consecutive day with Frank.

6. If Anna is seen on Wednesday, then for how many students do you know the exact days that they learn tetherball?
   (A) three
   (B) four
   (C) five
   (D) six
   (E) seven

SOLUTION STEPS

1. Transcribe the Constraints

1. **Box Rule—** A B
2. **Sequencing Rule—** 
3. **Sequencing Rule—** A < G
4. **Box Rule—** B __ E

You should notice that the two box rules can be added in order to make the following box rule, which is very *"burdensome,"* that is, it greatly restricts the number of possible arrangements of the variables.

A B __ E

The two sequencing rules can be consolidated to form:

A < G < D

2. Draw the Scenarios

Is there a burdensome constraint?

Yes, there is. So you should keep in mind that **four** spots are taken by the A, B, and E box in a game with only **seven** positions. You should now draw the four possible scenarios:

A B _ E _ _ _

_ A B _ E _ _

_ _ A B _ E _

_ _ _ A B _ E

3. Write Out the Vacancy-Occupancy Rules

Draw in vacancy rules for each possible scenario.

A B _ E _ _ _ (~~D~~ under the third position)

_ A B _ E _ _ (~~D~~ ~~G~~ under the first position; ~~D~~ under the fourth position)

_ _ A B _ E _ (~~D~~ ~~G~~ under the first and second positions; ~~D~~ under the fifth position)

_ _ _ A B _ E (~~D~~ ~~G~~ under the first, second, and third positions; ~~D~~ under the sixth position)

Draw in double possibilities and other occupancy rules.

In the third scenario, it is clear that D must go on Sunday and G must go on Friday since there is nowhere else for them to go. This leaves only two places for C and F, so draw in that double possibility.

In the fourth scenario, there is nowhere for D to go, so it becomes apparent that this scenario is impossible and that A cannot go later than Wednesday.

Eliminate repetitive rules.

You should now clean up your diagram by eliminating the vacancy rules for D and G in scenario 3, since you know where D and G are in that scenario. Also, you should delete scenario 4 entirely.

4. Make Deductions from the Diagram. There are no deductions that you can make from this diagram. Just be sure to have the final diagram handy when answering the questions.

1. A B _ E _ _ _ (~~D~~ under the third position)

2. _ A B _ E _ _ (~~D~~ ~~G~~ under the first position; ~~D~~ under the fourth position)

3. C/F F/C A B G E D

Answering the Questions

Question 1: Which of the following could be an order in which the students are seen from Monday to Sunday?

(C) The order has to correspond to one of the three scenarios above. This one corresponds to scenario 2.

(A) Dana cannot go before Garry.
(B) Only one person can be between Ben and Evan.
(D) Ben must immediately follow Anna.
(E) Ben must immediately follow Anna.

Question 2: If Ben is seen on Wednesday, then which of the following must be true?

(D) If this happens, you are in scenario 2, and Evan must be seen on Friday.

Question 3: If Evan is seen on Saturday, then which of the following must be true?

(B) This occurs in scenario 3, in which Dana is seen on Sunday.

Question 4: Which is the latest day in the week that Anna can be seen?

(B) This corresponds to scenario 3, which shows that Anna can be seen on Wednesday. If you did not draw in your vacancy rules correctly, then you might not have deduced that scenario 4 is impossible.

Question 5: If Ben is seen on Wednesday, then which of the following must NOT be true?

(B) If Ben is seen on Wednesday, then you are in scenario 2. If Chris and Frank are both seen on the weekend, then Dana would be forced into a position that would break a constraint.

Question 6: If Anna is seen on Wednesday, then for how many students do you know the exact days that they learn tetherball?

(C) This corresponds to scenario 3, where you know the exact positions of Anna, Ben, Garry, Evan, and Dana.

LINEAR GAME 2

Jason and his Argonauts pilot their boat toward Athens. In order to maximize rowing efficiency, Jason has organized his Argonauts—Anna, Ben, Chris, Dana, Evan, Frank, and Garry—along the rowing positions from the front to the back of the boat. The seat at the front of the boat is ranked first, and the seat farthest back is ranked seventh. The rowing position of each Argonaut is determined by the following:

If Chris rows fourth, then Garry rows in seventh position and Ben rows in fifth.
If Anna does not row second, then Ben rows in sixth position and Dana rows in second.
Frank rows in the position immediately after Ben.

1. Which of the following could be an order of the Argonauts?
   (A) Anna, Dana, Evan, Chris, Garry, Ben, Frank.
   (B) Ben, Anna, Garry, Chris, Evan, Frank, Dana.
   (C) Evan, Anna, Dana, Ben, Frank, Garry, Chris.
   (D) Dana, Anna, Evan, Chris, Garry, Ben, Frank.
   (E) None of the above.

2. If Chris does not row fourth, then which of the following must be true?
   (A) Ben rows sixth.
   (B) Anna rows second.
   (C) Evan rows first or second.
   (D) Dana rows fifth or sixth.
   (E) None of the above.

3. If Chris rows fourth, then which of the following must be true?
   (A) Anna rows second.
   (B) Dana rows third.
   (C) Evan rows first.
   (D) Garry rows third.
   (E) None of the above.

4. If Evan and Dana row before Anna, then which of the following must NOT be true?
   (A) Garry rows first and Chris rows fifth.
   (B) Anna rows third and Garry rows fifth.
   (C) Ben rows sixth and Frank rows seventh.
   (D) Evan rows first and Dana rows second.
   (E) None of the above.

5. Which position could the fewest number of people potentially go in?
   (A) 1
   (B) 2
   (C) 3
   (D) 5
   (E) 7

6. If Evan rows first and Dana rows third, then how many possible configurations of the Argonauts are there?
   (A) two
   (B) three
   (C) four
   (D) five
   (E) six

SOLUTION STEPS

1. Transcribe the Constraints

1. The first two constraints can be transcribed as sufficient-necessary statements and their contrapositives:
   a. $C_4 \rightarrow G_7$; b. $\not{G}_7 \rightarrow \not{C}_4$
   a. $C_4 \rightarrow B_5$; b. $\not{B}_5 \rightarrow \not{C}_4$
2. a. $\not{A}_2 \rightarrow B_6$; b. $\not{B}_6 \rightarrow A_2$
   a. $\not{A}_2 \rightarrow D_2$; b. $\not{D}_2 \rightarrow A_2$
3. The third constraint can be transcribed as a box rule: [B F]

2. Draw the Scenarios

Is there a burdensome constraint?

Yes, there are very burdensome sufficient-necessary rules, and these should be mapped out underneath the linear continuum. For every sufficient condition, you should put an asterisk underneath the slot where the condition would be invoked. Take a look at the following example. If A is not in slot 2, as stated in 3.a. and 4.a., then a condition will be invoked. If C is in slot 4, as stated in 1.a. and 2.a., then a sufficient-necessary condition will be invoked. You should note these statements in the following fashion:

— *A — *C — — —

It is also a good idea to note the sufficient conditions of the contrapositives:

___	*~~A~~ *~~D~~	___	*C	*~~B~~	*~~B~~	*~~G~~

Now you will be able to remember what conditions will occur due to the placement of the variables within the game.

3. Write Out the Vacancy-Occupancy Rules. *Draw in vacancy rules for each possible scenario.*

Looking at the sufficient-necessary constraint regarding variable A and slot 2, you can see that if A is not in slot 2, then D must be in slot 2. This means that either A or D must be in slot 2. This can be noted with a double possibility or by drawing the two scenarios. In this case, do the latter.

Draw in double possibilities and other occupancy rules.

___	A	___	___	___	___	___
	*~~A~~ *~~D~~		*C	*~~B~~	*~~B~~	*~~G~~
___	D	___	___	___	B	F
	*~~A~~ *~~D~~		*C ~~C~~	*~~B~~	*~~B~~	*~~G~~

You know that F goes last in the second scenario because of your box rule. *Eliminate repetitive rules.*

Since you have found the places of several variables in each scenario, you can delete several sufficient-necessary notes in each scenario. Additionally, you have learned of a vacancy rule for the second scenario—C cannot go fourth when D is second. So delete the irrelevancies:

___	A	___	___	___	___	___
			*C	*~~B~~		*~~G~~
___	D	___	___	___	B	F
			~~C~~			

Sit back and think of why each deleted condition is now irrelevant. After doing several of these problems, you will be able to make these deletions intuitively.

4. Make Deductions from the Diagram. Unfortunately, there are no more deductions that you can make from our diagram at this point. You will have to wait for constraints within questions to find variables' exact positions.

Answering the Questions

Question 1: Which of the following could be an order of the Argonauts?

(C) This configuration is possible.

(A) If Chris is fourth, then Garry is seventh and Ben is fifth.

(B) Frank must go immediately after Ben.

(D) If Chris is fourth, then Garry is seventh and Ben is fifth.

(E) **C** is the correct answer.

Question 2: If Chris does not row fourth, then which of the following must be true?

(E) Chris not rowing fourth does not tell you anything about the rest of the game.

Question 3: If Chris rows fourth, then which of the following must be true?

(A) If Chris rows fourth, then Anna must row second, Ben must row fifth, Frank sixth, and Garry seventh.

Question 4: If Evan and Dana row before Anna, then which of the following must NOT be true?

(B) This constraint means that Anna cannot row second, so Dana must row second. This occurs in the second scenario. In this scenario, if Anna rowed third and Garry rowed fifth, then that would force Evan to row first. The only space left for Chris would be the fourth position, which would force the game to a contradiction.

Question 5: Which position could the fewest number of people potentially go in?

(B) This is the second position—only Anna or Dana could go there.

Question 6: If Evan rows first and Dana rows third, then how many possible configurations of the Argonauts are there?

(D) This constraint puts you in the first scenario. You should draw out the configurations for the BF box after putting what you know into the diagram.

E	A	D	B	F	C/G	G/C
			*C	*~~B~~		*~~G~~
E	A	D	C/G	B	F	G/C
			*C	*~~B~~		*~~G~~
E	A	D	G	C	B	F
			*C	*~~B~~		*~~G~~

Counting up the possible configurations of the diagram, you find that there are five possible scenarios. Each scenario with a double possibility counts twice.

LINEAR GAME 3

A number of secret agents desire to be sent on a mission to Kazakhstan. The agents' names are Anna, Ben, Chris, Dana, Evan, Frank, and Garry. Each agent is required to schedule an interview this week from Monday to Sunday in order to have a background check. Only one agent can receive a background check per day, and all agents will receive background checks this week. The order in which the agents are seen is determined by the following:

Chris is seen on Wednesday.
Dana is seen on a day consecutive with Evan.
If Garry is seen later in the week than Dana, then Frank is seen on Saturday and Ben is seen on Sunday.
If Anna is seen earlier in the week than Evan, then Ben is seen on Saturday and Frank is seen on Sunday.
Garry is seen on a day consecutive with Anna.

1. Which of the following is an order in which the agents could be seen?
   (A) Dana, Evan, Chris, Anna, Garry, Ben, Frank.
   (B) Anna, Garry, Chris, Evan, Dana, Ben, Frank.
   (C) Dana, Chris, Evan, Garry, Anna, Frank, Ben.
   (D) Garry, Anna, Chris, Dana, Ben, Evan, Frank.
   (E) Frank, Ben, Dana, Evan, Chris, Garry, Anna.

2. If Garry is seen on Friday, then for how many people do you know the exact day they are seen?
   (A) two
   (B) three
   (C) four
   (D) five
   (E) six

3. If Ben is seen before Frank, then which of the following must be true?
   (A) Garry is seen earlier in the week than Dana.
   (B) Anna is seen on Monday and Garry is seen on Tuesday.
   (C) Chris is seen earlier in the week than Anna.
   (D) Ben and Dana are seen on consecutive days.
   (E) Garry and Anna are not seen on consecutive days.

4. Which of the following is a pair of people either of whom could be seen on Thursday?
   (A) Frank, Garry
   (B) Evan, Ben
   (C) Anna, Dana
   (D) Chris, Evan
   (E) Ben, Frank

5. If Garry is seen earlier in the week than Anna, then which of the following could be true?
   (A) Garry is seen on Friday.
   (B) Anna is seen on Monday.
   (C) Garry is seen on Tuesday.
   (D) Anna is seen on Thursday.
   (E) Ben is seen on Sunday.

6. If Chris is seen on days consecutive with Anna and Dana, then which of the following must NOT be true?
   (A) Ben is seen on Sunday.
   (B) Anna is seen on Friday.
   (C) Frank is seen on Sunday.
   (D) Dana is seen on Tuesday.
   (E) Garry is seen on Monday.

SOLUTION STEPS

1. Transcribe the Constraints

1. **Direct Placement:** C = Wednesday
2. **Box Rule:** $\boxed{D\ E}$
3. **Box Rule:** $\boxed{G\ A}$
4. **Sufficient-Necessary:**
   $D < G \rightarrow F_{Sat}$; $\not{F}_{Sat} \rightarrow G < D$
   $D < G \rightarrow B_{Sun}$; $\not{B}_{Sun} \rightarrow G < D$

In a contrapositive that includes sequencing, the sequencing is reversed instead of the sign being switched.

5. **Sufficient-Necessary:**
   $A < E \rightarrow B_{Sat}$; $\not{B}_{Sat} \rightarrow E < A$
   $A < E \rightarrow F_{Sun}$; $\not{F}_{Sun} \rightarrow E < A$

2. Draw the Scenarios. *Is there a burdensome constraint?*

Yes. Box rules, especially when they are placed in the mix with direct placement constraints, almost always mean that the game has a limited number of scenarios, which you can figure out quickly and which will be instrumental in finding the answers to the questions. Here are the scenarios that you should immediately draw out:

1. A/G G/A C D/E E/D B F
2. D/E E/D C A/G G/A F B
3. B/F F/B C A/G G/A D/E E/D
4. B/F F/B C D/E E/D G/A A/G

When you analyze the above scenarios with your sufficient-necessary conditions, you realize that one of the two boxes has to go before C. This makes scenarios 3 and 4 impossible. Here is why: In scenario 3, A < E, but B and F cannot go on the weekends to complete the mandates of the constraint. In scenario 4, D < G, but B and F cannot go on the weekends here either to fulfill the sufficient-necessary constraint's requirements. Therefore, the only two possibilities for the game are the first two scenarios.

3. Write Out the Vacancy-Occupancy Rules. You have already drawn in the occupancy rules through the use of double possibilities. Therefore, it is not necessary to write out any vacancy rules.

4. Make Deductions from the Diagram. Your diagram corresponds to the following:

A/G G/A C D/E E/D B F

D/E E/D C A/G G/A F B

There are no deductions left for you to make. It would be a bad idea to rely on anything in these circumstances. If you haven't found the answer and there are no more deductions to make, then it would be wise to rework the problem.

Answering the Questions

Question 1: Which of the following is an order in which the agents could be seen?

(B) This is a possible order.

(A) If Frank is not seen on Saturday, then Garry must be seen before Dana.
(C) Chris must be seen on Wednesday.
(D) If Ben is not seen on Saturday, then Evan must be seen before Anna.
(E) Chris must be seen on Wednesday.

Question 2: If Garry is seen on Friday, then for how many people do you know the exact day they are seen?

(D) This is possible only in scenario 2. We know the position of C, A, G, F, and B.

Question 3: If Ben is seen before Frank, then which of the following must be true?

(A) This constraint puts Ben on Saturday and Frank on Sunday, which occurs in scenario 1. Garry must be seen earlier in the week than Dana.

Question 4: Which of the following is a pair of people either of whom could be seen on Thursday?

(C) The variables D, E, A, and G could all be seen on Thursday. F, B, and C cannot be seen that day.

Question 5: If Garry is seen earlier in the week than Anna, then which of the following could be true?

(E) This constraint can occur in either scenario, so you must look for an answer choice that does not conflict with your diagrams and the question's constraint of G < A.

Question 6: If Chris is seen on days consecutive with Anna and Dana, then which of the following must NOT be true?

(B) Anna must be seen on Thursday or Tuesday to be consecutive with Chris, who can be seen only on Wednesday.

LINEAR GAME 4

A veterinarian lines up a group of puppies in order to groom them. The names of the puppies are Anna, Ben, Chris, Dana, Evan, Frank, and Garry. The order in which the puppies are groomed comports with the following constraints:

Ben is groomed second.
Evan is groomed fourth.
Anna is groomed before Dana.
Frank is groomed consecutively with Garry.
One puppy is groomed in between Dana and Anna.

1. Which of the following could be the order in which the puppies are groomed, from first to last?
   (A) Anna, Ben, Dana, Evan, Chris, Garry, Frank.
   (B) Chris, Ben, Evan, Anna, Dana, Frank, Garry.
   (C) Anna, Ben, Dana, Evan, Frank, Chris, Garry.
   (D) Chris, Ben, Anna, Evan, Frank, Garry, Dana.
   (E) Chris, Frank, Garry, Evan, Dana, Ben, Anna.

2. Which of the following is a complete list of the puppies that could be groomed fifth?
   (A) Garry, Frank
   (B) Frank, Garry, Anna
   (C) Chris, Dana, Anna
   (D) Chris, Garry, Frank, Dana
   (E) Frank, Dana, Anna, Chris, Garry

3. In how many different places in the line could Chris be groomed?
   (A) one
   (B) two
   (C) three
   (D) four
   (E) five

4. Which of the following is a pair of puppies either of which could be groomed seventh?
   (A) Garry, Dana
   (B) Anna, Garry
   (C) Dana, Frank
   (D) Evan, Ben
   (E) Frank, Chris

5. If Frank is groomed seventh, then which of the following must be true?
   (A) Dana is groomed fifth.
   (B) Anna is groomed first.
   (C) Chris is groomed fifth.
   (D) Garry is groomed sixth.
   (E) Dana is groomed third.

6. In how many different possible orders can the dogs be groomed?
   (A) four
   (B) six
   (C) eight
   (D) ten
   (E) twelve

SOLUTION STEPS

1. Transcribe the Constraints

1. **Direct Placement: B = 2**
2. **Direct Placement: E = 4**
3. **Sequencing: A < D**
4. **Switching Box Rule:** [F G]
5. **Switching Expanded Box Rule:**

[A ___ D]

Notice that the box rule in constraint 5 and the sequencing constraint in constraint 3 can be combined to form the following expanded box:

[A ___ D]

2. Draw the Scenarios

Is there a burdensome constraint?

Yes, the AD constraint is large and can go in only a couple of places in the game.

A B D E ___ ___ ___

C B A E D F/G G/F

___ B ___ E A ___ D

You will notice that scenario 3 is not possible, since the FG switching box would have nowhere to go.

3. Write Out the Vacancy-Occupancy Rules. A double possibility is included in the second scenario through the FG box. Another double possibility could be drawn in the first scenario. Think of where it should be drawn and with which variables. Remember that F and G must be consecutive.

4. Make Deductions from the Diagram. Your final diagram is this:

A B D E __ F/G __

C B A E D F/G G/F

Notice that there are **two** possible scenarios from the second line and **four** possible scenarios from the first line. Why not six? Because G and F have to be consecutive.

Answering the Questions

Question 1: Which of the following could be the order in which the puppies are groomed, from first to last?

(A) This is possible in the first scenario.

(B) This is not possible in either scenario, because Evan precedes Anna.
(C) Frank and Garry are not consecutive.
(D) Dana must go fifth in the second scenario.
(E) This answer is very far from being the correct one.

Question 2: Which of the following is a complete list of the puppies that could be groomed fifth?

(D) In the second scenario, Dana goes fifth, and in the first, Chris, Garry, or Frank could go fifth. This is four puppies.

Question 3: In how many different places in the line could Chris be groomed?

(C) Chris has to go first in the second scenario but could go fifth or seventh in the first scenario.

Question 4: Which of the following is a pair of puppies either of which could be groomed seventh?

(E) Garry, Frank, or Chris could all be groomed seventh.

Question 5: If Frank is groomed seventh, then which of the following must be true?

(D) If Frank is groomed seventh, then Garry must be groomed sixth for them to be groomed consecutively. Notice that Frank could be groomed in this position in either diagram.

Dana could be groomed either third or fifth. Therefore, answer choice A does not have to be true.

Question 6: In how many different possible orders can the dogs be groomed?

(B) You figured this out in step 4 when you were making deductions based on the diagram. The correct answer is six—two from the second scenario and four from the first.

On Your Own

LINEAR GAME 5

A crocodile hunter lines up seven crocodiles in order to determine which ones would be most fit to go on television with him. The crocodiles' names are Anna, Ben, Chris, Dana, Evan, Frank, and Garry. The crocodile hunter decides that the best idea would be for all of the crocodiles to go on television with him one at a time. The order in which they go on is determined by the following constraints:

Chris goes on second.
Exactly two crocodiles go on between Garry and Anna.
Garry goes on before Anna.
Frank goes on before Evan.
Ben goes on before Anna.

1. Which of the following could be the order in which the crocodiles go on?
   (A) Frank, Chris, Garry, Ben, Dana, Anna, Evan.
   (B) Garry, Chris, Ben, Anna, Evan, Frank, Dana.
   (C) Frank, Chris, Garry, Ben, Dana, Evan, Anna.
   (D) Ben, Chris, Anna, Dana, Frank, Evan, Garry.
   (E) None of the above.

2. If Garry goes first, then which of the following must be true?
   (A) Frank goes fifth.
   (B) Evan goes sixth.
   (C) Ben goes third.
   (D) Anna goes second.
   (E) None of the above.

3. In how many different places could Evan go on?
   (A) three
   (B) four
   (C) five
   (D) six
   (E) seven

4. If Garry goes third, then which of the following must NOT be true?
   (A) Evan goes on fourth and Dana goes on fifth.
   (B) Anna goes on sixth and Chris goes on second.
   (C) Ben goes on fourth and Dana goes on first.
   (D) Evan goes on seventh and Frank goes on fifth.
   (E) None of the above.

5. Which of the following is a complete list of the crocodiles that could go on last?
   (A) Dana, Evan
   (B) Ben, Dana, Evan, Frank, Anna
   (C) Anna, Dana, Evan
   (D) Dana, Frank, Anna, Evan
   (E) None of the above.

6. If Anna goes on fourth, then in how many possible orders could the crocodiles go on?
   (A) two
   (B) three
   (C) four
   (D) five
   (E) six

LINEAR GAME 6

A TV game show has lined up a number of potential contestants in the order in which they will go on the show to try to win one million dollars. The contestants' names are Anna, Ben, Chris, Dana, Evan, Frank, and Garry. Their order is determined by the following conditions:

Two contestants go on between Evan and Ben.
Anna does not go on consecutively with Evan or Ben.
Chris does not go on consecutively with Anna.
Garry goes on immediately after Evan.

1. Which of the following could be an order in which the contestants go on the show?
   - (A) Ben, Evan, Chris, Dana, Anna, Frank, Garry.
   - (B) Chris, Ben, Frank, Garry, Evan, Dana, Anna.
   - (C) Anna, Frank, Evan, Garry, Ben, Chris, Dana.
   - (D) Anna, Evan, Garry, Chris, Ben, Dana, Frank.
   - (E) Evan, Garry, Frank, Ben, Chris, Dana, Anna.

2. If Anna goes first and Chris goes sixth, then which of the following must be true?
   - (A) Dana goes second.
   - (B) Ben goes fourth.
   - (C) Frank goes third.
   - (D) Garry goes fifth.
   - (E) Ben goes third.

3. If Evan goes third, then which of the following could NOT be true?
   - (A) Chris goes second.
   - (B) Frank goes fifth.
   - (C) Dana goes seventh.
   - (D) Garry goes fourth.
   - (E) Anna goes first.

4. If Garry goes third, then which of the following must be true?
   - (A) Evan goes on before Dana.
   - (B) Chris goes on before Frank.
   - (C) Garry goes on after Chris.
   - (D) Dana goes on before Anna.
   - (E) Frank goes on after Dana.

5. If Anna goes on sixth, then which of the following could be true?
   - (A) Dana goes on fourth.
   - (B) Chris goes on third.
   - (C) Frank goes on first.
   - (D) Chris goes on fifth.
   - (E) Garry goes on third.

6. In how many different places in the order could Anna go on?
   - (A) three
   - (B) four
   - (C) five
   - (D) six
   - (E) seven

LINEAR GAME 7

In the local swim meet, six swimmers named Anna, Ben, Chris, Dana, Evan, and Frank are lined up in their lanes in order to compete in the 400-meter freestyle race. The lane assignments are determined by the following conditions:

Ben and Dana swim in consecutive lanes.
Anna and Evan swim in consecutive lanes.
Chris and Frank swim in consecutive lanes.
If Evan swims in a lower-numbered lane than Ben, then Frank swims in lane 4.

1. Which of the following could be the order of the lane assignments, from first to last?
   (A) Evan, Anna, Chris, Frank, Dana, Ben.
   (B) Frank, Dana, Chris, Ben, Anna, Evan.
   (C) Dana, Ben, Frank, Anna, Evan, Chris.
   (D) Frank, Chris, Anna, Evan, Ben, Dana.
   (E) None of the above.

2. In which lane can Chris NOT swim?
   (A) 2
   (B) 3
   (C) 4
   (D) 5
   (E) None of the above

3. If Evan swims in lane 2, then which of the following must be true?
   (A) Dana swims in lane 6.
   (B) Chris swims in lane 4.
   (C) Ben swims in lane 5.
   (D) Frank swims in lane 4.
   (E) None of the above.

4. If Anna swims in lane 6, then which of the following must be true?
   (A) Dana swims in the lane numbered just below Ben's lane.
   (B) Frank swims in a lower-numbered lane than Dana.
   (C) Chris swims in a higher-numbered lane than Anna.
   (D) Evan swims in a higher-numbered lane than Dana.
   (E) Frank swims in a lower-numbered lane than Chris.

5. If Chris swims in lane 3, then which of the following must be true?
   (A) Evan swims in a lower-numbered lane than Ben.
   (B) Dana swims in a higher-numbered lane than Ben.
   (C) Anna swims in lane 6 and Evan swims in lane 7.
   (D) Evan swims in a lower-numbered lane than Frank.
   (E) None of the above.

6. If Dana swims in lane 5, then for how many people do we know the exact lane numbers?
   (A) two
   (B) three
   (C) four
   (D) five
   (E) six

LINEAR GAME 8

The planes of several major airlines are lined up waiting to take off down the runway. The pilots of the planes are named Anna, Ben, Chris, Dana, Evan, Frank, and Garry. The order in which they will take off is determined by the following constraints:

If Chris does not take off third, then he takes off sixth.
Ben does not take off consecutively with Dana.
If Anna takes off second, then Ben takes off sixth.
One pilot takes off in between Chris and Dana.
Evan does not take off consecutively with Ben.

1. Which of the following could be the order in which the pilots take off?
   (A) Ben, Anna, Chris, Frank, Dana, Evan, Garry.
   (B) Garry, Frank, Anna, Dana, Ben, Chris, Evan.
   (C) Dana, Frank, Chris, Ben, Evan, Anna, Garry.
   (D) Dana, Anna, Chris, Evan, Frank, Ben, Garry.
   (E) Garry, Anna, Frank, Dana, Evan, Chris, Ben.

2. If Dana takes off fourth, then which of the following must NOT be true?
   (A) Ben takes off seventh.
   (B) Anna takes off second.
   (C) Frank takes off first.
   (D) Evan takes off fifth.
   (E) Garry takes off second.

3. If Anna takes off second, then which of the following must be true?
   (A) Garry takes off sixth.
   (B) Ben takes off fifth.
   (C) Frank takes off fourth.
   (D) Evan takes off seventh.
   (E) Dana takes off first.

4. In which place can Ben never take off?
   (A) Second
   (B) Third
   (C) Fourth
   (D) Fifth
   (E) Sixth

5. If Anna takes off consecutively with Ben and Dana takes off fifth, then which of the following could be true?
   (A) Anna takes off seventh.
   (B) Chris takes off fourth.
   (C) Garry takes off sixth.
   (D) Ben takes off first.
   (E) Frank takes off third.

6. If Ben takes off fifth, then which of the following must NOT be true?
   (A) Anna does not take off fourth or sixth.
   (B) Frank takes off either seventh or fourth.
   (C) Garry takes off second, fourth, sixth, or seventh.
   (D) Evan does not take off second or seventh.
   (E) Ben does not take off consecutively with either Evan or Anna.

ANSWERS AND EXPLANATIONS

Game 5

Initial Setup:

1	2	3	4	5	6	7
G	C	B	A			
				~~E~~		~~F~~

1	2	3	4	5	6	7
	C	G			A	
~~E~~						~~BF~~

1	2	3	4	5	6	7
	C		G			A
~~E~~						~~F~~

Question 1: Which of the following could be the order in which the crocodiles go on?

(A) This is a possible order for the variables.

(B) Evan cannot go fifth in scenario 1.
(C) Anna must go sixth in scenario 2.
(D) This is not close to any scenario.
(E) **A** is the correct answer.

Question 2: If Garry goes first, then which of the following must be true?

(C) This occurs in scenario 1. You can see that Ben must go third.

Question 3: In how many different places could Evan go on?

(C) Evan could go third, fourth, fifth, sixth, or seventh.

Question 4: If Garry goes on third, then which of the following must NOT be true?

(A) This constraint occurs in scenario 2. If Evan went on fourth and Dana went on fifth, then that would cause Ben to go on first, since Ben must precede Anna. This leaves no room for Frank to precede Evan.

Question 5: Which of the following is a complete list of the crocodiles that could go on last?

(C) Anna, Dana, and Evan could all go last.

Question 6: If Anna goes on fourth, then in how many possible orders could the crocodiles go on?

(B) This constraint occurs in the first scenario, where Frank could go on fifth or sixth. Based on Frank's position, Evan could be in either one or two positions, making three total possible orders.

Game 6

Initial Setup:

1.

1	2	3	4	5	6	7
E/B			B/E			
	~~A~~	~~A~~		~~A~~		

2.

1	2	3	4	5	6	7
	E/B			B/E		A
~~A~~		~~A~~	~~A~~		~~A~~ ~~C~~	

3.

1	2	3	4	5	6	7
A		E/B			B/E	
	~~A~~ ~~C~~		~~A~~	~~A~~		~~A~~

4.

1	2	3	4	5	6	7
			E	G		B
~~C~~	~~C~~	~~A~~			~~A~~	

In the fourth scenario, the double possibility is eliminated. Evan must go on fourth, because Garry cannot follow him if Evan goes on seventh.

Question 1: Which of the following could be an order in which the contestants go on the show?

(E) This is a possible order.

(A) Ben and Evan must be separated by two people.
(B) Garry must go on immediately after Evan.
(C) Ben and Evan must be separated by two people.
(D) Anna cannot go on consecutively with Evan.

Question 2: If Anna goes on first and Chris goes on sixth, then which of the following must be true?

(D) This constraint can occur in scenario 4, in which Evan goes on fourth, Garry fifth, and Ben seventh.

Question 3: If Evan goes on third, then which of the following could NOT be true?

(A) This constraint can occur in the third scenario. Chris cannot go on second here, and Garry must go on fourth.

Question 4: If Garry goes on third, then which of the following must be true?

(D) If Garry goes on third, then Evan must go on second due to the box rule, and Ben must go on fifth due to the other box rule:

1	2	3	4	5	6	7
	E	G		B		A
					~~C~~	

You can see that Dana must go before Anna, since Anna is last.

Question 5: If Anna goes on sixth, then which of the following could be true?

(B) This constraint is possible only in the first scenario, in which it is possible for Chris to go third.

(A) Evan or Ben must go on fourth.
(C) Evan or Ben must go on first.
(D) This would make Chris go on consecutively with Anna, which is disallowed by the third constraint.
(E) This would make it impossible for Garry to immediately follow Evan as required by the fourth constraint.

Question 6: In how many different places in the order could Anna go on?

(B) Anna could go on first, second, sixth, or seventh.

Game 7

Initial Setup:

There are six different scenarios for the box rules to go in; you should start by writing all of them out. You will find that two scenarios are impossible because of the $E < B \rightarrow F_4$ constraint. The ones that remain are the following:

A/E E/A C F B/D D/B

B/D D/B C/F F/C A/E E/A

B/D D/B A/E E/A C/F F/C

C/F F/C B/D D/B A/E E/A

Question 1: Which of the following could be the order of the lane assignments, from first to last?
(A) This is a possible order.

(B) Frank and Chris must swim in consecutive lanes, as must Dana and Ben.
(C) Frank and Chris must swim in consecutive lanes.
(D) This scenario is impossible because of the $E < B \rightarrow F_4$ sufficient-necessary constraint.
(E) **A** is the correct answer.

Question 2: In which lane can Chris NOT swim?
(E) Chris can be assigned to any of the lanes.

Question 3: If Evan swims in lane 2, then which of the following must be true?

(D) This constraint is possible in scenario 1. Frank must swim in lane 4, and Chris must swim in lane 3.

Question 4: If Anna swims in lane 6, then which of the following must be true?

(D) This constraint can occur in scenario 2 or 4. In both scenarios, because of the AE box rule, Evan must swim in lane 5. Since you already know lane 6 is occupied by Anna, Evan will swim in a higher-numbered lane than Dana.

Question 5: If Chris swims in lane 3, then which of the following must be true?

(E) This constraint is possible in both scenario 1 and scenario 3.

Question 6: If Dana swims in lane 5, then for how many people do we know the exact lane position?

(C) This constraint is possible in scenario 1, in which Chris swims in lane 3, Frank swims in lane 4, and Ben swims in lane 6 if Dana swims in lane 5.

Game 8

Initial Setup:

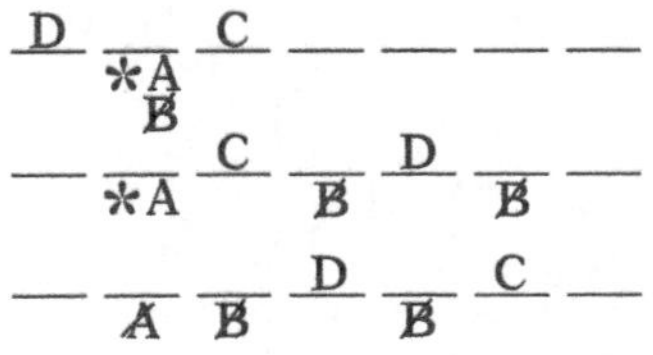

Question 1: Which of the following could be the order in which the pilots take off?

(D) This is a possible order of the variables.

(A) If Anna is second, then Ben is sixth.
(B) Ben cannot go next to Dana.
(C) Ben and Evan cannot go next to each other.
(E) If Anna is second, then Ben is sixth.

Question 2: If Dana takes off fourth, then which of the following must NOT be true?

(B) If Dana takes off fourth, then this puts you in the third scenario. Your vacancy rules tell you that Anna cannot go second and that Ben cannot go third or fifth, and your box rules tell you that Evan cannot go consecutively with Ben.

Question 3: If Anna takes off second, then which of the following must be true?

(E) This constraint could happen only in scenario 1. It appears that scenario 2 would also work, but it does not, because that would force Ben to go consecutively with Dana, which violates a constraint. The diagram for scenario 1 when Anna takes off second is as follows:

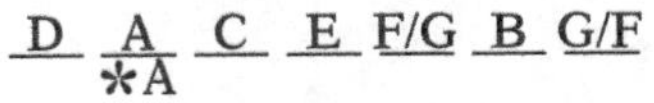

You can see that Dana must take off first.

Question 4: In which place can Ben never take off?

(B) Ben can never take off in the third position because C is usually there, and in the third scenario, he cannot go there.

Question 5: If Anna takes off consecutively with Ben and Dana takes off fifth, then which of the following could be true?

The following is the diagram for this question:

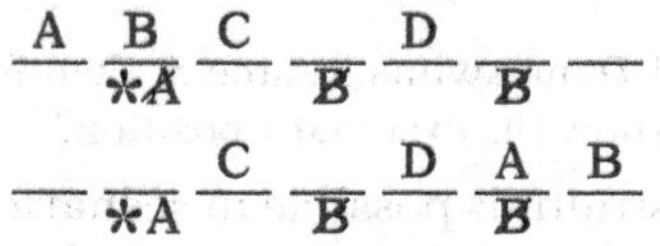

(C) Garry could go sixth in the upper scenario.

Question 6: If Ben takes off fifth, then which of the following must NOT be true?

(D) This constraint is possible only in scenario 1. The following diagram represents this question:

Evan must go second or seventh.

CHAPTER 4

COMPLEX LINEAR GAMES

Complex linear games use the same types of logic tools that regular linear games use. However, complex linear games are two-dimensional and need to be diagrammed using a two-dimensional grid instead of the straight-line continuum that is used to map regular linear games. Therefore, the logic tools that you used in the past will still be valid, but you will need to tweak them a little in order to apply them to the two-dimensional diagrams in complex linear games.

Typical Fact Pattern

> The doctor will see ten patients this week from Monday to Friday. He will see one patient each morning and one patient each afternoon. Anna, Ben, Chris, Dana, and Evan all work mornings and therefore can be seen only in the afternoon. Frank, Garry, Hillary, Iris, and Julian all work afternoons and can be seen only in the morning.
>
> Ben is seen on the same day as Julian.
> Evan is seen on Wednesday.
> Dana is seen on the day before Anna.
> Iris is seen on the same day as Anna.
> Chris is seen before the day Julian is seen.

Logic Tools

General

A typical diagram for this problem is the following:

	M	T	W	Th	F
A–E					
F–J					

You can see that A–E can go only in the top part of the day, which represents the afternoon, and F–J can go only in the bottom, which represents the morning. Everything else is the same as in linear games, except for minor changes in box rules and the addition of new box rules.

Box Rules

Constraint
Ben is seen on the same day as Julian.

Box Rule:
Write on your paper:

B
J

Box Rule Addition

Constraint
Iris is seen on the same day as Anna.

Box Rule:
Write on your paper:

A
I

Constraint
Dana is seen on the day before Anna.

Box Rule:
Write on your paper:

D	A

The variable A is common to these two boxes, so the box rules can be consolidated into the following:

D	A
	I

This box should be moved throughout the diagram of the game to create a number of scenarios for the variables.

Fact Pattern Organization Heuristics

The fact pattern organization heuristic for complex linear games is the same as the heuristic for linear games:

1. **Transcribe** the constraints.
2. Draw the complex linear scenarios.
   a. Is there a **burdensome constraint**?
   b. Draw in other evident constraints.
3. Write out the **vacancy-occupancy** rules.
   a. Draw in **vacancy** rules.
   b. Draw in **double possibilities** and other occupancy rules.
   c. Eliminate **repetitive rules.**
4. Make **deductions** from the diagram.

Review

In this section, you have learned all of the following:

1. How to draw a typical diagram for complex linear games.
2. How to use box rules for complex linear games.
3. How to add linear box rules together to make complex linear box rules.

Now you are ready to walk through the resolution of a couple of actual games. Take them slowly and pay attention to how the constraints that you have learned previously—sequencing constraints, direct placement, and formal logic constraints—function in these two-dimensional games.

Complex Linear Games Explained

COMPLEX LINEAR GAME I

Four newscasters named Anna, Ben, Chris, and Dana are scheduled to interview four athletes named Evan, Frank, Garry, and Hillary. There are four time slots for interviews, each of which will be occupied by one newscaster and one athlete. The people who are paired together in each time slot are determined by the following:

Dana does not interview Hillary or Frank.
Chris interviews Evan.
If Garry is not interviewed first, then he is interviewed last.
Hillary is interviewed in the time slot immediately before Evan's.

1. Which of the following could be the order in which the athletes are interviewed, from first to last?

    (A) Hillary, Evan, Frank, Garry.
    (B) Evan, Frank, Hillary, Garry.
    (C) Hillary, Garry, Evan, Frank.
    (D) Evan, Hillary, Frank, Garry.
    (E) Garry, Frank, Evan, Hillary.

2. If Frank is interviewed fourth, then which of the following must be true?

    (A) Dana interviews fourth.
    (B) Ben interviews second.
    (C) Chris interviews third.
    (D) Anna interviews first.
    (E) Evan is interviewed second.

3. If Anna interviews third, then which of the following must NOT be true?

    (A) Chris interviews second.
    (B) Frank is interviewed fourth.
    (C) Chris interviews fourth.
    (D) Ben interviews first.
    (E) Hillary is interviewed first.

4. If Dana interviews in a time slot consecutive with the one in which Chris interviews, then which of the following must be true?

    (A) Anna interviews second.
    (B) Frank is interviewed first.
    (C) Ben interviews second.
    (D) Garry is interviewed first.
    (E) Evan is interviewed second.

5. How many people cannot interview or be interviewed last?

    (A) one
    (B) two
    (C) three
    (D) four
    (E) five

6. If Anna and Ben interview in consecutive time slots, then which of the following must be true?

    (A) Dana interviews Garry in time slot 3.
    (B) Ben interviews Garry before Evan is interviewed.
    (C) Chris does not interview in a time slot consecutive with the one in which Hillary is interviewed.
    (D) Garry is interviewed first, and Hillary is interviewed second.
    (E) Hillary does not interview in a time slot before the one in which Frank is interviewed.

SOLUTION STEPS

1. Transcribe the Constraints

1. **Sufficient-Necessary:**
   $\not{G}_1 \rightarrow G_4$; $\not{G}_4 \rightarrow G_1$

2. **Box Rule:** D / F (separated by a diagonal line)

3. **Box Rule:** D / H (separated by a diagonal line)

4. **Box Rule:**

C
E

5. **Box Rule:**

H	E

Notice that box rules 4 and 5 can be added to make the following more comprehensive box rule:

	C
H	E

2. Draw the Complex Linear Scenarios. *Is there a burdensome constraint?* Yes, the CEH box is very restrictive and can go in only three places, so you should draw out these scenarios:

			C
		H	E

		C	
	H	E	

	C		
H	E		

Draw in other evident constraints.

The sufficient-necessary constraint tells you that G can go only first or last, so you should note this in your diagram. There are only four variables in the bottom, so if you learn the place of G in any of the diagrams, then you will also know the place of F.

			C
G	F	H	E

		C	
G/F	H	E	F/G

	C		
H	E	F	G

3. Write Out the Vacancy-Occupancy Rules. *Draw in vacancy rules for each possible scenario.* You know that Dana cannot interview Frank or Hillary—or Evan, since Chris must interview him—so you can determine the place of Dana in a couple of scenarios, or at least find a vacancy rule:

D			C
G	F	H	E

	~~D~~	C	
G/F	H	E	F/G

	C		D
H	E	F	G

Draw in double possibilities and other occupancy rules.

Notice how the vacancy rule in the second scenario leads you to write in a double possibility here:

D	A/B	B/A	C
G	F	H	E

	A/B	C	
G/F	H	E	F/G

A/B	C	A/B	D
H	E	F	G

4. Make Deductions from the Diagram. There are no more deductions that can be made here, but it is always good as a habit to question whether there are. This sometimes will show you more deductions and always will force you to process the game on a deeper level and therefore remember more of it when it is necessary.

ANSWERING THE QUESTIONS

Question 1: Which of the following could be the order in which the athletes are interviewed, from first to last?

(A) This order can happen in the third scenario.

Question 2: If Frank is interviewed fourth, then which of the following must be true?

(C) This constraint must occur in the second scenario, and it would cause Garry to be interviewed first. Chris interviews third in this scenario.

Question 3: If Anna interviews third, then which of the following must NOT be true?

(B) This constraint can happen in either the first or the third scenario. Frank cannot be interviewed fourth in either of these scenarios.

Question 4: If Dana interviews in a time slot consecutive with the one in which Chris interviews, then which of the following must be true?

(B) This constraint is possible only in the second scenario. Dana would interview fourth to be consecutive with Chris, and since she cannot interview Frank due to the no-box rule, Frank must be interviewed first.

Question 5: How many people cannot interview or be interviewed last?

(A) Frank, Garry, and Evan can be interviewed last. Anna, Ben, Chris, and Dana can interview last. This leaves Hillary as the only person not able to go last.

Question 6: If Anna and Ben interview in consecutive time slots, then which of the following must be true?

(E) This constraint can happen in the first or the second scenario. It seems that Hillary can be interviewed before Frank in the second scenario, but if Anna and Ben are consecutive, then they occupy the first two time slots, forcing Dana to slot 4. Frank cannot be interviewed by Dana, so that forces him to slot 1. This slot precedes Hillary's, which is slot 2.

COMPLEX LINEAR GAME 2

At an animal therapy session, a group of dogs named Anna, Ben, Chris, Dana, and Evan are each paired with one of the following cats: Frank, Garry, Hillary, Iris, and Julian. During the session, one dog will be isolated with one cat for several hours in each of the therapy rooms—1 through 5. The purpose of the session is to breed harmony and engender camaraderie between the species. The pairs and room assignments are governed by the following constraints:

Dana is in room 3.
Chris is paired with Garry.
Frank is paired with Ben.
Anna is in a lower-numbered therapy room than Dana and Garry.
Julian is in room 2.

1. Which of the following could NOT be two animals that are paired together?
   (A) Ben, Frank.
   (B) Julian, Evan.
   (C) Iris, Dana.
   (D) Hillary, Chris.
   (E) Anna, Iris.

2. Which of the following could be the list of the cats in the rooms from first to last?
   (A) Frank, Julian, Iris, Hillary, Garry.
   (B) Frank, Iris, Julian, Garry, Hillary.
   (C) Hillary, Garry, Iris, Julian, Frank.
   (D) Frank, Julian, Garry, Hillary, Iris.
   (E) Hillary, Julian, Frank, Iris, Garry.

3. How many different cats could Anna potentially be paired with?
   (A) one
   (B) two
   (C) three
   (D) four
   (E) five

4. If Iris is in therapy room 4, then which of the following must be true?
   (A) Garry is in therapy room 3.
   (B) Hillary is in therapy room 2.
   (C) Frank is in therapy room 1.
   (D) Chris is in therapy room 2.
   (E) Ben is in therapy room 5.

5. Which of the following could be true?
   (A) Chris is paired with Hillary.
   (B) Anna is in a higher-numbered room than Dana.
   (C) Anna is in a higher-numbered room than Julian.
   (D) Iris is paired with Dana.
   (E) Frank is in therapy room 3.

6. Which of the following must NOT be true?
   (A) Chris is in a lower-numbered room than Iris.
   (B) Dana is in a higher-numbered room than Garry.
   (C) Ben is not in a room that is consecutively numbered with Evan's room.
   (D) Julian is in a room that is consecutively numbered with Iris's room.
   (E) Garry and Hillary are not in consecutively numbered rooms.

SOLUTION STEPS

1. Transcribe the Constraints

1. **Direct Placement:** **D = 3**
2. **Direct Placement:** **J = 2**
3. **Box Rule:** C / G (boxed together)
4. **Box Rule:** B / F (boxed together)
5. **Sequencing Rule:** **A < D**
6. **Sequencing Rule:** **A < G**

2. Draw the Complex Linear Scenarios. *Is there a burdensome constraint?* There does not yet appear to be a burdensome constraint.

	1	2	3	4	5
A–E			D		
F–J		J			

3. Write Out the Vacancy-Occupancy Rules. *Draw in vacancy rules.* The sequential constraints impose some restraint on the CG box, because Anna must be in a lower-numbered room than Garry. This means that Chris and Garry cannot go in the first room. Anna must also go in a room with a lower number than Dana's, leaving Anna the option of going in only the first or the second room.

~~C~~		D	~~A~~	~~A~~
~~G~~	J			

Looking further into the diagram, you can see that the CG box can go only in the fourth or the fifth room. This would leave the BF box able to go in either the first or in one of the last two rooms that the CG box does not occupy. This makes a total of four scenarios that you can draw in:

		D	B	C
	J		F	G

		D	C	B
	J		G	F

B		D	~~A~~	C
F	J			G

B		D	C	~~A~~
F	J		G	

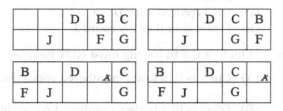

Draw in double possibilities and other occupancy rules. In the bottom two scenarios, you can deduce where the variables must go in the top row. In all other places in the game, you can write in double possibilities:

A/E	E/A	D	B	C
H/I	J	I/H	F	G

A/E	E/A	D	C	B
H/I	J	I/H	G	F

B	A	D	E	C
F	J	H/I	I/H	G

B	A	D	C	E
F	J	H/I	G	I/H

4. Make Deductions from the Diagram. There are no deductions left to make. As you improve at spotting different scenarios for the variables, there will be some occasions in the future when you will recognize that there are a limited number of scenarios but that you might not need to write them all out because you can remember them in your head. In the meantime, it is best to take things slowly and write them out as your brain exercises and accustoms itself to assimilating these techniques.

ANSWERING THE QUESTIONS

Question 1: Which of the following could NOT be two animals that are paired together?

(D) Chris must always be paired with Garry.

(A) Ben and Frank must always be paired.

(B) Julian and Evan could be paired in either of the top two scenarios.

(C) Iris and Dana could be paired in all four scenarios.

(E) Anna and Iris could be paired in either of the top two scenarios.

The LSAT is a confusing test. Taking scenarios to this level of analysis would be unnecessarily time-consuming and therefore a poor choice when you have only eight minutes to get through each game. Learning to understand generalized scenarios is an important skill this book practices.

Question 2: Which of the following could be the list of the cats in the rooms, from first to last?

(A) This order is possible in the bottom left scenario.

Question 3: How many different cats could Anna potentially be paired with?

(C) Anna could be paired with Hillary, Iris, or Julian.

Question 4: If Iris is in therapy room 4, then which of the following must be true?

(C) This constraint is possible only in the bottom left scenario, in which Frank must be in the first room.

Question 5: Which of the following could be true?

(D) This answer choice could occur in any scenario.

(A) Chris is always paired with Garry.

(B) Anna must always be in a lower-numbered room than Dana.

(C) Anna must always be in the same room as or in a lower-numbered room than Julian.

(E) Frank can never be in therapy room 3, because he has to be paired with Ben, and Dana is assigned to room 3.

Question 6: Which of the following must NOT be true?

(B) Dana must never be in a higher-numbered room than Garry, because Garry can never go in therapy room 1 or 2.

COMPLEX LINEAR GAME 3

At a Ping-Pong exhibition, players from the United States named Anna, Ben, Chris, Dana, and Evan are matched up with players from Canada named Frank, Garry, Hillary, Iris, and Julian at tables numbered 1 through 5. All people will play, and no person will play someone from his or her own country. The matchups and the tables at which the players will play are determined by the following constraints:

The number of Ben's table is two greater than the number of Dana's.
The number of Hillary's table is two less than the number of Julian's.
If Chris does not play on the table numbered one less than Anna's table, then Garry plays on the table numbered one less than Iris's table.
Ben does not play Hillary or Julian.
Dana does not play Hillary or Julian.

1. Which of the following could be the order in which the Canadian players play, from the lowest-numbered to the highest-numbered table?
   (A) Frank, Julian, Garry, Iris, Hillary.
   (B) Iris, Garry, Hillary, Frank, Julian.
   (C) Hillary, Frank, Julian, Garry, Iris.
   (D) Iris, Hillary, Garry, Frank, Julian.
   (E) None of the above.

2. If Chris plays on table 4, then which of the following must be true?
   (A) Evan plays on table 2.
   (B) Iris plays on table 3.
   (C) Garry plays on table 5.
   (D) Anna plays on table 3.
   (E) None of the above.

3. If Ben plays with Frank, then which of the following could be true?
   (A) Iris plays on table 4.
   (B) Garry plays on table 2.
   (C) Garry plays on table 4.
   (D) Ben plays with Julian.
   (E) None of the above.

4. Which table could Garry NOT play on?
   (A) 1
   (B) 2
   (C) 3
   (D) 4
   (E) 5

5. Which of the following players could never be paired together?
   (A) Ben, Garry.
   (B) Iris, Anna.
   (C) Garry, Chris.
   (D) Dana, Julian.
   (E) None of the above.

6. If Hillary plays on table 2, then how many different configurations of the players in the tournament are possible?
   (A) six
   (B) eight
   (C) ten
   (D) twelve
   (E) fourteen

SOLUTION STEPS

1. Transcribe the Constraints

1. **Box Rule:** D/H
2. **Box Rule:** D/J
3. **Box Rule:** B/H
4. **Box Rule:** B/J
5. **Box Rule:** D __ B
6. **Box Rule:** H __ J
7. **Sufficient-Necessary:**

C/A → G/I ; G/I → C/A

Ask yourself what this constraint means. It essentially says that either GI is a box or CA is a box—if one is not a box, then the other must be. Of course, both are concurrently possible.

2. Draw the Complex Linear Scenarios. *Is there a burdensome constraint?* Yes; when you combine the activity of the DB box with that of the HJ box, then only a couple of scenarios arise for the game. The DB box can go in three places, and its placement will dictate the position of the HJ box, since neither Dana nor Ben can play Hillary or Julian.

D		B		
	H		J	

		D		B
	H		J	

	D		B	
H		J		

	D		B	
		H		J

Draw in other evident constraints.

You should now remember your sufficient-necessary constraints. They require that Chris play immediately before Anna or Garry play immediately before Iris.

D		B	C	A
	H		J	

C	A	D		B
	H		J	

	D		B	
H		J	G	I

	D		B	
G	I	H		J

Since you know where four variables are in some rows, you automatically know where the fifth is:

D	E	B	C	A
	H		J	

C	A	D	E	B
	H		J	

	D		B	
H	F	J	G	I

	D		B	
G	I	H	F	J

3. Write Out the Vacancy-Occupancy Rules. In this instance, there are no more rules that can be drawn. Regardless, you should still consider this step, since often in games there are more variables to be drawn in or there are rules that you might have forgotten to include. Just to be safe, always include the consideration of this step.

4. Make Deductions from the Diagram. The deductions are that the DB box can go in any of three places and that the HJ box's placement is entirely dependent on the DB box's position.

ANSWERING THE QUESTIONS

Question 1: Which of the following could be the order in which the Canadian players play, from the lowest-numbered to the highest-numbered table?

(C) This order is possible in the bottom left scenario.

Question 2: If Chris plays on table 4, then which of the following must be true?

(A) This constraint can happen only in the upper left scenario, in which Evan must play on table 2.

Question 3: If Ben plays with Frank, then which of the following could be true?

(E) None of these scenarios is possible.

Question 4: Which table could Garry not play on?

(B) Garry cannot play on table 2 in any scenario.

Question 5: Which of the following players could never be paired together?

(D) The initial constraints tell you that Dana and Julian cannot face each other.

(A) Ben can be paired with Garry in the bottom left scenario.
(B) Iris and Anna could be paired in both of the left scenarios.
(C) Garry and Chris could be paired in both of the right scenarios.
(E) **D** is the correct answer.

Question 6: If Hillary plays on table 2, then how many different configurations of the players in the tournament are possible?

(D) This constraint is possible in the following two scenarios:

D	E	B	C	A
	H		J	

C	A	D	E	B
	H		J	

How many different places could F, G, and I go in either scenario? They could go:

1. FGI
2. FIG
3. GFI
4. GIF
5. IGF
6. IFG

There are six possibilities for each game, making a total of twelve.

COMPLEX LINEAR GAME 4

Many people claim that over time, pets and their owners come to have similar facial characteristics. Scientists wanting to test this theory have decided to give five people five houses to live in with five different dogs for six months. Each person will live in one house, numbered from 1 to 5, with one of the five dogs. The people are named Anna, Ben, Chris, Dana, and Evan, and the dogs are named Frank, Garry, Hillary, Iris, and Julian. People are given pets and houses based on the following conditions:

If Anna is not in house 5, then Anna is in house 2 and Hillary is in a higher-numbered house than Ben.

If Hillary is not in house 5, then Hillary is in house 3, Chris is in house 1, and Julian is in house 1.

Ben and Evan are in consecutively numbered houses.

Hillary and Iris are in consecutively numbered houses.

1. Which of the following could be the order of the pet owners in their houses, from the lowest-numbered house to the highest?
   (A) Dana, Chris, Anna, Ben, Evan.
   (B) Chris, Dana, Evan, Ben, Anna.
   (C) Chris, Ben, Dana, Evan, Anna.
   (D) Dana, Anna, Evan, Chris, Ben.
   (E) Chris, Anna, Dana, Evan, Ben.

2. Which of the following is a complete list of the dogs that Anna could be paired with?
   (A) Iris, Hillary.
   (B) Frank, Garry, Hillary.
   (C) Garry, Julian, Frank.
   (D) Hillary, Frank, Garry, Julian.
   (E) Frank, Garry, Hillary, Iris, Julian.

3. If Hillary is in house 3, then which of the following must NOT be true?
   (A) Dana is in house 2.
   (B) Iris is not in house 5.
   (C) Chris is in house 1.
   (D) Dana is in house 3.
   (E) Evan is in house 4.

4. If Anna is in house 2, then which of the following must NOT be true?
   (A) Frank is in house 3.
   (B) Evan is in house 1.
   (C) Julian is in house 2.
   (D) Dana shares a house with Frank.
   (E) Garry shares a house with Anna.

5. Which of the following could potentially live in the greatest number of houses?
   (A) Ben
   (B) Julian
   (C) Hillary
   (D) Frank
   (E) Iris

6. How many different houses could Julian live in?
   (A) one
   (B) two
   (C) three
   (D) four
   (E) five

SOLUTION STEPS

1. Transcribe the Constraints

1. **Sufficient-Necessary:** $\cancel{A_5} \rightarrow A_2$; $\cancel{A_2} \rightarrow A_5$
2. **Sufficient-Necessary:** $\cancel{A_5} \rightarrow B < H$;
   $H \leq B \rightarrow A_5$
3. **Sufficient-Necessary:** $\cancel{H_5} \rightarrow H_3$; $\cancel{H_3} \rightarrow H_5$
4. **Sufficient-Necessary:** $\cancel{H_5} \rightarrow C_1$; $\cancel{C_1} \rightarrow H_5$
5. **Sufficient-Necessary:** $\cancel{H_5} \rightarrow J_1$; $\cancel{J_1} \rightarrow H_5$
6. **Box Rule** [B E]
7. **Box Rule** [H I]

2. Draw the Complex Linear Scenarios. *Is there a burdensome constraint?* There are not really any burdensome constraints. However, the sufficient-necessary variables should be drawn in. These are the fact that Anna can go only in house 2 or 5 and the fact that Hillary can go only in house 3 or 5. You should test to see what kind of implications these facts have on the rest of the game:

				A
				H

	A			
				H

				A
		H		

	A			
		H		

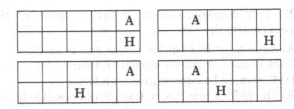

Remember that when Anna is not in house 5, Ben has to be in a lower-numbered house than Hillary, which is why, when Anna is in house 2, Hillary cannot be in house 3 because Chris has to be in house 1 when Hillary is in 3. Also, note that when Hillary is in house 3, Chris is in house 1 and Julian is in house 1. You should draw all this information into the diagram:

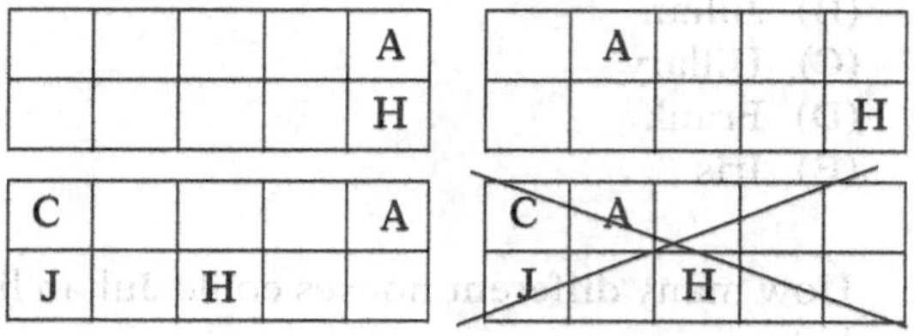

Draw in other evident constraints.

Draw in the information that you know from the box rules:

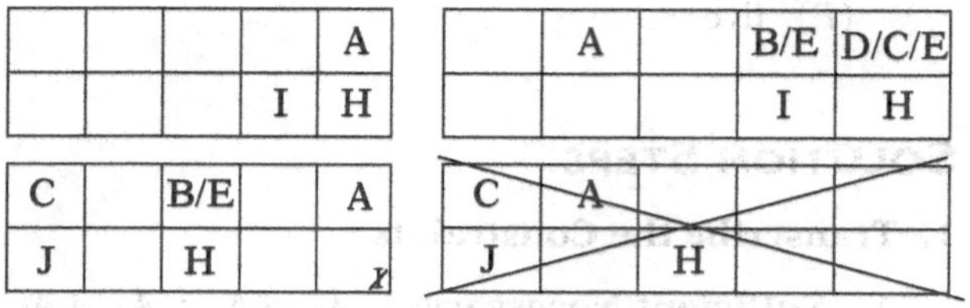

3. Write Out the Vacancy-Occupancy Rules. This was done in the previous step—you know that Evan must be consecutive with Ben, so Chris or Dana must go in house 1 in the upper left scenario.

4. Make Deductions from the Diagram. Notice that Hillary can go in house 3 in only one scenario. Other than that, realize that these diagrams will be very helpful when solving problems, but currently, they are all pretty similar and open. Dana can go in numerous places along with most of the variables on the bottom. Keep this in mind because you will have to do a little diagramming on top of these diagrams when answering questions.

Answering the Questions

Question 1: Which of the following could be the order of the pet owners in their houses, from the lowest-numbered house to the highest?

(B) This constraint could occur in either of the scenarios on the left.

(A) Anna must be in either house 2 or house 5.
(C) Ben must be consecutive with Evan.
(D) Ben must be consecutive with Evan.
(E) The order Chris, Anna, Dana is not possible in any scenario.

Question 2: Which of the following is a complete list of the dogs that Anna could be paired with?

(D) Anna can never be paired with Iris. You will notice that in the bottom left diagram, Hillary's being in house 3 prevents Iris from being in house 5 due to the box rule.

Question 3: If Hillary is in house 3, then which of the following must NOT be true?

(D) This constraint occurs only in the bottom left scenario. Everything could be true except for Dana's being in house 3, because Dana's being in house 3 would split up the BE box.

Question 4: If Anna is in house 2, then which of the following must NOT be true?

(B) This constraint occurs in the right scenario, and Evan cannot be in house 1 in any of the scenarios because Evan must be consecutive with Ben.

Question 5: Which of the following could potentially live in the greatest number of houses?

(D) Frank could live in any of the five houses.

(A) Ben could be in four houses.
(B) Julian could be in three houses.
(C) Hillary could live in two houses.
(E) Iris could live in three houses.

Question 6: How many different houses could Julian live in?

(C) The three scenarios demonstrate that Julian could live in three different houses.

On Your Own

COMPLEX LINEAR GAME 5

At a job orientation, coworkers are paired and then put in rooms in order to talk and get to know each other better. One senior adviser is always paired with one junior associate. The senior advisers are Anna, Ben, Chris, and Dana, and the junior associates are named Evan, Frank, Garry, and Hillary. The rooms are numbered from 1 to 4, and only one pair will be in each room. The room assignments and pairings are governed by the following constraints:

Dana is in a lower-numbered room than Anna.
If Evan is in room 1, then Dana is in room 3.
Hillary is not in a room with Chris or Anna.
If Chris is in room 2, then Anna is in room 3.
Ben is paired with Evan.

1. Whom must Dana be paired with?
   (A) Evan
   (B) Frank
   (C) Garry
   (D) Hillary
   (E) None of the above

2. Which of the following is a possible order of the senior advisers, from room 1 to room 4?
   (A) Ben, Chris, Anna, Dana.
   (B) Anna, Chris, Dana, Ben.
   (C) Chris, Dana, Ben, Anna.
   (D) Ben, Chris, Dana, Anna.
   (E) None of the above.

3. If Hillary is in room 1, then which of the following must be true?
   (A) Anna shares a room with Garry.
   (B) Chris shares a room with Frank.
   (C) Chris is in room 2.
   (D) Ben is in a room consecutive with Chris's room.
   (E) None of the above.

4. If Chris is in room 2, then which of the following must be true?
   (A) Frank is in room 3.
   (B) Frank is in room 2.
   (C) Evan is in room 4.
   (D) Hillary is in room 2.
   (E) None of the above.

5. If Anna is in a room consecutively numbered with the rooms of both Dana and Chris, then which of the following could NOT be true?
   (A) Hillary is paired with Dana in room 2.
   (B) Chris is not paired with Frank in room 1.
   (C) Frank is paired with Anna in room 2.
   (D) Evan is paired with Ben in room 4.
   (E) None of the above.

6. Which room could Ben never be in?
   (A) 1
   (B) 2
   (C) 3
   (D) 4
   (E) None of the above

COMPLEX LINEAR GAME 6

In four showrooms, numbered 1 through 4, tigers are being shown and sold to zookeepers by salespeople. In every room there is exactly one tiger and one salesperson. The names of the tigers are Anna, Ben, Chris, and Dana, and the names of the salespeople are Evan, Frank, Garry, and Hillary. The rooms where the tigers are shown and the salespeople are showing them are determined by the following constraints:

Chris is not in a showroom with Frank or Hillary.
If Ben is shown by Frank, then Anna is shown by Garry.
If Dana is shown by Frank, then Anna is shown by Hillary.
Frank is in showroom 3.
Chris is in a higher-numbered room than Anna.
Garry is in a lower-numbered room than Hillary.

1. Which tiger can NOT be in showroom 3?

    (A) Anna
    (B) Ben
    (C) Chris
    (D) Dana
    (E) None of the above

2. Which of the following could NOT be true?

    (A) Dana is shown in showroom 3 by Frank.
    (B) Anna is shown in showroom 2 by Garry.
    (C) Chris is shown in showroom 4 by Evan.
    (D) Ben is shown in showroom 1 by Garry.
    (E) None of the above.

3. If Ben is shown in showroom 3, then which of the following must be true?

    (A) Evan shows Chris in showroom 2.
    (B) Frank shows Anna in showroom 4.
    (C) Hillary shows Dana in showroom 2.
    (D) Garry shows Anna in showroom 1.
    (E) None of the above.

4. If Frank shows Dana, then which of the following must NOT be true?

    (A) Garry shows Ben in showroom 1.
    (B) Evan shows Chris in showroom 4.
    (C) Hillary shows Anna in showroom 2.
    (D) Frank shows Dana in showroom 3.
    (E) None of the above.

5. If Anna is shown in showroom 2, then which of the following must NOT be true?

    (A) Chris is shown in showroom 4.
    (B) Ben is shown in showroom 3.
    (C) Evan shows in showroom 4.
    (D) Garry does not show in showroom 2.
    (E) None of the above.

6. If Ben is shown by Frank, then how many possible configurations of the variables are there?

    (A) two
    (B) four
    (C) six
    (D) eight
    (E) None of the above

COMPLEX LINEAR GAME 7

Five models are selected to hand out medals and thank-you cards to Olympic athletes returning home. The Welcoming Committee flies each of the five athletes, named Anna, Ben, Chris, Dana, and Evan, home in a different plane and sends one model from among Frank, Garry, Hillary, Iris, and Julian to welcome each plane. Each model welcomes only one athlete, and all athletes receive only one greeting. The planes that carry the athletes and the models who greet them are determined by the following constraints:

Anna is in plane 3.
Evan is in a plane with a lower number than the plane that Julian greets.
Anna does not fly in a plane that is numbered consecutively with Chris's plane.
If Ben flies in plane 2, then Frank greets plane 2.
Evan does not fly in a plane that is numbered consecutively with Anna's plane.
Garry greets a plane that is numbered consecutively with Chris's plane.

1. Which of the following could be the order of the athletes in the planes, from 1 to 5?
   (A) Chris, Ben, Anna, Dana, Evan.
   (B) Evan, Chris, Anna, Dana, Ben.
   (C) Evan, Ben, Anna, Dana, Chris.
   (D) Ben, Dana, Anna, Evan, Chris.
   (E) Dana, Chris, Evan, Anna, Ben.

2. Who must greet plane 4?
   (A) Frank
   (B) Garry
   (C) Hillary
   (D) Iris
   (E) Julian

3. Which of the following is a pair of people either of whom could greet Ben?
   (A) Hillary, Garry.
   (B) Iris, Frank.
   (C) Hillary, Julian.
   (D) Garry, Frank.
   (E) Julian, Iris.

4. If Frank greets plane 2, then which of the following must be true?
   (A) Ben flies in plane 2.
   (B) Hillary greets plane 3.
   (C) Garry greets Ben in plane 4.
   (D) Frank greets a lower-numbered plane than the one Iris greets.
   (E) Julian does not greet plane 1.

5. If Frank greets Anna, then which of the following must be true?
   (A) Dana flies in plane 2.
   (B) Hillary greets plane 1.
   (C) Julian greets plane 5.
   (D) Ben is greeted by Julian.
   (E) Chris is greeted by Hillary.

6. If Ben flies in plane 2 and Hillary greets Chris, then which of the following must be true?
   (A) Frank greets Chris.
   (B) Julian greets Ben.
   (C) Iris greets Evan.
   (D) Garry does not greet Dana.
   (E) Hillary greets Anna.

COMPLEX LINEAR GAME 8

At a rock concert, there are five band members named Anna, Ben, Chris, Dana, and Evan. The auditorium assigns a dressing room to each star, along with one attendant. The dressing rooms are numbered 1 through 5, and the attendants are named Frank, Garry, Hillary, Iris, and Julian. Each rock star gets one room and one attendant, but which rock star gets which attendant and which room is dictated by the following constraints:

Julian attends the room that is numbered one less than the room Garry attends.
Dana is in the room that is numbered one less than the room Julian attends.
Ben is in room 5.
Evan is not in a room numbered consecutively with Chris's or Anna's room.
Frank does not attend a room numbered consecutively with the room Hillary attends.

1. Which of the following is a possible order of the rock stars, from room 1 to room 5?
   (A) Evan, Dana, Chris, Ben, Anna.
   (B) Dana, Anna, Chris, Evan, Ben.
   (C) Evan, Anna, Dana, Chris, Ben.
   (D) Chris, Anna, Dana, Evan, Ben.
   (E) None of the above.

2. If Evan is in room 4, then which of the following must be true?
   (A) Chris is in room 2.
   (B) Frank attends room 3.
   (C) Anna is in room 2.
   (D) Iris attends room 2.
   (E) None of the above.

3. Which of the following must NOT be true?
   (A) Julian attends room 4.
   (B) Dana is in room 1.
   (C) Garry attends Ben.
   (D) Hillary attends Dana.
   (E) None of the above.

4. If Anna is in room 3, then which of the following must NOT be true?
   (A) Iris attends room 1.
   (B) Hillary attends room 5.
   (C) Hillary attends room 2.
   (D) Chris is attended by Garry.
   (E) None of the above.

5. If Chris is in room 1, then how many different possible configurations of the variables are there?
   (A) two
   (B) four
   (C) six
   (D) eight
   (E) ten

6. Which of the following is a pair neither of whom could be attended by Garry?
   (A) Anna, Dana.
   (B) Chris, Ben.
   (C) Dana, Evan.
   (D) Chris, Anna.
   (E) None of the above.

ANSWERS AND EXPLANATIONS

Game 5

Initial Setup:

This game is fairly open, so you should transcribe all of your constraints. Notice that since Hillary cannot be paired with Chris or Anna or with Ben (since Ben is paired with Evan), there is a DH box. From that we can surmise three scenarios where the DH box can go. Its placement is limited, since Dana's room number must precede Anna's.

D	*C		
H			

C	D	A/B	B/A
F/G	H		

C	B	D	A
F/G	E	H	G/F

The most difficult deduction of the game is figuring out that Chris must be in room 1 in scenario 2. You know that Evan cannot be in room 1, since that would force Dana to be in room 3. Therefore, Ben cannot be in room 1, since the box rule would force Evan to be in room 1 too. We know that Anna cannot be in room 1, since Dana must be in a lower-numbered room than Anna. Therefore, Chris must be in room 1, with the double possibility on the lower row.

Question 1: Whom must Dana be paired with?

(D) This is a pivotal deduction in the game. D must be paired with H.

Question 2: Which of the following is a possible order of the senior advisers, from room 1 to room 4?

(C) This order is possible in scenario 2.

(A) Ben can never be in room 1.
(B) Anna's room can never have a number lower than Dana's.
(D) Ben can never be in room 1.
(E) **C** is the correct answer.

Question 3: If Hillary is in room 1, then which of the following must be true?

(E) This constraint is possible only in the first scenario, a scenario that tells you nothing else about the game except for the fact that Dana must also be in room 1.

Question 4: If Chris is in room 2, then which of the following must be true?

(C) This constraint is possible only in the first scenario, and it will impose a sufficient-necessary constraint on the game. Dana is in room 1, and if Chris is in room 2, then the sufficient-necessary constraint says that Anna must be in room 3, which leaves only one place in the top row for Ben to be in, which is room 4. Evan is paired with Ben, so he must also be in room 4.

Question 5: If Anna is in a room consecutively numbered with the rooms of both Dana and Chris, then which of the following could NOT be true?

(A) This constraint means that Anna must be between Dana and Chris. This is possible only in the first scenario. The order of the advisers must be Dana, Anna, Chris, Ben. This puts Evan in room 4 and Hillary in room 1.

Question 6: Which room could Ben never be in?

(A) Ben is in room 2 in the third scenario, and he could be in room 3 or 4 in the second scenario. He could never be in room 1 in any of the scenarios.

Game 6

Initial Setup:

If you fill in all of the vacancy-occupancy rules, then you will see that certain variables must go in certain places.

A–D	~~C~~		~~C~~	~~A~~
E–H	~~H~~		F	~~G~~

After you do this, you should see that Chris can go in only two places. Draw these scenarios and see if you can make deductions from them:

A–D	A	C	B	D
E–H	G	E	F	H

			C
G ~~H~~	H	F	E ~~G~~

You see the several deductions that can be made based on Anna having to be in a lower room than Chris and the constraints that arise when certain variables are paired with Frank.

Question 1: Which tiger can NOT be in showroom 3?

(C) In neither scenario can Chris go in showroom 3.

Question 2: Which of the following could NOT be true?

(B) Garry can never show Anna in showroom 2.

(A) Dana can be shown by Frank in the second scenario.
(C) Chris can be shown in showroom 4 by Evan in the second scenario.
(D) Ben can be shown in showroom 1 by Garry in the second scenario.
(E) **B** is the correct answer.

Question 3: If Ben is shown in showroom 3, then which of the following must be true?

(D) This constraint is possible in both scenarios. Frank is also in showroom 3 in both, so Garry must show Anna in showroom 1.

(A) Evan can show Chris in showroom 2 only in the first scenario.
(B) Frank cannot show Anna in showroom 4 in any scenario.
(C) Hillary can show Dana in showroom 2 only in the second scenario.
(E) **D** is the correct answer.

Question 4: If Frank shows Dana, then which of the following must NOT be true?

This constraint is possible only in the second scenario, which would cause the following configuration of variables:

B	A	D	C
G	H	F	E

(E) All of the answer choices are possible.

Question 5: If Anna is shown in showroom 2, then which of the following must NOT be true?

(B) The diagram for the previous question shows the only possible scenario in which this constraint can happen. Ben cannot be paired with Frank, because that would force Anna to pair with Garry in showroom 1.

Question 6: If Ben is shown by Frank, then how many possible configurations of the variables are there?

(A) You should draw out the possible iterations of both scenarios:

A	C	B	D
G	E	F	H

A	D	B	C
G	H	F	E

Game 7

Initial Setup:

	1	2	3	4	5
A–E	E	*B/D	A	D/B	C
F–J	~~J~~			G	

Evan must be in plane 1. Evan's plane cannot be numbered consecutively with Anna's, which would force Evan to fly in plane 1 or plane 5. But since his plane's number must be less than Julian's, he must be in plane 1.

Question 1: Which of the following could be the order of the athletes in the planes, from 1 to 5?

(C) This is a possible order of the athletes.

(A) Evan must be in plane 1.
(B) Chris's plane cannot be numbered consecutively with Anna's.
(D) Evan must be in plane 1.
(E) Evan must be in plane 1.

Question 2: Who must greet plane 4?

(B) Garry must, because he greets a plane numbered consecutively with Chris's, and Chris must be in plane 5.

Question 3: Which of the following is a pair of people either of whom could greet Ben?

(D) This question is tricky, because if you forget the sufficient-necessary rule, then it would seem that anyone would be able to greet Ben. However, this rule is still in place, so Garry and Frank are the correct answer.

Question 4: If Frank greets plane 2, then which of the following must be true?

(E) This constraint does not tell you anything about the game that you did not already know. Julian still cannot greet plane 1, because he must greet a higher-numbered plane than the one that Evan is in.

(A) Frank's greeting plane 2 does not force Ben to fly in it, nor does it disqualify him from doing so.

Question 5: If Frank greets Anna, then which of the following must be true?

(A) This constraint means that Ben cannot fly in plane 2, because Frank would be unavailable to greet him. Therefore, Dana must fly in plane 2 and Ben must fly in plane 4.

Question 6: If Ben flies in plane 2 and Hillary greets Chris, then which of the following must be true?

This is the configuration of the variables under these constraints:

E	B	A	D	C
I	F	J	G	H

(C) Iris must greet Evan.

Game 8

Initial Setup:

E	D	A/C	C/A	B
		J	G	F/H

A/C	C/A	D	E	B
F/H	I	H/F	J	G

Question 1: Which of the following is a possible order of the rock stars, from room 1 to room 5?

(D) This is a possible order.

(A) Ben must be in room 5.
(B) Dana cannot be in room 1.
(C) Evan and Anna cannot be in consecutively numbered rooms.
(E) **D** is the correct answer.

Question 2: If Evan is in room 4, then which of the following must be true?

(D) This occurs in scenario 2. You can see that Iris must attend room 2 because she has to be between Frank and Hillary.

Question 3: Which of the following must NOT be true?

(B) Dana can never be in room 1.

(A) Julian can attend room 4 in scenario 2.
(C) Garry can attend Ben in scenario 2.
(D) Hillary can attend Dana in either scenario.
(E) **B** is the correct answer.

Question 4: If Anna is in room 3, then which of the following can NOT be true?

(E) This constraint can occur only in the first scenario, in which all of the answer choices are very possible.

Question 5: If Chris is in room 1, then how many different possible configurations of the variables are there?

(A) This constraint can occur in the second scenario, restricting Anna to room 2 and leaving Frank and Hillary free to be in either of two different rooms.

Question 6: Which of the following is a pair neither of whom could be attended by Garry?

(C) Garry can attend only Anna, Chris, or Ben. Therefore, Evan and Dana cannot be attended by Garry.

CHAPTER 5

GROUPING GAMES

Grouping games are some of the most common and most difficult logic games in the LSAT. Often these games do not give you many constraints until you reach the questions, leaving you in the dark until you need to scramble for the answers. Grouping games use all of the logic tools that we have highlighted previously, along with special **grouping constraints** that are easy to interpret and will be outlined in this chapter.

Typical Fact Pattern

> Three groups of shoppers go to the mall; group 1 goes in the morning, group 2 goes in the afternoon, and group 3 goes at night. Each group has exactly three people. The shoppers' names are Anna, Ben, Chris, Dana, Evan, Frank, Garry, Hillary, and Iris. No shopper goes to the mall twice, and every shopper goes to the mall. The members of each group are determined by the following constraints:
>
> Ben goes in group 2.
> Iris goes in the same group as Dana.
> Iris goes earlier in the day than Evan.
> Hillary does not go in the same group as Ben.
> Frank goes in group 3.
> Evan cannot shop with Frank.

Logic Tools

General

A typical diagram for grouping games is as follows:

1	2	3
___	___	___
___	___	___
___	___	___

There are three spots for each of the three shoppers that must go in each group. Vacancy rules are written underneath each group, or beside certain positions within a group when necessary.

Grouping

There are several grouping constraints in this example game. Generally, what would be a box rule in a linear game becomes a grouping rule in a grouping game.

Second Constraint:
Iris goes in the same group as Dana.

I = D

Fourth Constraint:
Hillary does not go in the same group as Ben.

H ≠ B

Sixth Constraint:
Evan cannot shop with Frank.

E ≠ F

Vacancy-Occupancy Rules

You should add your direct placement variables into the diagram immediately. Then, based on these variables, you should be able to add in vacancy-occupancy rules:

1	2	3
___	B	F
___	___	___
~~E~~	~~H~~	~~I~~ ~~E~~ ~~D~~

Based on these rules, you can make several deductions:

1	2	3
I	B	F
D	E	___
___	~~H~~	___

Fact Pattern Organization Heuristics

1. **Transcribe** the constraints.
2. Draw a **diagram**.
   a. Write out **vacancy-occupancy** rules.
   b. Is there a **burdensome constraint**?
3. Make a **hierarchy** of consolidated constraints.

You see that much of this heuristic is similar to that for complex linear games. We will go over the last step in more detail in the games that follow in this chapter.

Review

In this section you have learned:

1. How to make a typical diagram for a grouping game.
2. How to use logic tools that you have previously learned in grouping games.
3. How to recognize and transcribe grouping constraints.
4. The fact pattern organization heuristic for grouping games.

Grouping games are the most difficult games in the LSAT and also the most prevalent. Have patience with yourself as you go through them, and be sure to take everything slowly, because this is just the beginning of the learning process.

If you need more practice when you finish this lesson on grouping games or the lessons regarding any other type of game, Curvebreakers offers workbooks dedicated solely to specific logic game types. If you are still having trouble with grouping games after you finish this lesson or if you would just like more practice, then visit www.Curvebreakers.com, and look under the "Supplemental Materials," heading and then select whichever part of the LSAT you would like to gain additional experience with. For grouping games, after clicking "Logic Games," select the "Logic Games: Grouping" workbook. This workbook will offer you plenty of extra logic games to practice on while perfecting your solving technique.

Grouping Games Explained

GROUPING GAME I

In a local pet store, seven puppies wait to be introduced to their new owners. The puppies, named Anna, Ben, Chris, Dana, Evan, Frank, and Garry, are all kept in two pens. Pen 1 holds three puppies, and pen 2 holds four puppies. Each potential owner will choose a puppy from one of the two pens.

If Garry is kept in pen 1, then Dana is not kept in pen 2.
If Dana is not kept in pen 2, then Garry is kept in pen 1.
If Anna is kept in pen 2, then Ben is not kept in pen 2.
If Ben is kept in pen 1, then Anna is not kept in pen 1.

1. Which of the following groups of puppies could be in pen 2?
   (A) Garry, Dana, Chris, Evan.
   (B) Ben, Garry, Anna, Dana.
   (C) Anna, Garry, Dana.
   (D) Ben, Chris, Evan, Frank.
   (E) Garry, Anna, Frank, Evan.

2. If Evan shares a pen with Frank, then which of the following must be true?
   (A) Garry is in pen 1 with Dana.
   (B) Chris is in pen 2.
   (C) Ben is in pen 2 and Frank is in pen 1.
   (D) Evan is in pen 1.
   (E) Garry shares a pen with Ben.

3. If Evan and Frank are in different pens, then which of the following must NOT be true?
   (A) Frank shares a pen with Chris.
   (B) Garry shares a pen with Anna.
   (C) Evan is in a higher-numbered pen than Ben.
   (D) Ben shares pen 2 with Evan and Dana.
   (E) Chris is in a higher-numbered pen than Frank.

4. We would know the identities of all the puppies in pens 1 and 2 if we knew that which of the following puppies shared pen 1 with Ben?
   (A) Anna
   (B) Chris
   (C) Evan
   (D) Dana
   (E) Frank

5. If Evan shares a pen with Garry, then which of the following could be true?
   (A) Ben shares a pen with Anna.
   (B) Evan shares a pen with Frank.
   (C) Dana does not share a pen with Anna or Garry.
   (D) Frank shares a pen with Chris.
   (E) Ben shares pen 1 with Dana.

6. If Anna shares a pen with Garry, then which of the following could NOT be true?
   (A) Chris and Evan share pen 2.
   (B) Frank shares pen 1 with Ben.
   (C) Dana shares pen 2 with Evan.
   (D) Evan shares pen 2 with Ben.
   (E) Anna shares pen 1 with Frank.

SOLUTION STEPS

1. Transcribe the Constraints

1. **Sufficient-Necessary:**

$$G_1 \rightarrow D_1 \quad ; \quad \not{D}_1 \rightarrow \not{G}_1$$

Notice that since there are only two groups for the variables to be placed in, $\not{D}_1 = D_2$. In the same way, $\not{G}_1 = G_2$. So this rule can be represented as follows:

$$G_1 \rightarrow D_1 \quad ; \quad D_2 \rightarrow G_2$$

Keep this in mind for all sufficient-necessary conditions in future grouping games. There are several more in this very game where this rule holds true.

2. **Sufficient-Necessary:**

$$D_1 \rightarrow G_1 \quad ; \quad G_2 \rightarrow D_2$$

3. **Sufficient-Necessary:**

$$A_2 \rightarrow B_1 \quad ; \quad B_2 \rightarrow A_1$$

4. **Sufficient-Necessary:**

$$B_1 \rightarrow A_2 \quad ; \quad A_1 \rightarrow B_2$$

The sufficient-necessary rules can all be added together to make two grouping rules. The sufficient-necessary rules regarding Garry and Dana basically make it so that when either Garry or Dana is in pen 1, the other is also in pen 1. The same is true of pen 2: whenever Garry or Dana is in pen 2, the other puppy must also be there. This leads to the following mapping constraint:

$$G = D$$

For the sufficient-necessary conditions regarding Anna and Ben, you see that whichever pen one puppy is in, the other must be in the other pen. This is equivalent to the following mapping constraint:

$$A \neq B$$

2. Draw a Diagram. *Write out the vacancy-occupancy rules.* The mapping constraint regarding AB allows you to draw in the following double possibility:

1	2
A/B	B/A
___	___
___	___
	___

Is there a burdensome constraint?

Not really, but you should see that there are only two places for the DG mapping constraint to go, so you should draw in these scenarios now, because they will be helpful and you will more than likely need to do so later in the game.

1	2	1	2
A/B	B/A	A/B	B/A
D	___	___	D
G	___	___	G
		___	___

3. Make a Hierarchy of Consolidated Constraints. In this case, you have already included all of your constraints in the two preceding scenarios. However, you see that you did consolidate the four sufficient-necessary constraints by turning them into two mapping constraints. If you were solving a game in which you were not able to include any of these mapping constraints in the diagram, then you would include them in this step to keep in mind for when you began answering the questions.

ANSWERING THE QUESTIONS

Question 1: Which of the following groups of puppies could be in pen 2?

(D) This grouping is possible in the first scenario.

(A) Anna and Ben cannot share pen 1.
(B) Anna and Ben cannot share pen 2.
(C) There must be four puppies in pen 2.
(E) Garry must share a pen with Dana.

Question 2: If Evan shares a pen with Frank, then which of the following must be true?

(B) This constraint could happen in either scenario, but in both cases, Chris must be in pen 2.

Question 3: If Evan and Frank are in different pens, then which of the following must NOT be true?

(E) This constraint is possible only in scenario 2. At most, Chris can share a pen with Frank or be in a lower-numbered pen.

Question 4: We would know the identities of all the puppies in pens 1 and 2 if we knew that which of the following puppies shared pen 1 with Ben?

(D) If Dana were in pen 1 with Ben, then you would know that Garry was in the same pen and all the other puppies were in pen 2.

Question 5: If Evan shares a pen with Garry, then which of the following could be true?

(D) This constraint is possible only in scenario 2:

1	2
A/B	B/A
C	D
F	G
	E

Question 6: If Anna shares a pen with Garry, then which of the following could NOT be true?

(E) If Anna shares pen 1 with Garry, then Dana would take the last space in pen 1 due to the FG mapping constraint, leaving no space for Frank.

GROUPING GAME 2

Three groups of children from the group Anna, Ben, Chris, Dana, Evan, Frank, Garry, Hillary, and Iris are assigned to three different lemonade stands. Each stand is staffed by exactly three children, and the compositions of the groups taking care of the stands are determined by the following constraints:

Dana is assigned to stand 3.
Evan is assigned to the same stand as Frank.
If Anna is assigned to stand 1, then Evan is assigned to stand 2 and Chris is assigned to stand 3.
If Ben is assigned to stand 2, then Garry is assigned to stand 1 and Chris is assigned to stand 1.
Garry is not assigned to the same stand as Dana.

1. Which of the following is not a group that could be assigned to stand 2?

(A) Garry, Hillary, Iris.
(B) Garry, Frank, Evan.
(C) Chris, Anna, Hillary.
(D) Evan, Ben, Garry.
(E) Hillary, Iris, Garry.

2. If Anna and Ben are assigned to stand 2, then which of the following must NOT be true?

(A) Evan is assigned to stand 1.
(B) Hillary is assigned to stand 1.
(C) Garry is assigned to stand 1.
(D) Iris is assigned to stand 1.
(E) Chris is assigned to stand 1.

3. If Frank is assigned to stand 1, then which of the following could NOT be true?

(A) Anna is assigned to stand 1.
(B) Ben is assigned to stand 3.
(C) Garry is assigned to stand 2.
(D) Chris is assigned to stand 1.
(E) Hillary is assigned to stand 2.

4. If Anna does not share a stand with Dana or Garry, then which of the following must be true?

(A) Anna shares a stand with Ben.
(B) Chris shares a stand with Evan.
(C) Iris shares a stand with Hillary.
(D) Hillary does not share a stand with Dana.
(E) Frank shares a stand with Evan.

5. If Frank shares a stand with Anna, then which of the following must be true?

(A) Anna is assigned to stand 3.
(B) Hillary is assigned to stand 2.
(C) Garry is assigned to stand 1.
(D) Iris is assigned to stand 3.
(E) Ben is assigned to stand 3.

6. If Iris and Hillary are assigned to stand 1, then which of the following could NOT be true?

(A) Chris is assigned to stand 1.
(B) Ben is assigned to stand 2.
(C) Evan is assigned to stand 3.
(D) Frank is assigned to stand 2.
(E) Garry is assigned to stand 1.

SOLUTION STEPS

1. Transcribe the Constraints

1. **Direct Placement:** $D = 3$
2. **Grouping:** $E = F$
3. **Grouping:** $G \neq D$
4. **Sufficient-Necessary:**

$A_1 \rightarrow E_2$; $\not{E}_{\not{2}} \rightarrow \not{A}_{\not{1}}$
$A_1 \rightarrow C_3$; $\not{C}_{\not{3}} \rightarrow \not{A}_{\not{1}}$

5. **Sufficient-Necessary:**

$B_2 \rightarrow G_1$; $\not{G}_{\not{1}} \rightarrow \not{B}_{\not{2}}$
$B_2 \rightarrow C_1$; $\not{C}_{\not{1}} \rightarrow \not{B}_{\not{2}}$

2. Draw a Diagram. *Write out the vacancy-occupancy rules.* In this game, the contrapositives of the sufficient-necessary constraints are not likely to be very influential; in fact, they yield repetitive information. For this reason, they are not included in the diagram. This will not always be true of contrapositives, but normally any sufficient-necessary constraint that has all negative variables will not be very influential on grouping games with *more than* two groups. If there were only two groups, then two negative variables could be translated to positive variables: $\not{D}_{\not{1}} \rightarrow \not{G}_{\not{1}} = D_2 \rightarrow G_2$. But otherwise, you should pay attention to sufficient-necessary chains only when at least one of the variables is positive; this will still allow you to stay apprised of all information. If both variables are negative, then just take the contrapositive with the positive variables and use that in your diagram.

1	2	3
___	___	D
___	___	___
*A	*B	~~G~~

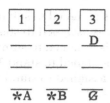

Is there a burdensome constraint?

Not really. This game is extremely open, so you should rank the constraints that are not adequately included on your diagram in the order of their probable influence.

3. Make a Hierarchy of Consolidated Constraints.

1. E = F
2. G ≠ D

The sufficient-necessary constraints have already been noted on the diagram, so you need to be sure to be aware of them if A goes in group 1 or if B goes in group 2.

Answering the Questions

Question 1: Which of the following is not a group that could be assigned to stand 2?

(D) If Ben is assigned to stand 2, then Garry must be assigned to stand 1, so Garry, Ben, and Evan cannot share stand 2 and Frank has to be at the same stand as Evan.

Question 2: If Anna and Ben are assigned to stand 2, then which of the following must NOT be true?

(A) Evan cannot be assigned to stand 1. Notice that Garry and Chris must be at stand 1 so Frank cannot be at that stand with Evan. Here is a diagram of this situation:

1	2	3
G	A	D
C	B	E
I/H	H/I	F
*A	*B	~~G~~

Question 3: If Frank is assigned to stand 1, then which of the following could NOT be true?

(A) Anna cannot be assigned to stand 1, because that would require Evan to be assigned to stand 2 instead of stand 1 with Frank.

1	2	3
F	___	D
E	___	___
~~A~~	~~B~~	~~G~~

Question 4: If Anna does not share a stand with Dana or Garry, then which of the following must be true?

(E) This temporary constraint means that there is a double possibility for Anna and Garry at stands 1 and 2. However, this tells you nothing about the game that you do not already know. Therefore, the question's constraint that Evan must share a group with Frank is the correct answer.

Question 5: If Frank shares a stand with Anna, then which of the following must be true?

(C) This constraint can happen only when Frank, Evan, and Anna all share stand 2. Remember that if they were assigned to stand 1, then Anna's sufficient-necessary condition would force Evan to go to stand 2, which would be impossible with Frank assigned to stand 1. Therefore, since Garry cannot be assigned to stand 3, the only space for him is at stand 1.

Question 6: If Iris and Hillary are assigned to stand 1, then which of the following could NOT be true?

This constraint could occur in two scenarios, which you should draw out:

1	2	3
I	F	D
H	E	___
*A	~~B~~	~~G~~

1	2	3
I	A	D
H	C	F
B	G	E
*A	*B	~~G~~

(B) Ben cannot be assigned to stand 2, because that would force Garry and Chris to be assigned to stand 1, thereby overcrowding it.

GROUPING GAME 3

At a park, there are three small picnic tables. Tables 1 and 2 each seat three people. Table 3 seats only one person, since two of its seats are broken. Anna, Ben, Chris, Dana, Evan, Frank, and Garry all sit at seats at these picnic tables. Who sits with whom and at which table are determined by the following constraints:

> Chris does not sit at the same table as Garry.
> Evan does not sit at the same table as Dana.
> Frank does not sit at the same table as Chris.
> Anna does not sit at the same table as Ben.
> Garry does not sit at the same table as Frank.

1. Which of the following is a list of people who could sit together at table 2?

   (A) Ben, Frank, Chris.
   (B) Garry, Evan, Anna.
   (C) Chris, Garry, Dana.
   (D) Frank, Dana, Evan.
   (E) Ben, Evan, Anna.

2. If Frank sits at table 3 and Dana sits at table 2, then which of the following pairs could share a table?

   (A) Anna, Ben.
   (B) Dana, Evan.
   (C) Chris, Frank.
   (D) Ben, Garry.
   (E) Anna, Frank.

3. If Chris cannot sit at a table with Ben or Anna, then which of the following must NOT be true?

   (A) Evan sits at table 2.
   (B) Anna sits with Garry.
   (C) Frank sits at table 3.
   (D) Garry sits with Ben.
   (E) Evan sits with Anna.

4. If Chris shares a table with Evan and Garry shares a table with Anna, then which of the following could be true?

   (A) Evan shares table 1 with Ben.
   (B) Garry shares table 2 with Evan.
   (C) Frank shares table 1 with Ben.
   (D) Ben shares table 3 with Anna.
   (E) Dana shares table 2 with Chris.

5. If Anna does not share a table with Dana or Garry, then which of the following could NOT be true?

   (A) Dana sits at table 1.
   (B) Garry sits at table 3.
   (C) Ben shares a table with Dana.
   (D) Garry shares a table with Evan.
   (E) Chris shares a table with Anna.

6. How many different people could potentially sit at table 3?

   (A) three
   (B) four
   (C) five
   (D) six
   (E) seven

SOLUTION STEPS

1. Transcribe the Constraints

1. Grouping: $C \neq G$
2. Grouping: $E \neq D$
3. Grouping: $F \neq C$
4. Grouping: $A \neq B$
5. Grouping: $G \neq F$

Notice that constraints 1, 3, and 5 can be consolidated:

$$C \neq G \neq F$$

This consolidated constraint demonstrates that none of these variables can be at the same table:

1	2	3
F/C/G	G/F/C	C/G/F
___	___	
___	___	

2. Draw a Diagram. *Write out the vacancy-occupancy rules.* Based on the triple possibility that you have drawn above, you can write in two double possibilities:

1	2	3
F/C/G	G/F/C	C/G/F
E/D	D/E	
A/B	B/A	

Is there a burdensome constraint?

The triple possibility constrains the game so far that you know where every variable in the game can go.

3. Make a Hierarchy of Consolidated Constraints. This is not necessary, since all of the variables are included in the game.

ANSWERING THE QUESTIONS

Question 1: Which of the following is a list of people who could sit together at table 2?

(B) Notice that the same people could sit at table 2 as could sit at table 1.

(A) Frank and Chris cannot be in the same group.
(C) Chris and Garry cannot be in the same group.
(D) Evan and Dana cannot be in the same group.
(E) Ben and Anna cannot be in the same a group.

Question 2: If Frank sits at table 3 and Dana sits at table 2, then which of the following pairs could share a table?

(D) Dana's sitting at table 2 makes Evan sit at table 1. Ben and Garry could share a table.

Question 3: If Chris cannot sit at a table with Evan or Anna, then which of the following must NOT be true?

(C) Anna and Ben cannot sit at the same table, so they must sit at tables 1 and 2. This makes Chris sit at table 3. Since table 3 holds only one person, Frank cannot sit at table 3.

Question 4: If Chris shares a table with Evan and Garry shares a table with Anna, then which of the following could be true?

(A) Here is a possibility for this scenario. Notice that the people sitting at table 1 could also sit at table 2, yielding two possibilities for this configuration of variables:

1	2	3
C	G	F
B	A	
E	D	

(B) Garry and Chris cannot share a table with the same person.
(C) Frank must sit at table 3.
(D) Table 3 has room for only one person.
(E) Chris cannot share a table with both Evan and Dana.

Question 5: If Anna does not share a table with Dana or Garry, then which of the following could NOT be true?

You cannot determine whether these people sit at table 1 or 2, so you should just draw out one scenario and be aware that tables 1 and 2 are interchangeable.

1	2	3
F/C	G/F/C	C/G/F
A	B	
E	D	

(D) You can see that Garry cannot share a table with Evan.

Question 6: How many different people could potentially sit at table 3?

(A) Only three people, Chris, Garry, or Frank, could sit at table 3.

GROUPING GAME 4

Two groups of students are selected to attend a paleontology conference at their state museum. The students selected are Anna, Ben, Chris, Dana, Evan, Frank, Garry, and Hillary. Four students will go in group 1, and three students will go in group 2. One student may go in both groups, and some students might not attend the conference. The composition of the groups is determined by the following constraints:

If Anna goes in group 1, then Chris goes in group 2 and does not go in group 1. If Hillary goes in group 2, then Frank goes in group 1.

If Chris goes in group 1, then Hillary goes in group 1.

If Dana attends the conference, then Garry and Evan go to the conference in the same group.

If someone goes in both groups, then Anna and Chris go in the same group at least once.

1. Which of the following groups of people could make up group 1?

(A) Dana, Garry, Chris, Ben.
(B) Anna, Chris, Evan, Ben.
(C) Hillary, Chris, Frank, Ben.
(D) Anna, Ben, Chris, Dana.
(E) Evan, Chris, Dana, Ben.

2. If Dana goes in group 1 with Chris, then which of the following must be true?

(A) Ben goes in group 2.
(B) Hillary goes in both groups.
(C) Garry goes in the same group as Frank.
(D) Hillary goes in group 1.
(E) Evan does not attend the conference.

3. If Hillary goes in both groups, then which of the following must NOT be true?

(A) Ben goes in group 1.
(B) Evan goes in group 1.
(C) Anna goes in group 2.
(D) Frank goes in group 1.
(E) Dana goes in group 1.

4. If Hillary goes in group 1 with Anna, then which of the following could be true?

(A) Dana goes to the conference and Garry does not.
(B) Chris does not go to the conference.
(C) Evan and Frank do not go to the conference.
(D) Chris goes in both groups.
(E) Ben goes in a group with Dana.

5. If Anna goes in group 2 with Ben and Hillary, then which of the following is a list of people who could make up group 1?

(A) Chris, Anna, Garry, Evan.
(B) Ben, Evan, Garry, Frank.
(C) Dana, Evan, Frank, Garry.
(D) Chris, Evan, Dana, Hillary.
(E) Dana, Chris, Garry, Anna.

6. If Dana, Anna, and Garry go in the same group, then which of the following could be true?

(A) Hillary goes in group 2.
(B) Anna goes in the same group with Chris.
(C) Garry goes in group 2.
(D) Evan goes in the same group with Chris.
(E) Chris does not go to the conference.

SOLUTION STEPS

1. Transcribe the Constraints

1. Sufficient-Necessary: $A_1 \rightarrow C_2$
2. Sufficient-Necessary: $A_1 \rightarrow \not{C}_1$
3. Sufficient-Necessary: $H_2 \rightarrow F_1$
4. Sufficient-Necessary: $C_1 \rightarrow H_1$
5. Sufficient-Necessary: $D \rightarrow E = G$
6. Sufficient-Necessary: Twice $\rightarrow A = C$

2. Draw a Diagram. This game is very typical of "maximized-variable grouping games." There are not many constraints that you can diagram up front, which means that you should have your constraints handy because the questions will force you to make diagrams.

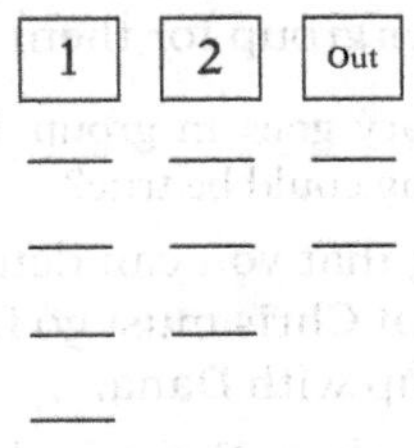

3. Make a Hierarchy of Consolidated Constraints

1. Twice $\rightarrow A = C$
2. $A_1 \rightarrow C_2$
3. $A_1 \rightarrow \not{C}_1$
4. $C_1 \rightarrow H_1$
5. $D \rightarrow E = G$
6. $H_2 \rightarrow F_1$

ANSWERING THE QUESTIONS

Question 1: Which of the following groups of people could make up group 1?

(C) Hillary, Chris, Frank, and Ben could make up group 1.

(A)–(E) If Chris is in group 1, then Hillary also must be in group 1.

Question 2: If Dana goes in group 1 with Chris, then which of the following must be true?

You should diagram this on your paper, keeping your constraints in mind, in the following way:

1	2	Out
D	E	___
C	G	___
H	___	
B/F		

(D) Hillary must go in group 1.

Question 3: If Hillary goes in both groups, then which of the following must NOT be true?

The diagram for this question is as follows:

1	2	Out
H	H	D
F	A	___
___	C	
___		

(E) Dana cannot go in group 1 or 2, because that would force Evan and Garry to go together, and there is no room in either group for them to do this.

Question 4: If Hillary goes in group 1 with Anna, then which of the following could be true?

(E) The only thing that you can determine from this configuration is that Chris must go in group 2. Ben is able to go in a group with Dana.

(A) If Dana goes, then Evan and Garry must go together in the same group.
(B) If Anna goes in group 1, then Chris must go in group 2.
(C) If Evan and Frank do not go, then Dana must go, which would require Evan and Garry to go to the conference in the same group.
(D) Anna goes in group 1, so Chris cannot also go in group 1.

Question 5: If Anna goes in group 2 with Ben and Hillary, then which of the following is a group of people that could make up group 1?

(C) This is a possible group.

(A) Frank must go in group 1, because Hillary is in group 2.
(B) Ben cannot go twice, because only one person can go twice and Anna cannot go in the same group with Chris in group 2.
(D) Frank must go in group 1, because Hillary is in group 2.
(E) Frank must go in group 1, because Hillary is in group 2.

Question 6: If Dana, Anna, and Garry go in the same group, then which of the following could be true?

If this constraint occurs, then these three students must go in group 1. Evan must also be in group 1 because Garry and Evan share a group when Dana is in a group. Since Anna is in group 1, then Chris must go in group 2. Hillary cannot go in group 2, because if she did, then Frank would have to go in group 1 where there is no room for him.

1	2	Out
D	C	H
A	___	___
G	___	
E		

(B) There is room for Anna to go in the same group with Chris in group 2.

(A) Hillary must sit out.
(C) No one can go twice besides Anna, because that would force Anna to also go twice.
(D) No one can go twice besides Anna, because that would force Anna to also go twice.
(E) Since Anna goes in group 1, Chris must go in group 2.

On Your Own

GROUPING GAME 5

Two canoes filled with three people each leave from summer camp at midnight. Seven young trouble-makers, Anna, Ben, Chris, Dana, Evan, Frank, and Garry, decide whether or not to depart for the other side of the lake. One person will be unable to go, because there will not be enough room in the canoes, but the other six people will each take positions in the canoes. The canoes each have three positions: front, middle, and back. The order of people in the canoes is determined by the following:

If Dana goes, then she goes in a canoe with Chris.
Garry sits in the front of a canoe.
Anna sits in the back of canoe 1.
If Ben sits in canoe 2, then Evan sits in the middle of canoe 2.
Frank does not sit in the front or the back of a canoe.

1. Which of the following groups could be the people who go in canoe 1, from front to back?

   (A) Garry, Dana, Chris.
   (B) Frank, Chris, Anna.
   (C) Garry, Frank, Anna.
   (D) Dana, Ben, Anna.
   (E) None of the above.

2. If Dana sits in the front of canoe 2, then which of the following must NOT be true?

   (A) Ben goes in the back of canoe 2.
   (B) Frank goes in the middle of canoe 1.
   (C) Garry goes in the front of canoe 1.
   (D) Chris goes in the middle of canoe 2.
   (E) None of the above.

3. If Dana goes in a canoe with Garry, then which of the following could be true?

   (A) Frank sits in the front of canoe 1.
   (B) Frank shares a canoe with Dana.
   (C) Dana sits in the front of canoe 2.
   (D) Ben sits in the back of canoe 1.
   (E) None of the above.

4. If Garry sits in a canoe with Anna, then which of the following must NOT be true?

   (A) Ben sits in the front of canoe 2.
   (B) Frank does not go in a canoe.
   (C) Dana goes in the middle of canoe 1.
   (D) Chris goes in the back of canoe 2.
   (E) None of the above.

5. If Dana does not go, then which of the following could NOT be true?

   (A) Chris goes in the front of canoe 1.
   (B) Ben goes in the middle of canoe 2.
   (C) Frank goes in the middle of canoe 1.
   (D) Garry goes in the front of canoe 2.
   (E) None of the above.

6. If Ben does not go in a canoe with Anna or Evan, then who must sit out?

   (A) Ben
   (B) Chris
   (C) Dana
   (D) Evan
   (E) None of the above

GROUPING GAME 6

Jamie has invited five guests for dinner and is planning a menu of broccoli, chicken, eggs, and ham. His guests are Anna, Ben, Chris, Dana, and Evan. Each guest eats two different dishes, subject to the following conditions:

No two guests eat the same two dishes.
If Anna eats chicken or ham, Dana has eggs.
Ben has one dish that Chris has, and Chris has one dish that Dana has.
If Evan has ham, Anna has eggs.
If Chris has broccoli or ham, then Evan shares that dish with Chris.

1. If Ben and Chris both have broccoli, what could Dana have?
   (A) Broccoli and chicken.
   (B) Broccoli and eggs.
   (C) Broccoli and ham.
   (D) Chicken and ham.
   (E) Eggs and ham.

2. If Chris has eggs and ham, what could Anna have?
   (A) Broccoli and chicken.
   (B) Broccoli and eggs.
   (C) Broccoli and ham.
   (D) Chicken and ham.
   (E) Eggs and ham.

3. If Anna and Dana both have chicken, what could Chris have?
   (A) Broccoli and chicken.
   (B) Chicken and eggs.
   (C) Broccoli and ham.
   (D) Chicken and ham.
   (E) Eggs and ham.

4. Which of the following is a group of all the people who can all have ham at the same time?
   (A) Anna, Ben, and Chris.
   (B) Anna, Ben, and Evan.
   (C) Anna, Chris, and Dana.
   (D) Anna, Dana, and Evan.
   (E) Ben, Chris, and Dana.

5. If Dana has chicken and ham, what could Ben NOT have?
   (A) Broccoli and chicken.
   (B) Broccoli and eggs.
   (C) Broccoli and ham.
   (D) Chicken and eggs.
   (E) Eggs and ham.

6. How many people, at most, could have eggs?
   (A) one
   (B) two
   (C) three
   (D) four
   (E) five

7. If only Chris and Evan have ham, what could Anna have?
   (A) Broccoli and chicken.
   (B) Broccoli and eggs.
   (C) Chicken and eggs.
   (D) Chicken and ham.
   (E) Eggs and ham.

GROUPING GAME 7

Sam the stockbroker just got a hot tip on four stocks—Aphid Corp., Beta Corp., Cappa Corp., and Datita Corp. He passes along the tips to three of his customers—Garry, Hillary, and Iris—subject to the following conditions:

No two customers receive the same set of stock tips, and every customer gets at least one tip.

Sam tells each stock tip to at least one customer.

Sam tells Hillary every stock tip that he tells Garry.

If Sam tells Iris about Cappa or Datita, he tells Garry about Beta.

If Sam tells Iris exactly three stock tips, he tells Hillary about Aphid.

If Sam tells Garry about Aphid or Datita, he tells Iris about neither.

1. If Sam tells Garry about Aphid, Beta, and Cappa, which of the following must be true?

   (A) Sam does not tell Hillary about Datita.
   (B) Sam does not tell Iris about Datita.
   (C) Hillary receives exactly three stock tips.
   (D) Iris receives exactly three stock tips.
   (E) Iris receives exactly two stock tips.

2. If Sam tells Iris only about Aphid, Beta, and Datita, at least how many stock tips does Hillary receive?

   (A) none
   (B) one
   (C) two
   (D) three
   (E) four

3. If Sam does not tell Iris any stock tips he tells Hillary, which of the following can NOT be true?

   (A) Sam tells Iris exactly three stock tips.
   (B) Sam tells Iris one stock tip.
   (C) Sam tells Garry about Aphid.
   (D) Sam tells Garry about Beta and Datita.
   (E) Sam tells Hillary about Beta and Cappa.

4. If Sam tells Garry three stock tips, which of the following can NOT be true?

   (A) Sam tells Garry about Aphid.
   (B) Sam tells Iris the same number of stock tips he tells Hillary.
   (C) Sam does not tell Garry about Beta.
   (D) Sam tells Iris one stock tip.
   (E) Sam does not tell Garry about Cappa.

5. If Sam tells Garry about Aphid, what stocks must he tell Hillary about?

   (A) Aphid, Beta.
   (B) Aphid, Beta, Datita.
   (C) Aphid, Datita.
   (D) Beta, Cappa, Datita.
   (E) Cappa, Datita.

6. If Sam tells Hillary only two stock tips, what stocks can he NOT tell Hillary about?

   (A) Aphid, Beta.
   (B) Aphid, Cappa.
   (C) Beta, Cappa.
   (D) Beta, Datita.
   (E) Cappa, Datita.

GROUPING GAME 8

General Ozymandias is scheduling flights for his airline based out of Naples, Italy. His crew includes Anna, Ben, Chris, Dana, and Evan. He needs to plan flights to Bologna and Rome—subject to the following conditions:

Each flight needs a pilot, a copilot, and a navigator.
One and only one crew member will serve on both flights.
Dana will serve only as pilot.
Chris must serve on the flight to Rome.
Evan will not serve as copilot on a flight if Chris or Ben is the pilot or navigator of that flight.
Ben will serve as navigator on a flight only if Anna is the pilot of that flight.

1. If Chris pilots the flight to Rome, which of the following must be true?
   (A) Anna copilots the flight to Bologna.
   (B) Dana copilots the flight to Rome.
   (C) Ben serves on the flight to Bologna.
   (D) Chris navigates the flight to Rome.
   (E) Ben serves as copilot.

2. If Ben navigates the flight to Bologna, who must serve on both flights?
   (A) Anna
   (B) Ben
   (C) Chris
   (D) Dana
   (E) Evan

3. If Ben navigates the flight to Rome, which of the following can NOT be true?
   (A) Ben serves on both flights.
   (B) Dana serves on both flights.
   (C) Evan copilots the flight to Bologna.
   (D) Anna serves on both flights.
   (E) Chris copilots at least one flight.

4. If Dana serves on both flights, then which of the following must be true?
   (A) Dana serves as copilot on the flight to Rome.
   (B) Chris serves as pilot on the flight to Bologna.
   (C) Ben does not serve as navigator on the flight to Bologna.
   (D) Anna does not serve as navigator.
   (E) Evan does not fly on the same flight as Ben.

5. If Ben serves as pilot on the flight to Bologna and Chris serves as navigator on the flight to Rome, then how many different people could potentially serve on both flights?
   (A) one
   (B) two
   (C) three
   (D) four
   (E) five

6. If Evan is the copilot on the Bologna flight, then which of the following could be true?
   (A) Evan serves as copilot on the flight to Rome.
   (B) Ben serves as pilot on the flight to Bologna.
   (C) Anna does not serve as navigator on the flight to Bologna.
   (D) Ben serves as navigator on the flight to Rome.
   (E) Chris serves as navigator on the flight to Bologna.

ANSWERS AND EXPLANATIONS

Game 5

Initial Setup:

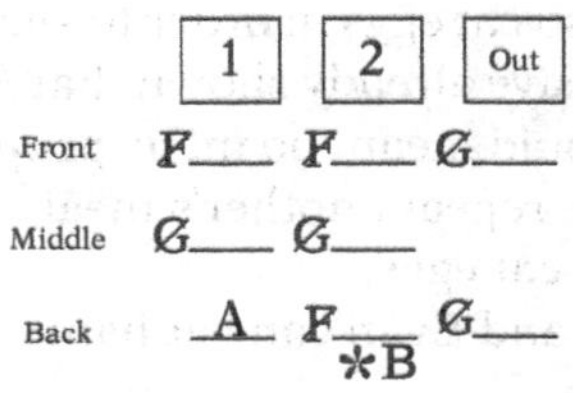

Question 1: Which of the following groups could be the people who go in canoe 1 from front to back?

(C) This is a possible order for canoe 1.

(A) Anna must sit in the back of canoe 1.
(B) Frank cannot sit in the front of a canoe.
(D) If Dana goes, then she must share a canoe with Chris.
(E) **C** is the correct answer.

Question 2: If Dana sits in the front of canoe 2, then which of the following must NOT be true?

(A) If this constraint occurs, then Chris must also be in canoe 2. This leaves no room for Ben to go in canoe 2, because that would require Evan to go in the middle of canoe 2.

Question 3: If Dana goes in a canoe with Garry, then which of the following could be true?

(E) Dana cannot go in canoe 1 with Garry, because then there would be no room for Chris to also go, since Anna sits in the back. However, they could go together in canoe 2:

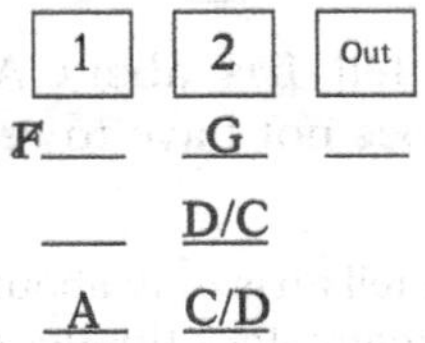

(A) Frank can never sit in the front of a canoe.
(B) Chris must go in the same canoe as Dana, so there is no room left in canoe 2 for Frank.
(C) This is where Garry must sit, since Garry and Dana cannot share canoe 1.
(D) Anna must sit in the back of canoe 1.

Question 4: If Garry sits in a canoe with Anna, then which of the following must NOT be true?

(C) Dana cannot sit in canoe 1 with two people already in the canoe, because that would leave no place for Chris to sit in that canoe.

Question 5: If Dana does not go, then which of the following could NOT be true?

(B) Dana's not going does not reveal anything extra to us about the game, so you should look for a contradiction within an answer choice. Ben cannot sit in the middle of canoe 2, because when he goes in canoe 2, this requires Evan to sit in the middle of canoe 2.

Question 6: If Ben does not go in a canoe with Anna or Evan, then who must sit out?

(A) If Ben does not go in a canoe with Anna, then he cannot go in canoe 1. If Ben does not go in a canoe with Evan, then he cannot go in canoe 2. Therefore, Ben must sit out.

Game 6

Initial Setup:

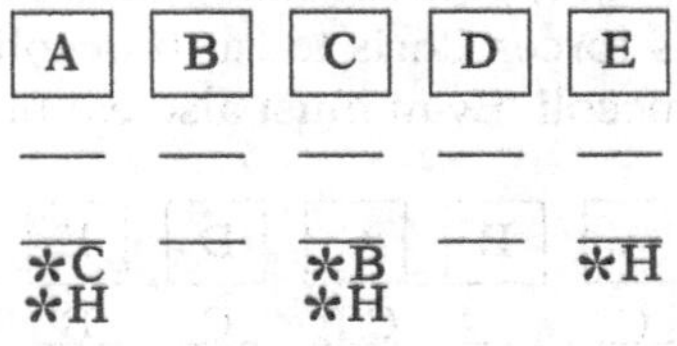

The key to solving this game is noticing that there are five people who are eating. There are four dishes, of which each person will have two. No person can have the same two dishes. Therefore, the possible meals are limited to six:

BC	CE	EH
BE	CH	
BH		

So each person will eat one meal from the above list, but one meal will be left over.

Question 1: If Ben and Chris both have broccoli, what could Dana have?

(E) If Chris has broccoli, then Evan must also have broccoli. This means that three people are eating broccoli, so no other person could have broccoli—Dana cannot eat broccoli. This means that every meal left has chicken or ham in it. This in turn means that Anna must eat a meal with chicken or ham, thereby enacting the sufficient-necessary condition that forces Dana to eat eggs.

(A) There are no broccoli meals left for Dana.
(B) There are no broccoli meals left for Dana.
(C) There are no broccoli meals left for Dana.
(D) Dana cannot eat a meal without eggs, because Anna is forced to eat a meal with chicken or ham in it.

Question 2: If Chris has eggs and ham, what could Anna have?

(B) If Chris has eggs and ham, the sufficient-necessary rule forces Evan to eat ham also. Evan's eating ham forces Anna to eat eggs, by another sufficient-necessary rule. Anna clearly cannot eat both eggs and ham, since that would give her the same dishes as Chris. The only possible option among those listed is that Anna eats eggs and broccoli.

Question 3: If Anna and Dana both have chicken, what could Chris have?

(A) If Anna has chicken, then Dana must eat eggs. This makes Dana's meal eggs and chicken. Dana must share one dish with Chris, so Chris must eat eggs or chicken. This means that Anna must have ham or broccoli with her chicken, because Dana took the eggs and they cannot both have the same meal. This means that Evan must not eat ham, because if he did, it would force Anna to eat eggs. Therefore, Chris cannot eat ham either, because that would force Evan to eat ham. This forces Chris to eat broccoli, and since Chris eats broccoli, Evan must also eat broccoli.

A	B	C	D	E
C	___	C/E	C	B
B/H	___	B ~~H~~	E	C/E ~~H~~

Question 4: Which of the following is a group of all the people who can all have ham at the same time?

(B) Anna, Ben, and Evan can all have ham.

(A) If Chris has ham, then Evan must also have ham.
(C) If Chris has ham, then Evan must also have ham.
(D) If Anna has ham, then Dana must have eggs. If Evan has ham, then Anna must have eggs. This leaves you with two people eating the same thing.
(E) If Chris has ham, then Evan must also have ham.

Question 5: If Dana has chicken and ham, what could Ben NOT have?

(B) If Dana has chicken and ham, then Anna cannot have chicken or ham, because that would require Dana to eat eggs. This leaves Anna with only one meal: eggs and broccoli. Since this meal cannot be eaten by two people, Ben cannot have eggs and broccoli.

Question 6: How many people, at most, could have eggs?

(C) The most people that could have any one particular meal is three.

Question 7: If only Chris and Evan have ham, what could Anna have?

This would mean that Chris cannot have broccoli, because that would force Evan to also eat broccoli and ham. Since Evan eats ham, Anna must eat eggs.

(B) Anna could have broccoli and eggs.

(A) Anna must eat eggs.
(C) If Anna had chicken and eggs, then Dana would have to eat eggs. This would force Chris to also eat eggs in order to share a dish with Dana. This would force Ben to also eat eggs in order to share a dish with Chris. But we have already shown that Anna must eat eggs, so this would mean too many people eating eggs to not have one repeat another's meal.
(D) Anna must eat eggs.
(E) Only Chris and Evan can eat ham.

Game 7

Initial Setup:

G	H	I
___	___	___
___	___	___
___	___	___
	___	___

Notice that Garry can have three tips at the most, because Hillary cannot receive the same set of tips as Garry, and therefore must receive more than he does.

Question 1: If Sam tells Garry about Aphid, Beta, and Cappa, which of the following must be true?

G	H	I
A	A	___
B	B	___ ~~A~~ ~~D~~
C	C	
	D	

(B) Sam cannot tell Iris about Aphid or Datita. Notice that Iris does not have to receive more than one stock tip.

Question 2: If Sam tells Iris only about Aphid, Beta, and Datita, at least how many stock tips does Hillary receive?

(D) If Iris is told three stock tips, then Hillary is told about Aphid. If Iris is told about Datita, then Garry is told about Beta, which makes Hillary also hear about Beta. Cappa must still be told to Garry or Hillary, and since Hillary hears about every stock that Garry hears about, Hillary must hear about at least three tips.

Question 3: If Sam does not tell Iris any stock tips he tells Hillary, which of the following can NOT be true?

(A) Hillary must hear at least two tips, since she cannot hear the same set of tips as Garry but hears at least what he hears. This means that it would be impossible for Iris to hear three tips because due to the constraint, Iris cannot hear any tip that Hillary hears and Hillary must hear at least two.

Question 4: If Sam tells Garry three stock tips, which of the following can NOT be true?

(B) Hillary must hear four tips if Garry hears three because Hillary hears all the tips that Garry hears but cannot hear the same number as he does and there are only four tips to hear. If Iris also hears four, then it would be impossible for Garry to hear three, because he would have to hear about Aphid or Datita, which would disqualify Iris from hearing about either, thereby dropping her down to hearing only two tips.

Question 5: If Sam tells Garry about Aphid, what stocks must he tell Hillary about?

(C) Here are the partially solved possible scenarios. In each one Hillary has to hear about Aphid and Datita. Hillary must hear about Datita because Iris cannot hear about Datita since Garry hears about Aphid. Therefore, Garry or Hillary must hear about Datita since someone must hear about Datita. If Garry hears about Datita, then so does Hillary. If Garry does not hear about Datita, then Hillary must hear about Datita since no one else does.

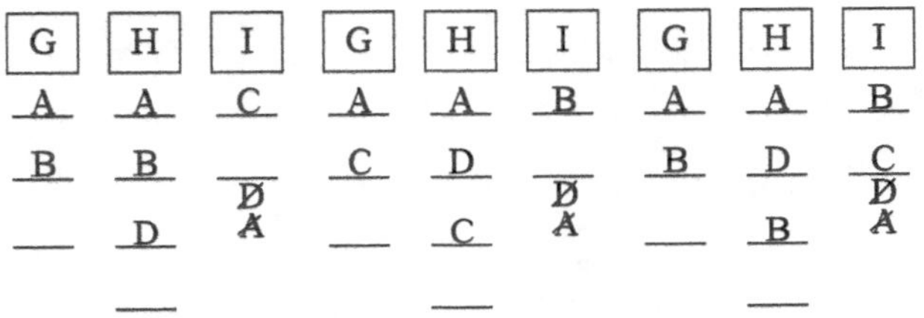

Question 6: If Sam tells Hillary only two stock tips, what tips can he NOT tell Hillary about?

(B) If Hillary is given tips only about Aphid and Cappa, then Garry must be given a tip about either Aphid or Cappa, but not both—since Hillary must hear every tip given to Garry, and they cannot have an identical set of tips. In either case, whether Garry gets a tip either about Aphid or about Cappa, Iris must get at least both of the remaining two tips, i.e., Beta as well as Datita, because we know that Sam gives out all four tips. But we know that if Sam tells Iris about Datita, he must tell Garry about Beta, but this is not possible, since we have just established that Garry can hear only one tip, and that too only about either Aphid or Cappa.

Game 8

Initial Setup:

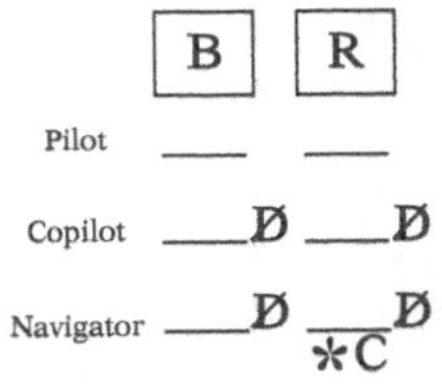

Question 1: If Chris pilots the flight to Rome, which of the following must be true?

(E) If Chris pilots the flight to Rome, then Dana must pilot the flight to Bologna. Therefore, Anna cannot pilot a flight. This means that Ben cannot be a navigator and must be a copilot on a flight.

Question 2: If Ben navigates the flight to Bologna, who must serve on both flights?

(C) Chris must serve on both flights, since Dana cannot serve as copilot and Evan cannot be copilot when Ben is navigator.

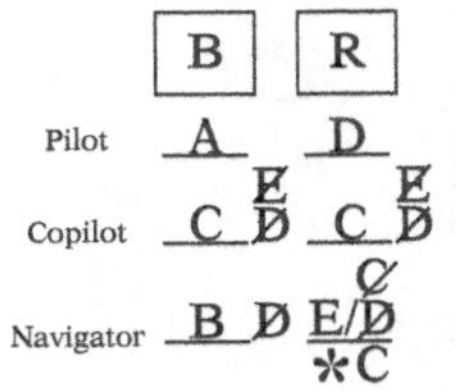

Question 3: If Ben navigates the flight to Rome, which of the following can NOT be true?

(B) If Ben navigates the flight, then Anna must be the pilot. Chris must travel on the flight to Rome, so he must be the copilot. Dana must pilot the flight to Bologna, because she can only be the pilot. Dana cannot serve on both flights, because Anna is the pilot on the flight to Rome.

Question 4: If Dana serves on both flights, then which of the following must be true?

(C) This constraint means that Ben cannot be the navigator of either flight, because if Dana serves as pilot on both flights, Anna cannot pilot either of them.

Question 5: If Ben serves as pilot on the flight to Bologna and Chris serves as navigator on the flight to Rome, then how many different people could potentially serve on both flights?

(C) Anna, Ben, and Chris could serve on both flights. Dana must serve as pilot, so she can be only on the flight to Rome. Evan cannot be the copilot on the flight to Rome, since Chris is the navigator. Evan cannot be the navigator on the flight to Bologna, since Ben is piloting it.

Question 6: If Evan is the copilot on the Bologna flight, then which of the following could be true?

(D) This constraint means that neither Chris nor Ben could be on the flight to Bologna. That means that Dana must pilot the flight to Bologna and Anna must navigate. This allows Ben to serve as navigator on the flight to Rome.

CHAPTER 6

MAPPING GAMES

Mapping games involve all of the types of constraints and logic tools that you have previously encountered. However, the constraints are applied to diagrams that are varied and more complex than those in linear or grouping diagrams. Sometimes the correct diagram is supplied for you by the fact pattern, but in general, you must sit back and think about the best way to go about diagramming the game. By going through this lesson, you will be introduced to all the different options for diagramming mapping games, including circular games, Venn diagram games, and more traditional mapping game types.

Typical Fact Pattern

At a country fair, a farmer is trying to sell six tractors. The tractors are numbered 1 through 6 and are arranged in the following way:

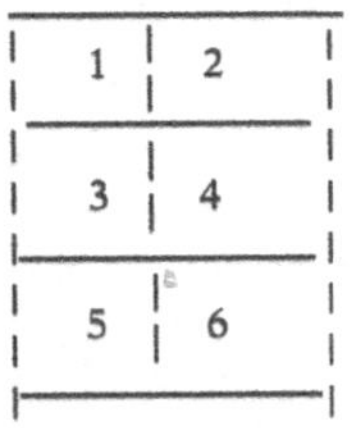

The tractors are either red or green.
The tractors are either big or small.
Tractor 4 is a small green tractor.
All green tractors are adjacent only to red tractors.

Logic Tools

General

Your diagram here should be roughly equivalent to that of the picture provided in the fact pattern. However, note that it includes six hash marks to denote that there are two variables that you need to remember about each tractor. When there are two variables per location, we call this **double positioning**. This is different from double possibility because two different variable types are present per location instead of there being two variables possible in only one location.

Mapping

The mapping constraint that you had was the following: "All green tractors are adjacent only to red tractors." This constraint allows you to infer several things about the tractors adjacent to tractor 4. Tractors 2, 3, and 6 are all adjacent to tractor 4, so they must be red tractors.

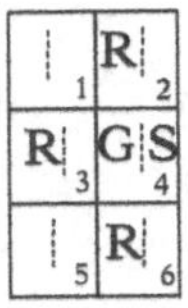

Mapping constraints are generally that simple, as long as you are able to determine the **direction** of the constraints. "Adjacent" always means any space that shares a border with another space. Be careful when you arrive at mapping constraints that use the phrases "next to" or "across from," because these imply that there are certain rows and columns in the game that you should be aware of. For example, the phrase "next to" can refer to spaces that are on the same side of a hypothetical street. The phrase "across from" generally refers to spaces that are on the opposite side of the street or row. The definition of each of these **directional phrases** changes based on the cues of the game, so you should be alert and make sure that you are adhering to the specific game's definition of its orienting phrases.

Fact Pattern Organization Heuristics

The heuristic steps to solving mapping games are exactly the same as the steps involved in solving grouping games:

1. **Transcribe** the constraints.
2. Draw a **representative diagram**.
   a. Use constraints to gain information.
3. Make a **hierarchy** of consolidated constraints.

Review

In this section you have learned:

1. About the versatility of diagrams required for mapping games.
2. About a typical mapping constraint.
3. The importance of the **directional phrases** inherent in mapping constraints.
4. The fact pattern heuristics used to solve mapping games.

Students often find mapping games to be difficult, because there is no one specific diagram that is the best for these games. Instead, you are required to look at the individual characteristics of the game and to create a diagram that most accurately represents that particular game. Working carefully through each individual mapping game in this chapter will help you solve this problem, because you will quickly learn which type of diagram is best for which type of game. If you feel you need additional practice with mapping games, a mapping game workbook is available on the Curvebreakers Web site, www.Curvebreakers.com.

Mapping Games Explained

MAPPING GAME I

The city of Nod is constructing a zoo in order to provide entertainment for its citizens. The zoo will possess six cages that are situated in two rows, with each cage directly across from the cage in the opposite row. The position of the cages is represented by the following diagram:

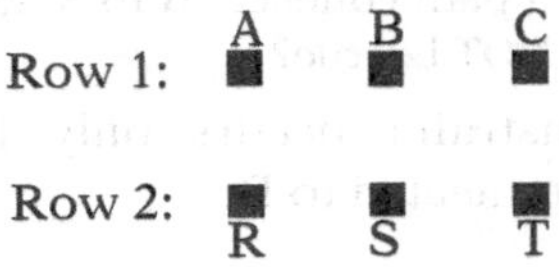

In order for people to walk to each cage, the zoo will have to build straight-line paths made of gold connecting the cages. However, the city wants to limit the number of gold paths that it constructs, because they are expensive. Therefore, the construction of the paths is governed by the following constraints:

Each cage is connected to no more than two paths.
Each cage is connected to a path, and all the paths are continuous.
The paths do not intersect in any spot.
One path connects B and R.
One path connects S and T.

1. If no path connects a cage in one row to a cage directly across from it, then which of the following must be true?

   (A) R is connected to C.
   (B) S is connected to R.
   (C) T is connected to B.
   (D) A is connected to R.
   (E) None of the above.

2. If a path connects B to C, then which of the following must be true?

   (A) A path connects S to C.
   (B) A path connects B to S.
   (C) A path connects C to T.
   (D) A path connects R to A.
   (E) None of the above.

3. If a path connects B to S, then which of the following must NOT be true?

   (A) R is connected to A.
   (B) C is connected to T.
   (C) A is connected to B.
   (D) S is connected to T.
   (E) None of the above.

4. If C is connected to two paths, then how many possible configurations are there for the paths?

   (A) two
   (B) four
   (C) six
   (D) eight
   (E) None of the above.

5. Which cage can never be connected to only one path?

   (A) A
   (B) B
   (C) C
   (D) S
   (E) T

6. If S is connected to C, then which of the following must be true?

   (A) C is connected to R.
   (B) A is connected to B.
   (C) B is connected to C.
   (D) R is connected to A.
   (E) None of the above.

SOLUTION STEPS

1. Transcribe the Constraints

1. **Mapping:** "Each cage is connected to no more than two paths."
2. **Mapping:** "Each cage is connected to at least one path."
3. **Mapping:** "The paths do not intersect."
4. **Direct Placement:** B and R are connected.
5. **Direct Placement:** S and T are connected.

2. Draw a Representative Diagram. *Use constraints to gain information.* The representative diagram is given to you in the fact pattern, so you should draw in the diagram, adding the direct placement constraints to gain information:

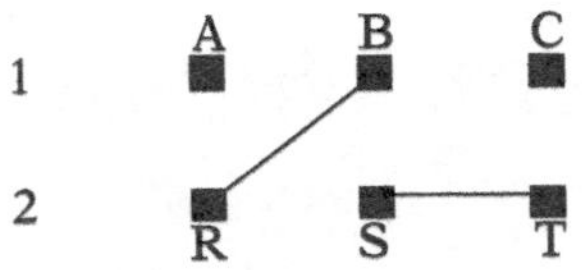

Looking at this base diagram, you know that each cage is connected to *no more than two paths* and *at least one path, no paths can cross*, and *all the paths are continuous*. This means that there are a limited number of configurations that can be made for this game. For instance, A must be connected to either B or R if it is to be connected to the rest of the cages, since a path from A cannot cross the BR path. Whichever way A is connected has different implications for the game. Here are all six possible configurations that you should come up with:

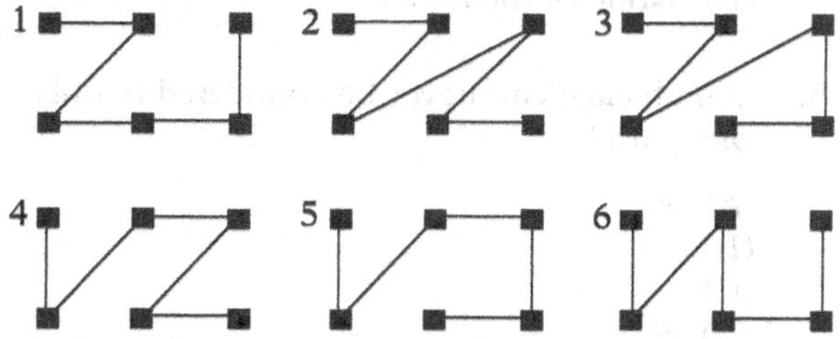

3. Make a Hierarchy of Consolidated Constraints. A hierarchy is not necessary, because you have already written out all of the possible scenarios.

Answering the Questions

Question 1: If no path connects a cage in one row to a cage directly across from it, then which of the following must be true?

(A) This constraint is possible only in scenario 2, in which R is connected to C.

Question 2: If a path connects B to C, then which of the following must be true?

(D) This constraint occurs in scenarios 4 and 5, in both of which A is connected to R.

Question 3: If a path connects B to S, then which of the following must NOT be true?

(C) This constraint occurs only in scenario 6. A cannot be connected to B.

Question 4: If C is connected to two paths, then how many possible configurations are there for the paths?

(B) C is connected to two paths in four scenarios.

Question 5: Which cage can never be connected to only one path?

(B) R and B are the only cages that must be connected to two paths.

Question 6: If S is connected to C, then which of the following must be true?

(E) This constraint occurs in scenarios 2 and 4, in which none of the answer choices is required to occur.

MAPPING GAME 2

A citywide beautification project is requiring all business owners to repaint their stores downtown. Each store must be painted red, blue, or green. As shown by the following diagram, stores 1 through 4 are on one side of the street and stores 5 through 8 are directly across from them on the opposite side of the street.

1	2	3	4
5	6	7	8

Stores *face* the store directly across from them in the opposite row.

Stores next to each other in the same row are *adjacent*.

Adjacent stores are painted different colors.

No green store faces another green store.

Store 2 is green.

Store 7 is blue.

No red store adjacent to a blue store can be adjacent to a green store.

1. Which of the following stores must be painted blue?
   (A) 1
   (B) 3
   (C) 4
   (D) 5
   (E) 8

2. What is the maximum number of blue stores that there could be?
   (A) two
   (B) three
   (C) four
   (D) five
   (E) six

3. Which of the following must be true if store 4 is painted green?
   (A) Store 3 is blue.
   (B) Store 1 is blue.
   (C) Store 8 is red.
   (D) Store 6 is blue.
   (E) Store 3 is red.

4. Which of the following must be true if store 3 is painted red?
   (A) Store 4 is green.
   (B) Store 8 is blue.
   (C) Store 1 is red.
   (D) Store 5 is green.
   (E) Store 6 is green.

5. Which store could NOT be painted blue?
   (A) 1
   (B) 3
   (C) 4
   (D) 5
   (E) 7

6. Which of the following does NOT have to be true if four stores are painted red?
   (A) Store 1 is red.
   (B) Store 8 is red.
   (C) Store 5 is blue.
   (D) Store 3 is red.
   (E) Store 6 is red.

SOLUTION STEPS

1. Transcribe the Constraints

1. **Direct Placement:** 2 = Green
2. **Direct Placement:** 7 = Blue
3. **Mapping:** "Adjacent stores are painted different colors."
4. **Mapping:** "No green store faces another green store."
5. **Mapping:** "No red store adjacent to a blue store can be adjacent to a green store."

2. Draw a Representative Diagram

1	2 G	3	4
5	6	7 B	8

Use constraints to gain information.

Let's go through this constraint by constraint:

Constraint 1: Adjacent stores are painted different colors.

Note that in this game "adjacent" means stores that are next to each other and not stores that are across from each other. This means that there is a double possibility in the stores adjacent to store 2 and store 7, since you know their colors.

1 R/B	2 G	3 R/B	4
5	6 G/R	7 B	8 G/R

Constraint 2: No green store faces another green store.

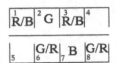

1 R/B	2 G	3 R/B	4
5	6 R	7 B	8 G/R

Constraint 3: No red store adjacent to a blue store can be adjacent to a green store.

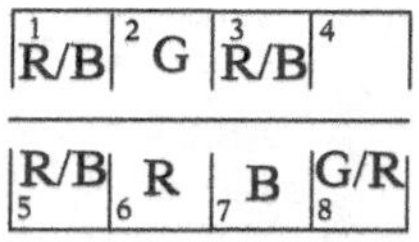

Remember constraint 1, which says that no store can be adjacent to a store that is the same color. Therefore, store 5 must be blue:

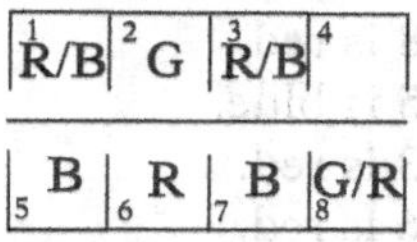

3. Make a Hierarchy of Consolidated Constraints. The consolidated constraints are just the mapping constraints that could still hold for the game:

1. Adjacent stores are painted different colors.
2. No green store faces another green store.
3. No red store adjacent to a blue store can be adjacent to a green store.

Answering the Questions

Question 1: Which of the following stores must be painted blue?

(D) Stores 5 and 7 must be painted blue.

Question 2: What is the maximum number of blue stores that there could be?

(C) Stores 5 and 7 must be blue, and stores 1 and 3 could both be blue. Store 4 cannot be blue because that would force store 3 to be red, which is not possible because a red store cannot be adjacent to both a blue store and a green store.

Question 3: Which of the following must be true if store 4 is painted green?

(C) This constraint would force store 8 to be red, since a green store cannot face another green store.

Question 4: Which of the following must be true if store 3 is painted red?

(A) This would force store 4 to be green, because if store 4 were blue, then store 3, since it is red, could not be adjacent to a green store.

Question 5: Which store could NOT be painted blue?

(C) Store 4 cannot be blue, because that would force store 3 to be red, and a red store that borders a blue store cannot also border a green store.

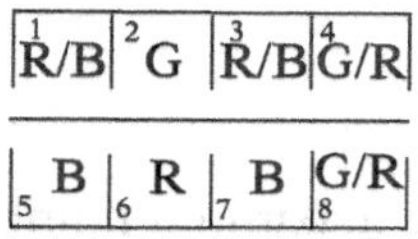

Question 6: Which of the following does NOT have to be true if four stores are painted red?

(D) Stores 1, 6, and 8 must all be red. Additionally, either store 3 or 4 could be red.

MAPPING GAME 3

At a United Nations summit, six diplomats sit around a circular table. The diplomats are named Anna, Ben, Chris, Dana, Evan, and Frank. The seating arrangements for the diplomats are determined by the following:

The six seats are numbered in sequential order.
Seat 6 is next to seat 1.
Ben sits directly across from Frank.
Frank does not sit next to Dana.
Chris sits directly across from Evan or Anna.

1. If Frank sits in seat 6, then who could sit in seats 1 and 5?

   (A) Evan, Ben.
   (B) Anna, Dana.
   (C) Ben, Dana.
   (D) Chris, Evan.
   (E) None of the above.

2. How many different people could potentially sit next to Frank?

   (A) two
   (B) three
   (C) four
   (D) five
   (E) six

3. Whom must Ben sit next to?

   (A) Dana
   (B) Chris
   (C) Anna
   (D) Evan
   (E) None of the above

4. If Evan sits in seat 4, then which of the following must be true?

   (A) Ben sits in seat 3.
   (B) Anna sits in seat 5.
   (C) Chris sits in seat 1.
   (D) Frank sits in seat 6.
   (E) None of the above.

5. If Ben sits in seat 1 and Dana sits in seat 6, then which of the following must be true?

   (A) Evan sits in seat 3.
   (B) Anna sits in seat 3.
   (C) Chris sits in seat 5.
   (D) Frank sits in seat 4.
   (E) None of the above.

6. If Ben sits in seat 1, then in how many different seats could Anna sit?

   (A) two
   (B) three
   (C) four
   (D) five
   (E) six

SOLUTION STEPS

1. Transcribe the Constraints

1. **Mapping:** Ben sits directly across from Frank.
2. **Mapping:** Frank does not sit next to Dana.
3. **Mapping:** Chris sits directly across from Evan or Anna.

2. Draw a Representative Diagram. For circular diagrams, you should always draw the diagram with spokes but no rim, instead of as a wheel or circle. This way you can easily keep track of who sits across from whom.

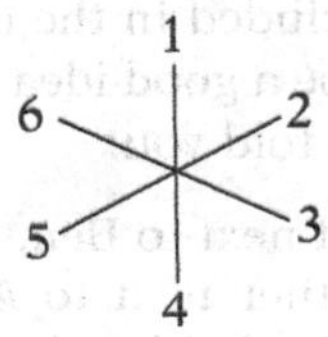

Use constraints to gain information.

The numbers here are arbitrary; seat 1 doesn't have to be at the top. It is all about who can sit next to or across from whom. If a question asks you about numbers, then the numbers are given to you only so that you can determine the ordering of the variables. Start out by placing a constraint on the diagram:

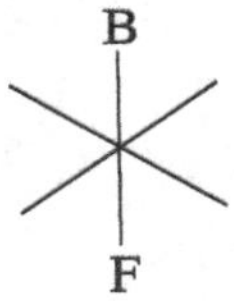

Next, think about the rules that this constraint would invoke. In this case, Dana cannot sit next to Frank:

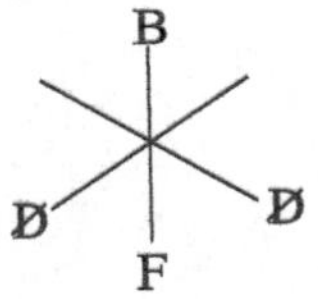

Now, there is one other constraint left to be added—the fact that Chris must sit across from either Anna or Evan. You see that there are two places for him to sit, so you would be wise to draw out these scenarios:

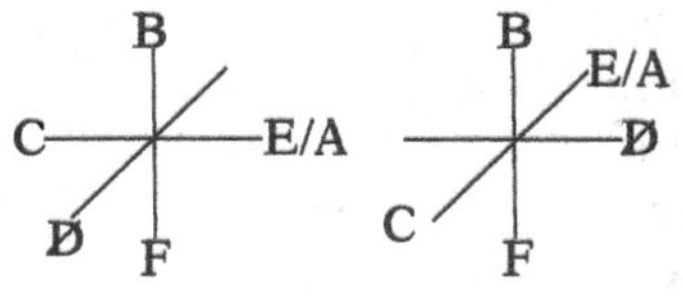

It seems that there are actually four places for Chris to sit, which could be obtained if you flip over the scenarios presented above. But if you do this, then you will see that the relative relationships of the variables are still the same, so there is no need to overcomplicate the diagram. Your final diagram should look like this:

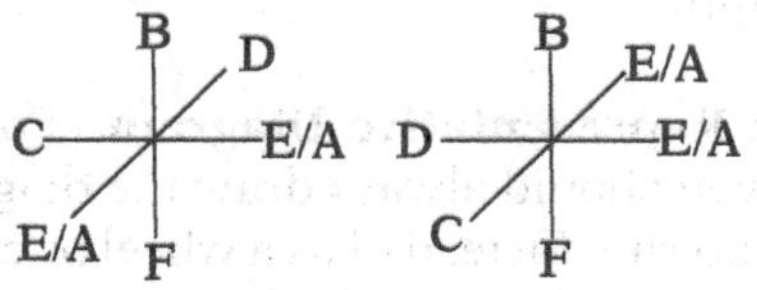

3. Make a Hierarchy of Consolidated Constraints. These have been included in the diagram, but since they have, it would be a good idea to think over what these diagrams have told you:

1. Dana must sit next to Ben.
2. Frank sits either next to Anna and Evan or next to Chris and either Anna or Evan.

Answering the Questions

Question 1: If Frank sits in seat 6, then who could sit in seats 1 and 5?

(D) Seats 1 and 5 are the two seats that are next to seat 6. Frank cannot sit next to Dana or Ben.

Question 2: How many different people could potentially sit next to Frank?

(B) Frank could sit next to Chris, Evan, or Anna.

Question 3: Whom must Ben sit next to?

(A) Ben must sit next to Dana.

Question 4: If Evan sits in seat 4, then which of the following must be true?

(E) None of the answer choices must be true, even though they all can be true.

(A) Ben does not have to sit next to Evan.
(B) Anna does not have to sit next to Evan.
(C) Chris could sit next to Evan.
(D) Frank could sit next to Evan.

Question 5: If Ben sits in seat 1 and Dana sits in seat 6, then which of the following must be true?

(D) If Ben sits in seat 1, then Frank must sit across from him in seat 4.

Question 6: If Ben sits in seat 1, then in how many different seats could Anna sit?

(C) Anna could sit in four seats: 2, 3, 5, and 6. You can see that she could sit in seats 5 and 6 in addition to 2 and 3 by flipping the diagram as we discussed in the beginning of the setup for this problem.

MAPPING GAME 4

The Navy performs security operations off the coast of the eastern seaboard. A total of four perfectly circular security areas are defined in the waters that the Navy surveys. Area A intersects area B. Area B intersects area C. Area C and area A do not intersect. Area D is completely encompassed by the part of area B that does not intersect any other area. At midnight, four ships, R, S, T, and U, are in the water in at least one of the areas. The positions of the ships are determined by the following:

R is in area A.
T is not in any security area that R is in.
S is in at least two security areas.
U is not in any security area that S is in.

1. Which of the following could NOT be true if R is in two areas?

(A) U is in area C.
(B) S is in area D and U is in area A.
(C) T is in area D.
(D) R and S are in areas A and B.
(E) None of the above.

2. If S and T are in the same two areas, then which of the following must be true?

(A) T is in area D.
(B) S is in areas B and C.
(C) U is in area A.
(D) R is not in area B.
(E) None of the above.

3. If R is in two areas, then which of the following must be true?

(A) S is in area D.
(B) U is in area D.
(C) T is in area B.
(D) R is in area C.
(E) None of the above.

4. Which of the following is a full list of the areas that U could be in?

(A) A
(B) C, A
(C) B, D
(D) B, A, D
(E) A, B, C, D

5. Which of the following is a pair of ships that could share area D?

(A) S, T
(B) R, U
(C) S, U
(D) T, R
(E) None of the above.

6. If T is not in any area that S is in, then which of the following must be true?

(A) S is in area D.
(B) U is in area C.
(C) S is in area A.
(D) T is in area C.
(E) None of the above.

SOLUTION STEPS

1. Transcribe the Constraints

1. **Direct Placement:** R = area A
2. **Mapping:** T ≠ R
3. **Mapping:** S = 2 areas
4. **Mapping:** U ≠ S

Since R is in area A and T cannot be in the same area that R is in, T cannot be in area A. Since S is in two areas and U cannot be in any area that S is also in, U must be in only one area. This means that U cannot be in area D or area B. Note that if any ship is in two areas, one of the areas must be area B.

2. Draw a Representative Diagram

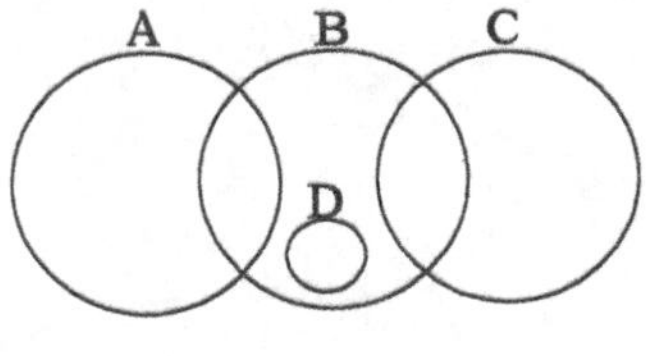

Use constraints to gain information.

There is not much information that you can gain here, except for the following:

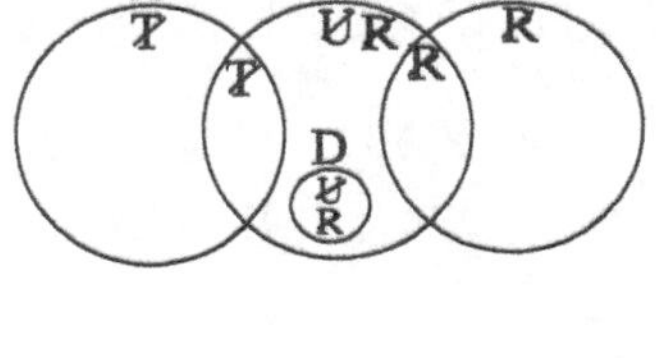

3. Make a Hierarchy of Consolidated Constraints. You should remember the constraints that are not included in your diagram:

1. R = area A
2. T ≠ R
3. S = 2 areas
4. U ≠ S

Answering the Questions

Question 1: Which of the following could NOT be true if R is in two areas?

(C) If R is in two areas, then one of them must be area B, so T cannot be in area B or area D.

Question 2: If S and T are in the same two areas, then which of the following must be true?

(D) If S and T are in the same two areas, then they must both be in area D or in the overlap between areas B and C. Otherwise, T would encroach in area A, which is not allowed, because R must be in that area. This also means that R cannot be in any part of area B, because that would mean T and R would be in the same area.

Question 3: If R is in two areas, then which of the following must be true?

(E) If R is in two areas, then they must be areas A and B. This would force T to be only in area C. However, this is not an answer choice, so the correct answer is "None of the above."

Question 4: Which of the following is a full list of the areas that U could be in?

(B) U can either be in area A or area C, because it cannot be in the same areas as S. S, since it must occupy two areas, must be in area B.

Question 5: Which of the following is a pair of ships that could share area D?

(A) U and R can never be in area D, but S and T both can.

Question 6: If T is not in any area that S is in, then which of the following must be true?

(D) If this constraint occurs, then T must be in only area C. This is because T cannot be in area A with S and S must be in area B.

On Your Own

MAPPING GAME 5

Nine travelers, Anna, Ben, Chris, Dana, Evan, Frank, Garry, Hillary, and Iris, are all flying on an airplane to Paris. The airplane seats that the travelers sit in are arranged as follows:

Row 1: 1 2 3
Row 2: 4 5 6
Row 3: 7 8 9

Each row of seats has an aisle at either end.

The seating arrangements are governed by the following conditions:

Iris does not sit in the same row as Anna.
Chris sits in the seat immediately behind Garry's.
Ben sits in the seat immediately to the right of Dana's.
Hillary sits immediately to the left of Chris.
Anna sits immediately in front of Dana.

1. Which of the following is a possible order for the travelers to sit in in seats 1, 2, and 3?

(A) Anna, Frank, Iris.
(B) Frank, Anna, Evan.
(C) Evan, Iris, Garry.
(D) Garry, Frank, Iris.
(E) Iris, Hillary, Chris.

2. If Frank sits in seat 2, then which of the following must be true?

(A) Iris sits in row 3.
(B) Evan sits in row 1.
(C) Ben and Garry sit in the same row.
(D) Evan sits in the same row as Ben.
(E) Hillary sits in the same row as Anna or Iris.

3. If Iris sits in seat 9, then which of the following must be true?

(A) Frank sits immediately in front of Anna.
(B) Garry sits immediately to the right of Evan.
(C) Hillary and Anna sit in the same row.
(D) Garry sits in the second row.
(E) Hillary sits behind Ben.

4. Which of the following is a pair of people who could sit in the same row?

(A) Iris, Anna.
(B) Hillary, Dana.
(C) Chris, Frank.
(D) Iris, Hillary.
(E) Anna, Dana.

5. If Ben and Garry sit in the same row, then which of the following must be true?

(A) Anna sits in seat 2.
(B) Iris sits in seat 7.
(C) Garry sits in seat 5.
(D) Frank sits in seat 9.
(E) Evan sits in seat 3.

6. If Iris does not sit in an aisle seat, then which of the following must be true?

(A) Hillary sits next to Iris.
(B) Evan sits next to Iris.
(C) Frank sits next to Iris.
(D) Ben sits behind Iris.
(E) Dana sits in front of Iris.

MAPPING GAME 6

In order to prevent litter, a city park is surrounded by trash cans. Some city council members favor steel trash cans, while others favor rubber, but both kinds are present on the border of the park. One trash can that is either rubber or steel is present at each point in the following diagram of the park:

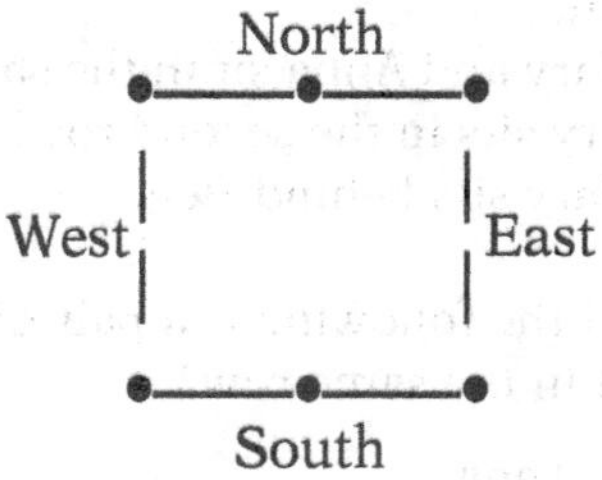

The type of trash can that is present at each of the six points is governed by the following conditions:

Each rubber trash can must be adjacent to at least one other rubber trash can.
Steel trash cans cannot have rubber trash cans on both sides of them.
The trash can on the southwest corner is steel.
The trash can in the middle of the north side is rubber.
At least two trash cans on the corners must be steel.
A steel trash can on a corner of the park must be adjacent to another steel trash can.

1. If the trash can in the middle of the south side is rubber, then which of the following must be true?
   (A) The trash can on the northeast corner is steel.
   (B) The trash can on the southeast corner is steel.
   (C) The trash can on the northwest corner is steel.
   (D) There are three steel trash cans.
   (E) None of the above.

2. If there are three steel trash cans on the corners of the park, then which of the following must be true?
   (A) The trash can on the northeast corner is steel.
   (B) The trash can on the southeast corner is steel.
   (C) The trash can on the northwest corner is steel.
   (D) There is a total of three steel trash cans.
   (E) None of the above.

3. What is the maximum number of rubber trash cans that can be present in the park?
   (A) one
   (B) two
   (C) three
   (D) four
   (E) None of the above

4. If the trash can on the northeast corner is steel, then which of the following must be true?
   (A) The trash can in the middle of the south side is steel.
   (B) The trash can on the northwest corner is not rubber.
   (C) The trash can on the southeast corner is rubber.
   (D) There is a total of three rubber trash cans.
   (E) None of the above.

5. If there are equal numbers of rubber and steel trash cans, then which of the following must NOT be true?
   (A) The trash can on the northeast corner is rubber.
   (B) The trash can on the northwest corner is rubber.
   (C) The trash can in the middle of the south side is steel.
   (D) The trash can on the southeast corner is steel.
   (E) None of the above.

6. Which of the following must NOT be true?
   (A) The trash can on the northeast corner is rubber, and the trash can on the northwest corner is steel.
   (B) The trash can in the middle of the south side is steel, and the trash can on the southeast corner is steel.
   (C) The trash can on the northwest corner is rubber, and the trash can in the middle of the south side is rubber.
   (D) The trash can in the middle of the north side is rubber, and the trash can in the middle of the south side is rubber.
   (E) None of the above.

MAPPING GAME 7

An Olympic athlete has put her medals up on the wall for everyone to admire. She has won six medals—two gold and four silver. The medals are from two Olympics, 2000 and 2004. The medals are arranged as shown:

1	2	3
4	5	6

Medal 2 is gold.
Both gold medals were won in the 2004 Olympics.
Medals 1 and 3 were won in 2000.
At most only three silver medals are on the corners.
All medals won in 2000 are hung adjacent to at least two medals won in 2004.

1. Which of the following could be the kinds of medals that 4, 5, and 6 are, respectively?
   (A) gold, silver, gold.
   (B) silver, gold, silver.
   (C) silver, silver, gold.
   (D) gold, gold, silver.
   (E) silver, silver, silver.

2. If medal 5 was won in 2000, then a total of how many medals were won in 2000?
   (A) two
   (B) three
   (C) four
   (D) five
   (E) six

3. If medal 6 is gold, then which of the following could be true?
   (A) Medal 4 is gold.
   (B) Medal 5 is gold.
   (C) Medal 3 was won in 2004.
   (D) Medal 1 is gold.
   (E) There are more medals from 2004 than from 2000.

4. If medal 4 is gold, then which of the following must be true?
   (A) Medal 6 is silver.
   (B) Medal 5 is gold.
   (C) Medal 5 is from 2004.
   (D) Medal 4 is from 2000.
   (E) There were only three medals won in 2004.

5. If the constraints are changed so that the four silver medals go on the corners, then which of the following must be true?
   (A) Medal 2 is from 2000.
   (B) Medal 6 is from 2000.
   (C) Medal 5 is from 2004.
   (D) Medal 1 is from 2004.
   (E) Medal 3 is from 2004.

6. If the constraints are changed so that the athlete could have won more or less than or exactly two gold medals and four silver medals, then which of the following could NOT be true?
   (A) Medal 4 is gold.
   (B) Medal 5 is from 2000.
   (C) The athlete has four gold medals.
   (D) The athlete has four medals from 2000.
   (E) The athlete has three silver medals.

MAPPING GAME 8

In the modern city of Atlantis, eight bubble domes, completely surrounding subdivisions and protecting them from water, are arranged into two rows as shown by the following diagram:

1	2	3	4
5	6	7	8

The mayor of the city will connect the subdivisions using waterproof tunnels. The arrangement of the tunnels is dictated by the following constraints:

Subdivision 3 is connected to subdivision 5.
Subdivision 6 is connected to subdivision 4.
No tunnel can intersect another tunnel.
Each tunnel is a perfectly straight line.
Each subdivision is connected to two tunnels at most.

1. If none of the subdivisions is connected to the subdivision directly across from it, then which of the following must be true?

(A) Subdivision 3 is connected to subdivision 6.
(B) Subdivision 4 is connected to subdivision 5.
(C) Subdivision 3 is connected to subdivision 4.
(D) Subdivision 6 is connected to subdivision 7.
(E) None of the above.

2. If subdivision 2 is connected to subdivision 3, then which of the following must NOT be true?

(A) Subdivision 1 is connected to subdivision 2.
(B) Subdivision 7 is connected to subdivision 8.
(C) Subdivision 6 is connected to subdivision 7.
(D) Subdivision 5 is connected to subdivision 4.
(E) None of the above.

3. If subdivision 7 is connected to subdivision 4, then which of the following must be true?

(A) Subdivision 5 is connected to subdivision 2.
(B) Subdivision 6 is connected to subdivision 3.
(C) Subdivision 1 is connected to subdivision 5.
(D) Subdivision 8 is connected to subdivision 7.
(E) None of the above.

4. If subdivision 2 is connected to subdivision 3, then which of the following could be true?

(A) Subdivision 5 is connected to subdivision 6.
(B) Subdivision 3 is connected to subdivision 6.
(C) Subdivision 2 is connected to subdivision 5.
(D) Subdivision 3 is connected to subdivision 8.
(E) None of the above.

5. If subdivision 3 is connected to subdivision 4, then which of the following must be true?

(A) Subdivision 5 is connected to subdivision 1.
(B) Subdivision 5 is connected to subdivision 4.
(C) Subdivision 7 is connected to subdivision 6.
(D) Subdivision 2 is connected to subdivision 5.
(E) None of the above.

6. How many different configurations for the tunnels are possible?

(A) four
(B) five
(C) six
(D) eight
(E) nine

ANSWERS AND EXPLANATIONS

Game 5

Initial Setup:

There are only two places where each of the constraining boxes (GCH and ADB) can go. This allows you to draw the two major scenarios:

1.			2.		
A	E/F	F/E	E/F/I	I/E/F	G
D	B	G	A	H	C
I	H	C	D	B	F/I/E

Question 1: Which of the following is a possible order for the travelers to sit in in seats 1, 2, and 3?

(C) Evan, Iris, and Garry can sit in that order in the first row in scenario number 2.

Question 2: If Frank sits in seat 2, then which of the following must be true?

(E) This can occur in either diagram. Hillary must share a row with Anna or Iris in both scenarios.

Question 3: If Iris sits in seat 9, then which of the following must be true?

(C) This constraint is possible only in scenario 2, in which Hillary and Anna sit in the same row.

Question 4: Which of the following is a pair of people who could sit in the same row?

(D) Hillary and Iris can both sit in the third row in the first scenario.

Question 5: If Ben and Garry sit in the same row, then which of the following must be true?

(B) This constraint occurs in the first scenario, in which Iris must sit in seat 7.

Question 6: If Iris does not sit in an aisle seat, then which of the following must be true?

(D) This constraint is possible only in scenario 2, in which Iris must sit in seat 2 in order to avoid sitting on an aisle. In that case, Ben must sit two rows behind Iris. Notice that the answer choice did not say "immediately behind," a constraint that would have required Ben to sit in seat 5.

Game 6

Initial Setup:

You can start out initially by diagramming the two direct placement variables in the problem:

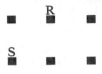

After careful inspection, you can see that there are five potential arrangements for all the variables:

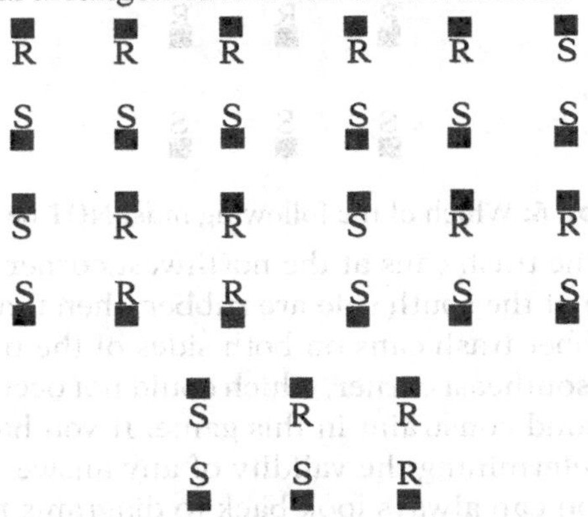

Question 1: If the trash can in the middle of the south side is rubber, then which of the following must be true?

(C) Here is a diagram for this situation:

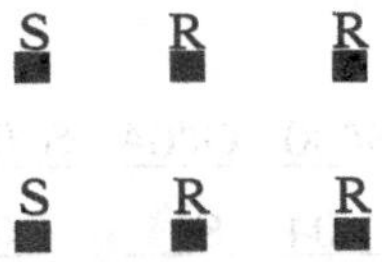

You see that the trash can on the northwest corner must be steel.

Question 2: If there are three steel trash cans on the corners of the park, then which of the following must be true?

(B) This constraint relegates us to one of the scenarios on the right-hand side. In both of them, the can at the southeast corner is steel.

Question 3: What is the maximum number of rubber trash cans that can be present in the park?

(D) Since there must be two steel trash cans on the corners, the diagram with the most rubber trash cans is as follows:

Question 4: If the northeast trash can is steel, then which of the following must be true?

(A) The diagram below represents this constraint.

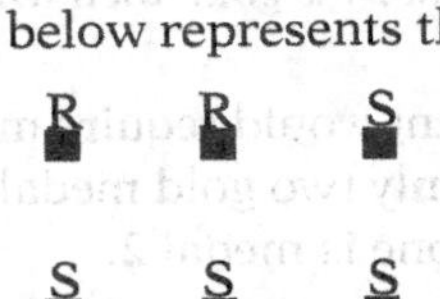

Question 5: If there are equal numbers of rubber and steel trash cans, then which of the following must NOT be true?

(E) For this constraint to happen, the configuration must be as follows:

Question 6: Which of the following must NOT be true?

(C) If the trash cans at the northwest corner and the middle of the south side are rubber, then that would put rubber trash cans on both sides of the trash can on the southeast corner, which could not occur under the second constraint in this game. If you had problems determining the validity of any answer choice, then you can always look back to diagrams that you have drawn for previous questions.

Game 7

Initial Setup:

S/'00 G/'04 S/'00

_/'04 S/_ _/'04

You know that the fifth medal must be silver, since there are only four silver medals and you know that at most, three of them can be hung on the corners.

Question 1: Which of the following could be the kinds of medals that 4, 5, and 6 are, respectively?

(C) The order could either be gold, silver, silver or silver, silver, gold.

Question 2: If medal 5 was won in 2000, then a total of how many medals were won in 2000?

(B) This would make three medals won in 2000.

Question 3: If medal 6 is gold, then which of the following could be true?

(E) If this constraint were true, then you would know what kind each of the other medals was. The only unknown left would be the year of medal 5. It could be from 2004, in which case there would be more medals won in 2004 than in 2000.

Question 4: If medal 4 is gold, then which of the following must be true?

(A) This constraint would require medal 6 to be silver, since there are only two gold medals and you already know the other one is medal 2.

Question 5: If the constraints are changed so that the four silver medals go on the corners, then which of the following must be true?

(C) This constraint would make the second gold medal number 5, and both gold medals were won in 2004. The diagram for the question would be as follows:

S/'00 G/'04 S/'00

S/'04 G/'04 S/'04

Question 6: If the constraints are changed so that the athlete could have won more or less than or exactly two gold medals and four silver medals, then which of the following could NOT be true?

(D) This constraint takes you back to your original setup, but now you cannot infer that medal 5 is silver, because there would be enough gold medals to go on the corners and in position 5. The most medals that the athlete could have won in 2000 would be three.

S/'00 G/'04 S/'00

_/'04 _/_ _/'04

Game 8

Initial Setup:

There are nine possible configurations for this game. The pairs of broken lines denote that a line could be drawn to either of two subdivisions in subsequent configurations based on the scenario. The numbers at the top of each scenario denote how many configurations could be drawn based on that scenario.

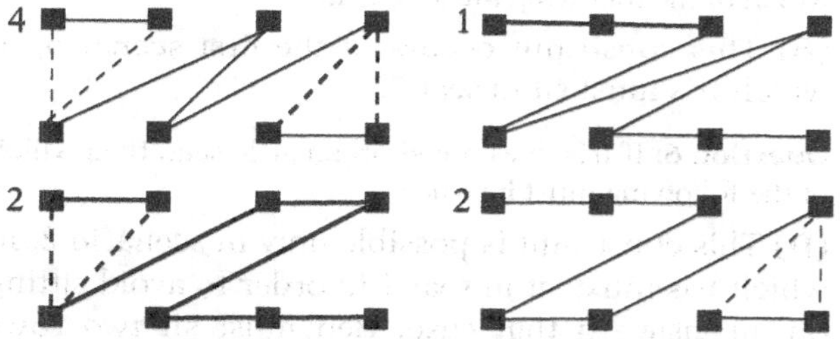

Question 1: If none of the subdivisions is connected to the subdivision directly across from it, then which of the following must be true?

(E) This constraint means that either subdivisions 2 and 5 are connected along with 7 and 8 or subdivisions 4 and 7 are connected along with 2 and 3, but it does not necessarily mean that one of these configurations occurs specifically.

Question 2: If subdivision 2 is connected to subdivision 3, then which of the following must NOT be true?

(E) Each answer choice could occur in at least one scenario.

Question 3: If subdivision 7 is connected to subdivision 4, then which of the following must be true?

(D) In every diagram, subdivision 8 must be connected to subdivision 7.

Question 4: If subdivision 2 is connected to subdivision 3, then which of the following could be true?

(A) This constraint is possible in configurations based on the bottom right scenario, in which subdivision 5 is connected to subdivision 6.

Question 5: If subdivision 3 is connected to subdivision 4, then which of the following must be true?

(C) This constraint occurs in configurations based on the bottom left scenario, in which subdivision 7 is connected to subdivision 6.

Question 6: How many different configurations for the tunnels are possible?

(E) Four configurations are possible from the top left scenario, one from the top right scenario, and two from each bottom scenario, making a total of nine.

CHAPTER 7

PATTERN GAMES

Pattern games are very rare on modern-day LSATs, but you should still be prepared in case one appears on your test by surprise. Regardless, the organization skills that you learn for pattern games will help you to solve other types of games. For pattern games, diagrams are difficult to draw. Sometimes they take the form of an expanded linear or grouping game. Other times there is not much of a diagram that you can draw, and the best that you can hope for is to make a list of constraints to remember while creating and dissecting the iterations of the game.

Typical Fact Pattern

> Anna, Ben, Chris, Dana, Evan, Frank, and Garry are all salespeople for Salescorp, LLC. Each year Salescorp sends three salespeople from this group to a conference. No salesperson is sent three years in a row. Every salesperson is sent at least once every three years. Who is sent to the conferences is governed by the following constraints:
>
> Anna does not go to conferences with Frank.
> Garry always attends conferences with Dana.
> Dana and Ben always attend conferences in consecutive years but never in the same year.
> Ben and Anna go to the conference in the first year.

Logic Tools

General

The general diagram for this question is theoretically infinite, but generally, pattern game questions do not question you past years five or six:

1 — — —
2 — — —
3 — — —
4 — — —
5 — — —

Pattern

Most logic tools for pattern games are very similar to those used in grouping games and complex linear games. We call them *pattern constraints*, since they are applied to games in which there is no end in sight to the diagram—in the previous fact pattern, people could attend conferences for years to come. The same type of theory can be applied to these games, because each year can be seen as one group in a grouping game.

Constraint 1: Anna does not go to conferences with Frank.

A ≠ F

Constraint 2: Garry always attends conferences with Dana.

G = D

Constraint 3: Dana and Ben always attend conferences in consecutive years but never in the same year.

Constraint 4: Ben and Anna go to the conference in the first year.

B = 1 A = 1

Diagram:

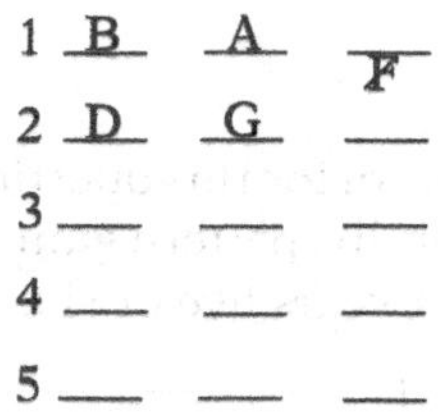

Fact Pattern Organization Heuristics

The heuristic steps are exactly the same as those for mapping games:

1. **Transcribe** the constraints.
2. Draw a **representative diagram.**
   a. Use constraints to gain information.
3. Make a **hierarchy** of consolidated constraints.

Review

In this section, you have learned:

1. How to diagram pattern games.
2. The traits of a typical fact pattern for pattern games.
3. How to apply previously learned logic tools to pattern games.
4. The fact pattern organization heuristic steps for solving pattern games.

Pattern Games Explained

PATTERN GAME 1

A groovy fence painter takes a day off from work to paint the fence outside of his house. His attention span is minimal, so we are unable to determine how many planks of his fence he will paint today. However, he will paint each plank red, blue, white, green, purple, or orange. The color that he chooses for each plank will be determined by the following constraints:

Every fifth plank painted will be blue.
If two adjacent planks are of the same color, then they are both red.
No blue plank can be adjacent to a green plank.
Every white plank must be adjacent to a red plank and a blue plank.
If an orange plank is next to a green plank, then the pair is bordered by two blue planks.

1. Which of the following could be an order of colors the planks are painted, from first to last?
   (A) green, red, red, red, blue, green, orange, blue.
   (B) red, white, blue, red, blue, blue, purple, blue.
   (C) red, blue, orange, purple, blue, white, red.
   (D) orange, purple, blue, red, blue, white, red, orange, red, red.
   (E) None of the above.

2. If a white plank is painted fourth, then which of the following could be the colors of a pair of planks that are painted second and third, respectively?
   (A) orange, blue.
   (B) purple, green.
   (C) white, orange.
   (D) green, red.
   (E) None of the above.

3. If the painter paints ten planks and the fourth plank is white and the sixth and seventh planks are orange and purple, respectively, then which is another plank that could be white?
   (A) first
   (B) second
   (C) eighth
   (D) fifth
   (E) None of the above

4. If the painter paints five planks and the third and fourth planks are orange and purple, respectively, then which of the following could be the color of the second plank?
   (A) orange
   (B) white
   (C) green
   (D) purple
   (E) None of the above

5. If the painter paints seven planks, then which of the following could be true?
   (A) The sixth plank is green.
   (B) The third and fourth planks are red.
   (C) The fourth plank is blue.
   (D) The third plank is blue and the fourth plank is white.
   (E) None of the above.

6. If the painter paints ten planks and the sixth and seventh planks are red and green, respectively, then which of the following could NOT be true?
   (A) The eighth and ninth planks are both red.
   (B) The eighth and ninth planks are purple and orange, respectively.
   (C) The eighth and ninth planks are red and white, respectively.
   (D) The eighth and ninth planks are purple and red, respectively.
   (E) None of the above.

SOLUTION STEPS

1. Transcribe the Constraints

Sufficient-Necessary:
Multiple of 5 → B

Sufficient-Necessary:
Consecutive Same Color → RR. This means: ~~OO~~, ~~BB~~, ~~WW~~, and ~~GG~~.

Sufficient-Necessary: W →

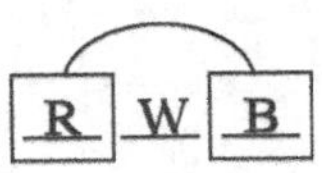

Box Rule:

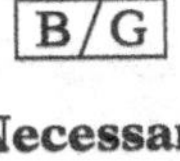

Sufficient-Necessary:

Orange cannot go next to green, because that would force green to go next to blue, which would violate the third constraint.

2. Draw a Representative Diagram. It is best to think of this game as one long linear game:

__ __ __ __ __ __ __ . . .
1 2 3 4 5 6 7

Use constraints to gain information.

As of yet, you cannot determine the placement of any variables except for one:

__ __ __ ~~BG~~ B ~~BG~~ __
1 2 3 4 5 6 7

3. Make a Hierarchy of Consolidated Constraints

Multiple of 5 → B

Consecutive Same Color → RR

W → [R] W [B]

[B/G]

[O/G]

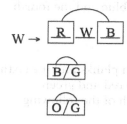

Answering the Questions

Question 1: Which of the following could be an order of colors the planks are painted, from first to last?

(C) This is a possible order.

(A) Green cannot go next to orange or blue.

(B) Blue cannot go consecutively with itself.

(D) The tenth plank must be blue.

(E) **C** is the correct answer.

Question 2: If a white plank is painted fourth, then which of the following could be the colors of a pair of planks that are painted second and third, respectively?

(D) White must be bordered by red and blue. Since the fifth plank must be blue, the third plank cannot be blue, as in answer choice A.

Question 3: If the painter paints ten planks and the fourth plank is white and the sixth and seventh planks are orange and purple, respectively, then which is another plank that could be white?

__ __ __ W B O P __ __ B
1 2 3 4 5 6 7 8 9 10

(B) It appears that the second and ninth planks could also be white. White could go ninth since there would be room for red to go eighth. White could go second since there would be room for red and blue to border it.

Question 4: If the painter paints five planks and the third and fourth planks are orange and purple, respectively, then which of the following could be the color of the second plank?

(D) This question boils down to "what could border an orange plank?" Green, orange, and white cannot, so it must be blue, purple, or red.

Question 5: If the painter paints seven planks, then which of the following could be true?

(B) Both the third and fourth planks could be red.

(A) A green plank cannot border the fifth plank, which is blue.

(C) The fourth plank cannot be blue, because the fifth plank is blue.

(D) White planks must be bordered by red and blue planks.

Question 6: If the painter paints ten planks and the sixth and seventh planks are red and green, respectively, then which of the following could NOT be true?

__ __ __ __ B R G P/R __ B
1 2 3 4 5 6 7 8 9 10

(E) All these configurations are possible.

PATTERN GAME 2

A kindergarten art teacher is making a tie-dyed T-shirt for her class. Some colors will be added more than once to create cool effects. The colors used are red, green, purple, orange, and yellow. In order to preserve the artistic nature of the shirt, the colors have to be added in certain orders that are dictated by the following constraints:

Colors can be added more than once in order to create certain effects.
All colors will be added to the shirt at least once.
The same color can be added consecutively in order to create strange effects.
If red is added, then orange is added immediately before it and yellow is added immediately after it.
Green is not added consecutively with either red or purple.
If yellow is added, then red is added immediately before it and orange is added immediately after it.

1. If the art teacher adds colors to the shirt six times, then which of the following could be the order in which the colors are added, from first to last?

   (A) orange, red, orange, yellow, purple, green.
   (B) green, orange, red, yellow, red, purple.
   (C) purple, orange, red, yellow, orange, purple.
   (D) orange, red, yellow, orange, green, purple.
   (E) green, orange, red, yellow, orange, purple.

2. What is the least number of times that the teacher could add colors and be able to add all of the colors available?

   (A) five
   (B) six
   (C) seven
   (D) eight
   (E) nine

3. If yellow and orange are added consecutively, then which of the following must be true?

   (A) Green is added immediately after orange is added.
   (B) Red is added immediately after purple is added.
   (C) Orange is added two colors before yellow is added.
   (D) Purple is added immediately before orange is added.
   (E) Orange is added immediately after orange is added.

4. Which of the following are both colors that can never be used to make consecutive same-color additions?

   (A) orange, green.
   (B) yellow, purple.
   (C) purple, green.
   (D) yellow, red.
   (E) red, green.

5. Which color could be added immediately before or after the largest variety of colors?

   (A) green
   (B) purple
   (C) orange
   (D) red
   (E) yellow

6. What is the minimum number of times that colors must be added to the shirt in order to use red exactly five times?

   (A) 16
   (B) 18
   (C) 20
   (D) 23
   (E) 25

SOLUTION STEPS

1. Transcribe the Constraints

Pattern: All colors will be added at least once.

Sufficient-Necessary: R → [O R Y]

Sufficient-Necessary: Y → [R Y O]

Box Rule: [G/P]

Notice that you already know that green cannot be added consecutively with red due to the second constraint. Also, you can add the second and third sufficient-necessary boxes to get the following rules:

R → [O R Y O]

Y → [O R Y O]

2. Draw a Representative Diagram. You can tell a little about the first couple of places in the game due to the box rules for R and Y:

RY Y __ __ __ __ __ __ __ __
1 2 3 4 5 6 7 8 9 10

3. Make a Hierarchy of Consolidated Constraints

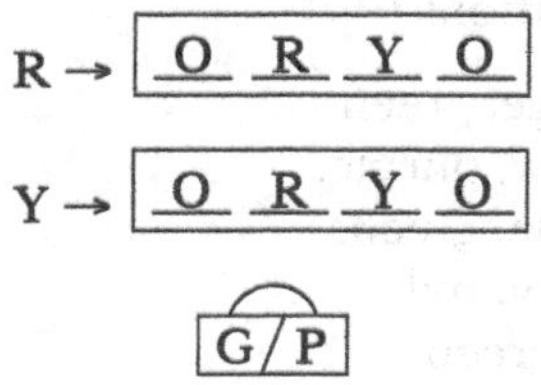

All colors will be added at least once.

ANSWERING THE QUESTIONS

Question 1: If the art teacher adds colors to the shirt six times, then which of the following could be the order in which the colors are added, from first to last?

(E) This could be the order.

(A) Red must be followed by yellow.
(B) Yellow must be followed by orange.
(C) Green must be added.
(D) Green cannot be next to purple.

Question 2: What is the least number of times that the teacher could add colors and be able to add all of the colors available?

(B) The teacher must add all five colors. If the teacher adds red or yellow, which she must, then she must add orange twice. This makes a total of six color additions as the minimum.

Question 3: If yellow and orange are added consecutively, then which of the following must be true?

(C) If yellow is added, then the ORYO box is activated, so red must precede yellow and orange must precede red.

Question 4: Which of the following are both colors that can never be used to make consecutive same-color additions?

(D) Red and yellow cannot be added twice in a row because of the box rule that is invoked whenever one of them is added.

Question 5: Which color could be added immediately before or after the largest variety of colors?

(C) Orange can go before or after any color.

(A) Green cannot go near purple, red, or yellow.
(B) Purple cannot go near green, red, or yellow.
(D) Red can only go near yellow and orange.
(E) Yellow can go only near red and orange.

Question 6: What is the minimum number of times that colors must be added to the shirt in order to use red exactly five times?

(B) Every time that red is used, two oranges and a yellow must also be used. However, one addition of orange can be counted for two chains. So the first time red is used four colors are required, but subsequent additions of red require only three colors to be added—RYO. $(1 \times 4) + (4 \times 3) = 16$ additions of colors required for red to be used five times. You must also add the other two colors, green and purple, to make sure that all of the colors are used. $16 + 2 = 18$. Either of these colors can be added in position 1 and the other in position 18 so that they are not added consecutively.

PATTERN GAME 3

A country has four diplomats—Anna, Ben, Chris, and Dana. Each year exactly three of these diplomats are sent to foreign countries in order to increase foreign appreciation of the country. The rules determining which diplomats are sent out in a particular year are set forth by the following:

Any diplomat who was not sent out in one year must be sent out in the next year.

A diplomatic term ends when at least one of the four diplomats has been sent out four times.

When a diplomatic term ends, the country does not send out any more diplomats in subsequent years.

1. If the diplomats participating in the first year are Chris, Dana, and Anna, then which of the following could not be the diplomats participating in the second year?

   (A) Dana, Anna, Ben
   (B) Ben, Chris, Dana
   (C) Dana, Chris, Anna
   (D) Ben, Anna, Chris
   (E) None of the above.

2. Which of the following must be true about three diplomats' participation each term?

   (A) Anna participates in years one, two, and four.
   (B) Ben participates in years one, two, and three.
   (C) Dana participates in years two, three, and four.
   (D) Dana participates for only three years.
   (E) None of the above.

3. How many years is the longest possible diplomatic term?

   (A) four
   (B) five
   (C) six
   (D) seven
   (E) eight

4. If Anna, Dana, and Chris are sent out in the first year and Chris, Dana, and Ben are sent out in the third year, then which of the following must be true?

   (A) Chris is sent out in three consecutive years.
   (B) Ben, Anna, and Dana are sent out in year two.
   (C) No diplomat is sent out in four consecutive years.
   (D) Anna is sent out in the second and fourth years.
   (E) None of the above.

5. If Chris is sent out in four consecutive years, then which of the following must be true?

   (A) No other diplomat is sent out in three consecutive years.
   (B) No other diplomat is sent out in four consecutive years.
   (C) Two diplomats are sent out only twice.
   (D) No diplomat is sent out only once.
   (E) None of the above.

6. If the diplomats sent out in year four are Ben, Anna, and Dana, then which of the following must be true?

   (A) Chris is sent out in year five.
   (B) Anna and Ben are sent out in year one.
   (C) Chris and Dana are sent out in year three.
   (D) Ben is sent out in year two.
   (E) None of the above.

SOLUTION STEPS

1. Transcribe the Constraints

Pattern: Any diplomat not sent out in one year must be sent out in the next year.

Pattern: A diplomatic term ends when a diplomat has been sent out four times.

Pattern: When a diplomatic term ends, no more diplomats are sent out.

2. Draw a Representative Diagram

				Out
1	___	___	___	___
2	___	___	___	___
3	___	___	___	___
4	___	___	___	___
5	___	___	___	___

3. Make a Hierarchy of Consolidated Constraints. These constraints are all that you have to determine the rules of the game:

Any diplomat not sent out in one year must be sent out in the next year.

A diplomatic term ends when a diplomat has been sent out four times.

In this example it might help you to visualize the problem by drawing out a representative term before answering the real questions.

ANSWERING THE QUESTIONS

Question 1: If the diplomats participating in the first year are Chris, Dana, and Anna, then which of the following could not be the diplomats participating in the second year?

(C) If Ben does not participate in the first year, then he must participate in the next year.

Question 2: Which of the following must be true about three diplomats' participation each term?

(E) All of these things could be true, but none of them must be true.

Question 3: How many years is the longest possible diplomatic term?

(B) The longest that a term could last is five years. You should test this out by drawing a sample term.

Question 4: If Anna, Dana, and Chris are sent out in the first year and Chris, Dana, and Ben are sent out in the third year, then which of the following must be true?

(D) Anna must be sent out in the second year, because if she is not, then she is not sent out twice in a row. She must be sent out in the fourth year, because she was not sent out in the third year.

Question 5: If Chris is sent out in four consecutive years, then which of the following must be true?

(D) It would be impossible to send out a diplomat only once in a four-year span, because then that diplomat would not be sent out for two years running.

Question 6: If the diplomats sent out in year four are Ben, Anna, and Dana, then which of the following must be true?

(E) If this constraint occurs, then Chris must go in year five and year three. This might appear to make choice A correct, except that it is possible for the diplomatic term to end before year five.

PATTERN GAME 4

A computer company sends members of its sales team to a convention each year. The members of the sales team are named Anna, Ben, Chris, Dana, Evan, and Frank. Each year exactly four members of the team go to the convention. Which people will make up the attending group in a given year is determined by the following rules:

Each person must go to the convention at least once in any two consecutive years.

No person goes to the convention in three consecutive years.

Each person has a partner and must attend the convention with the same partner every year that he or she attends.

Each person is partnered with exactly one person.

1. If Anna, Ben, Chris, and Dana attend the convention in the first year, then which of the following is a group that could NOT attend the convention in the third year?
   (A) Chris, Dana, Evan, Frank.
   (B) Evan, Frank, Chris, Dana.
   (C) Evan, Frank, Chris, Anna.
   (D) Anna, Ben, Frank, Dana.
   (E) Evan, Frank, Ben, Anna.

2. If Anna, Ben, Frank, and Dana attend the convention in the third year, then which of the following must be true?
   (A) Anna and Ben are partners.
   (B) Evan and Chris are partners.
   (C) Frank and Dana are partners.
   (D) Chris and Evan attend the convention in the first year.
   (E) Anna and Ben attend the convention in the first year.

3. If Evan, Anna, Ben, and Frank attend the convention in the fourth year and Ben and Evan attend the convention in the third year, then which of the following must be true?
   (A) Ben and Evan attend the convention in the second year.
   (B) Frank and Chris attend the convention in the first year.
   (C) Frank and Anna attend the convention in the third year.
   (D) Evan and Anna attend the convention in the third year.
   (E) Anna and Frank attend the convention in the first year.

4. If Anna, Chris, and Frank attend the convention in the first year and Anna, Ben, and Chris go to the convention in the third year, then which of the following must NOT be true?
   (A) Evan is partnered with Frank.
   (B) Evan is partnered with Dana.
   (C) Frank is partnered with Ben.
   (D) Dana goes to the convention in the first year.
   (E) Dana goes to the convention in the fourth year.

5. How many different pairs of people could be partners?
   (A) 8
   (B) 10
   (C) 15
   (D) 20
   (E) 25

6. If Anna, Chris, Frank, and Ben go to the convention in the second year and Frank, Evan, Anna, and Dana go to the convention in the fourth year, then which of the following could be true?
   (A) Evan and Dana do not go to the convention in the third year.
   (B) Frank and Ben go to the convention in the sixth year.
   (C) Frank and Chris go to the convention in the first year.
   (D) Anna and Frank go to the convention in the third year.
   (E) Chris and Anna go to the convention in the fifth year.

SOLUTION STEPS

1. Transcribe the Constraints

Pattern: Each person attends the convention with the same partner every year that he or she attends.

Pattern: No person goes to the convention three years in a row.

Pattern: No person sits out the convention two years in a row.

2. Draw a Representative Diagram

					Out	
1	___	___	___	___	___	___
2	___	___	___	___	___	___
3	___	___	___	___	___	___
4	___	___	___	___	___	___
5	___	___	___	___	___	___

3. Make a Hierarchy of Consolidated Constraints. These are the same as the original constraints. The constraint that everyone must have a partner exerts strong control over the game.

Each person attends the convention with the same partner every year.

No person goes to the convention three years in a row.

No person sits out the convention two years in a row.

ANSWERING THE QUESTIONS

Question 1: If Anna, Ben, Chris, and Dana attend the convention in the first year, then which of the following is a group that could NOT attend the convention in the third year?

(D) This constraint means two things. First, Evan and Frank must be partners, since they are the only two people who did not attend the convention in the first year. Evan cannot attend any convention without Frank, and Frank cannot attend any convention without Evan. Second, Evan and Frank must attend the convention in the second year.

Question 2: If Anna, Ben, Frank, and Dana attend the convention in the third year, then which of the following must be true?

(B) This constraint means that Evan and Chris are partners and that they both go to the convention in years two and four.

Question 3: If Evan, Anna, Ben, and Frank attend the convention in the fourth year and Ben and Evan attend the convention in the third year, then which of the following must be true?

If this constraint occurs, then you know that Ben and Evan are partners, Anna and Frank are partners, and Chris and Dana are partners. Based on this and the rule that no one can go to the convention three years in a row, you can determine the placement of all of the variables in the diagram up to year five and beyond.

					Out	
1	B	E	A	F	C	D
2	A	F	C	D	B	E
3	B	E	C	D	A	F
4	E	A	B	F	C	D
5	C	D	A	F	B	E

(E) Anna and Frank must attend the convention in the first year.

Question 4: If Anna, Chris, and Frank attend the convention in the first year and Anna, Ben, and Chris go to the convention in the third year, then which of the following must NOT be true?

If this occurs, then you know that Anna and Chris are partners and must sit out year two together. Based on that, you see everyone who goes to the convention in year two. Frank cannot go to the convention three years in a row, so he cannot go in year three. Ben cannot go to the convention three years running, so he cannot go in year one:

					Out	
1	A	C	F	___	B	___
2	F	B	D	E	A	C
3	A	B	C	___	F	___
4	___	___	___	___	B	___
5	___	___	___	___	___	___

(C) You know that Frank cannot be partnered with Ben because each sits out the same year that the other goes to the convention.

Question 5: How many different pairs of people could be partners?

This is a simple matter of determining who can go to the convention with whom. There are five people in the game, so the possible combinations are:

AB	AC	AD	AE	AF
BC	BD	BE	BF	
CD	CE	CF		
DE	DF			
EF				

(C) You must not count BA and AB twice. All in all, there are 15 different potential partnerships.

Question 6: If Anna, Chris, Frank, and Ben go to the convention in the second year and Frank, Evan, Anna, and Dana go to the convention in the fourth year, then which of the following could be true?

The following is the diagram for this scenario:

					Out	
1	A	F	D	E	C	B
2	C	B	A	F	D	E
3	C	B	D	E	A	F
4	A	F	D	E	C	B
5	C	B	A	F	D	E
6	D	E	C	B	A	F

(E) Chris and Anna's going to the convention in year five is the only answer choice that is possible.

On Your Own

PATTERN GAME 5

In a newly developed word game that very few people play, a sentence is formed by six words that are either real or nonsensical but that are in alphabetical order. The rules of the game are as follows:

Each word must have at least three letters.

The words in the sentence cannot all share the same starting letter.

Based on the first word in the sentence, each subsequent word is formed by exactly one of the following transformations: 1. Adding a letter. 2. Deleting a letter. 3. Replacing a letter with another letter.

In a sentence, each kind of transformation is used at least once, and the same kind of transformation is not used twice in a row.

1. Which of the following could be a sentence in the game?

   (A) greek reek sreek streek street treet.
   (B) beet meet mett sett bett zett.
   (C) hit kit kits kitt kitte kitten.
   (D) now snow sow tow tows tozs.
   (E) foam roam room zoom zzoom zzooz.

2. If the first word of a sentence has seven letters, what is the maximum number of letters that the final word of the sentence could have?

   (A) eight
   (B) nine
   (C) ten
   (D) eleven
   (E) twelve

3. If the third word in a sentence is "zambo," then which of the following could be the first word?

   (A) zmbo
   (B) smambos
   (C) zambo
   (D) zamz
   (E) lamb

4. If the first word in a sentence is "piper," then which of the following could NOT be the third word in the sentence?

   (A) zipper
   (B) sbiper
   (C) ppter
   (D) piterr
   (E) wipers

5. If "radio" is the first word of the sentence, then which of the following is a complete list of the positions that the word "radium" could occupy?

   (A) second
   (B) third
   (C) third, fifth, sixth
   (D) third, fourth, fifth, sixth
   (E) second, third, fourth, fifth, sixth

6. If the first word of the sentence is "algebra," then which of the following is the earliest possible letter of the alphabet that the sixth word can begin with?

   (A) A
   (B) B
   (C) D
   (D) F
   (E) Z

PATTERN GAME 6

In a newly developed number game that very few people play, a numerical series is formed by four different numbers. The only digits used in the game are 1 through 9; 0 is never used. The rules of the game are as follows:

Each number in the series must have at least four digits.

Based on the first number in the series, each subsequent number is formed by one of the following transformations: 1. Adding a digit. 2. Deleting a digit. 3. Replacing a digit with another digit.

In a series, the same kind of transformation is not used twice in a row.

1. Which of the following could be a series of numbers in the game?

   (A) 1234, 1334, 13345, 133457
   (B) 324, 3244, 3246, 32461
   (C) 4445, 44457, 4445, 444558
   (D) 2543, 2544, 25446, 2546
   (E) 8185, 8188, 81881, 8288

2. What is the smallest number that could be used to start a series?

   (A) 1
   (B) 1000
   (C) 111
   (D) 11
   (E) 1111

3. If the first number in the series is 9534, then what is the greatest number that could end the series?

   (A) 999934
   (B) 99534999
   (C) 993411
   (D) 9999534
   (E) 999539

4. If 3425 is the first number in the series, then which is the smallest number that could end the series?

   (A) 1315
   (B) 11125
   (C) 1142
   (D) 1125
   (E) 1111

5. If 52434 is the third number in the series, then which of the following could be the first number in the series?

   (A) 434
   (B) 56634
   (C) 52636
   (D) 5243452
   (E) 85234

6. If there are six digits in the first number, then what is the maximum number of digits that could be in any number in the series?

   (A) six
   (B) seven
   (C) eight
   (D) nine
   (E) ten

PATTERN GAME 7

In a particular word game, a word that is either real or nonsensical is formed using only the letters A, B, C, D, E, and F. No letter can be used more than twice in the word. Each word is formed according to the following constraints:

If D is used twice, then C is used twice.

If B is used twice, then A and E are each used twice.

If no letter is used twice, then C is used and must be bordered only by F. If D is not used, then B is not used.

If A is not used, then F is used.

B can be bordered only by A or C.

1. Which of the following could be a word in the game?
   (A) ABCD
   (B) BBAAEE
   (C) EFABCD
   (D) DDCCBA
   (E) BCCDE

2. What is the maximum number of letters that could be used in a word?
   (A) 10
   (B) 11
   (C) 12
   (D) 13
   (E) 14

3. What is the fewest number of letters that could be used to form a word?
   (A) 1
   (B) 2
   (C) 3
   (D) 4
   (E) 5

4. If no letter is used twice, then which of the following must be true?
   (A) F and A are used in the word.
   (B) B is either the first or the last letter in the word.
   (C) F must be used twice somewhere in the word.
   (D) Neither B nor D is used in the word.
   (E) C is either the first or the last letter in the word.

5. If no letter is used twice, all letters are used, and B is used before F, then which of the following might NOT be true?
   (A) F is the fifth letter.
   (B) D is the third letter.
   (C) A is the second letter.
   (D) C is the sixth letter.
   (E) B is the first letter.

6. If only three letters are used in the word, then which of the following could NOT be a pair of letters that are used?
   (A) C, F
   (B) A, D
   (C) E, C
   (D) A, F
   (E) B, F

PATTERN GAME 8

A church has six missionaries—Anna, Ben, Chris, Dana, Evan, and Frank. Each year exactly four of these missionaries are sent to foreign nations in order to do charitable acts. The rules determining which missionaries are sent out in a particular year are the following:

Any missionary who was not sent out in one year must be sent out in the next year.

A charitable term ends when all of the six missionaries have been sent out four times.

Evan cannot be sent out in years that Anna is sent out.

Ben cannot be sent out in years that Chris is sent out.

1. If Chris, Evan, Frank, and Dana are sent out in the first year, then which of the following could be the missionaries sent out in the second year?

   (A) Evan, Frank, Dana, Anna.
   (B) Ben, Chris, Frank, Anna.
   (C) Anna, Ben, Frank, Dana.
   (D) Dana, Frank, Evan, Chris.
   (E) None of the above.

2. How many years long is the shortest possible missionary term?

   (A) 2
   (B) 4
   (C) 6
   (D) 8
   (E) 10

3. Which of the following is a pair of missionaries who must always be sent out in the same years?

   (A) Chris, Evan.
   (B) Ben, Evan.
   (C) Dana, Frank.
   (D) Anna, Chris.
   (E) None of the above.

4. Which of the following missionaries will be sent out for the most years in a missionary term?

   (A) Anna
   (B) Ben
   (C) Chris
   (D) Dana
   (E) Evan

5. If Chris is sent out in the third year, then which of the following must be true?

   (A) Evan is sent out in the third year.
   (B) Evan is sent out in the fourth year.
   (C) Chris is sent out in the seventh year.
   (D) Ben and Anna are sent out in the same years.
   (E) Frank and Chris are not sent out in the same years.

6. If Frank and Ben are sent out in the fourth year, then which of the following must NOT be true?

   (A) Evan is sent out in years two and three.
   (B) Dana is sent out in years five and six.
   (C) Chris is sent out in years three and five.
   (D) Anna is sent out in years two and four.
   (E) Whenever Evan is sent out, Dana is also sent out.

Game 5

Initial Setup:

There is no real initial setup that helps for this game. Just be sure to remember the rules:

1. Each word must have at least three letters.
2. The words in the sentence cannot all share the same starting letter.
3. After the first word, each subsequent word is formed by exactly one of the following transformations:
   a. Adding a letter.
   b. Deleting a letter.
   c. Replacing a letter with another letter.
4. In a sentence:
   a. Each kind of transformation is used at least once.
   b. The same kind of transformation is not used twice in a row.

Question 1: Which of the following could be a sentence in the game?

(D) This could be a sentence in the game.

(A) This choice adds a letter twice in a row.
(B) This choice changes a letter twice in a row and the sentence is not alphabetical.
(C) This choice adds a letter twice in a row.
(E) This choice changes a letter twice in a row.

Question 2: If the first word of a sentence starts with seven letters, what is the maximum number of letters that the final word of the sentence could have?

(B) The sentence has six words and therefore five transformations. All transformations must be used and none of them consecutively. A possible series could be: 1. add, 2. change, 3. add, 4. delete, 5. add. This series would make a total of nine letters.

Question 3: If the third word in a sentence is "zambo," then which of the following could be the first word?

(E) "Lamb" could be the first word. "Zamb" could be second. "Zambo" could be third.

Question 4: If the first word in a sentence is "piper," then which of the following could NOT be the third word in the sentence?

(B) "Sbiper" could not be the third word because all transformations to make it from "piper" with only two changes would cause the sentence not to be alphabetical.

Question 5: If "radio" is the first word of the sentence, then which of the following is a complete list of the positions that the word "radium" could occupy?

(D) "Radium" could occupy the third, fourth, fifth, or sixth place in the sentence.

Third: radio→radiu→radium
Fourth: radio→radiu→radiul→radium
Fifth: radio→radios→radis→radiu→radium
Sixth: radio→radios→radiot→radit→radiu→radium

Question 6: If the first word of the sentence is "algebra," then which of the following is the earliest possible letter of the alphabet that the sixth word can begin with?

(B) The letter must be B, solely due to the rule that the words in the sentence cannot all have the same starting letter.

Game 6

Initial Setup:

The nature of this game is almost exactly like that of the previous one, so it too does not have a diagram. You should make sure that you understand the constraints:

1. A numerical series is formed by four different numbers.
2. Each number must have at least four digits.
3. After the first number, each subsequent number is formed from the previous one by one of the following transformations:
   a. Adding a digit.
   b. Deleting a digit.
   c. Replacing a digit with another digit.
4. In a series, the same kind of transformation is not used twice in a row.

Question 1: Which of the following could be a series of numbers in the game?

(D) This is a possible series.

(A) Addition is used twice in a row.
(B) All numbers must have at least four digits.
(C) The same number cannot appear twice.
(E) Getting from 81881 to 8288 requires more than one transformation.

Question 2: What is the smallest number that could be used to start a series?

(E) All numbers in this system must have four digits, and 0 is not allowed, so 1111 is the smallest number.

Question 3: If the first number in the series is 9534, then what is the greatest number that could end the series?

(A) You want to get the most 9s possible at the beginning of the last number, so add 9s or replace another number with 9: 9534; add a 9: 99534; change the 5 to a 9: 99934; add a 9: 999934.

Question 4: If 3425 is the first number in the series, then which is the smallest number that could end the series?

(D) 3425; change the 3 to a 1: 1425; add a 1: 11425; delete the 4: 1125.

Question 5: If 52434 is the third number in the series, then which of the following could be the first number in the series?

(E) 85234 can be transformed into 52434 with two transformations: a subtraction and an addition.

(A) Numbers must have at least four digits.
(B) 56634 is three transformations away, not two.
(C) 52636 is three transformations away, not two.
(D) Starting with a seven-digit number would require two subtractions in a row to get to a five-digit number by the third number.

Question 6: If there are six digits in the first number, then what is the maximum number of digits that could be in any number in the series?

(C) At most, you could add two digits and change one in between the additions, to end up with eight digits.

Game 7

Initial Setup:

You cannot draw a representative diagram without certain basic information, so it would be best to list the constraints:

1. DD → CC
2. BB → AA, EE
3. $\not{D} \rightarrow \not{B}$; B → D
4. $\not{A} \rightarrow$ F ; $\not{F} \rightarrow$ A
5. [B/F] [B/D] [B/E]
6. If **no** letter is used **twice** → C is next to no letter other than F

Question 1: Which of the following could be a word in the game?

(D) This is a possible word.

(A) If no letter is used twice, then C can border only F.
(B) If D is not used, then B is not used.
(C) If no letter is used twice, then C can border only F.
(E) If A is not used, then F is used.

Question 2: What is the maximum number of letters that could be used in a word?

(C) Every letter can be used no more than twice, so 12 is the answer.

Question 3: What is the fewest number of letters that could be used to form a word?

(B) There are several two-letter words that could be made: CF, FC, AA, FF.

Question 4: If no letters are used twice, then which of the following must be true?

(E) If no letters are used twice, then CF must be in the game somewhere. Since F cannot be used twice, C must be the first or the last letter in the word.

Question 5: If no letter is used twice, all letters are used, and B is used in the word before F, then which of the following might NOT be true?

(B) This constraint would mean that the word has six letters, of which C must be the last letter and F must be the second-to-last letter. In that case, B cannot border any letter other than A, so B must be first and A must be second. The only answer choice that might not be true is D being the third letter.

Question 6: If only three letters are used in the word, then which of the following could NOT be a pair of letters that is used?

(E) Having B in the word would require D to also be in the word. B cannot border D or F, so this configuration is impossible.

(A) C, F, E
(B) A, D, A
(C) E, C, F
(D) F, A, A

Game 8

Initial Setup:

You cannot draw a representative diagram without any information, so it would be best to list the constraints:

					Out	
1	___	___	___	___	___	___
2	___	___	___	___	___	___
3	___	___	___	___	___	___
4	___	___	___	___	___	___
5	___	___	___	___	___	___

1. Any missionary who was not sent out in one year must be sent out in the next year.
2. A charitable term ends when all of the five missionaries have been sent out four times.
3. E ≠ A
4. B ≠ C

Question 1: If Chris, Evan, Frank, and Dana are sent out in the first year, then which of the following could be the missionaries sent out in the second year?

(C) This constraint means that Anna and Ben were not sent out in the first year, so they must be sent out in the second year. Also, Chris and Evan cannot be sent out in the same year as Ben and Anna, respectively, so Anna, Ben, Frank, and Dana must be sent out in the second year.

Question 2: How many years long is the shortest possible missionary term?

(D) A term ends when all missionaries have been sent out four times. Since there are two missionaries who cannot go in the same year as two other missionaries, these "opposing" missionaries must be sent out every other year. In the previous question, for instance, Anna and Ben do not go in the first year, so Chris and Evan do not go in the second year. With these opposing missionaries going every other year, it takes at least 8 years for all six to complete their term.

Question 3: Which of the following is a pair of missionaries who must always be sent out in the same years?

(C) Since Evan cannot be sent out in the same year as Anna and Ben cannot be sent out in the same year as Chris, two of these people must sit out each year. Therefore, Dana and Frank must be sent out each year.

Question 4: Which of the following missionaries will be sent out for the most years in a missionary term?

(D) Since Dana and Frank must go out every year, it must be one of the two of them.

Question 5: If Chris is sent out in the third year, then which of the following must be true?

(C) This constraint tells you each year that Ben is sent out and each year that Chris is sent out. Chris is sent out in the first, fifth, and seventh years. Ben is sent out in the second, fourth, sixth, and eighth years.

Question 6: If Frank and Ben are sent out in the fourth year, then which of the following must NOT be true?

(A) None of the missionaries who cannot be sent out in the same years as another missionary—Evan, Chris, Anna, and Ben—could be sent out two years in a row.

CHAPTER 8

MINIMIZED- AND MAXIMIZED-VARIABLE GAMES

There are two additional ways to categorize LSAT logic games: as maximized-variable or minimized-variable games. These are not new types of games; they are variable types that exist in the types of games we have discussed previously in the book. Maximized-variable games are those in which, after the constraints from the fact pattern have been diagrammed, there are still numerous places and scenarios where each variable can exist. These games require you to make deductions solely based on the rules within the questions. Minimized-variable games, on the other hand, have very limited and constrained positioning options.

Solution Strategies

Minimized-Variable Games

You can tell that a game is a minimized-variable game if it includes a constraint that severely limits the number of scenarios in which the variables in the game can be placed. Burdensome constraints such as this are often large boxes, long sufficient-necessary chains, or extensive grouping rules. As soon as you recognize that a game has limited possibilities, you should try to map out all of the possibilities and then make as many deductions as you can for each scenario.

Maximized-Variable Games

A maximized-variable game does not offer much to diagram before the first question is reached. The constraints sometimes interplay, but never enough for you to make sweeping conclusions about the state of the variables in the game. In these games, you should focus on consolidating the constraints in the game through the use of the logic tools that you have learned in previous chapters. When you reach the first question, you will be quizzed on one of the constraints in the fact pattern. After answering it based on your list of consolidated constraints, you can move on to the next question, where you will be quizzed about a different constraint.

On Your Own

In the following section, Part A presents 8 minimized-variable games and Part B presents 8 maximized-variable games. The games are not arranged according to the game types you have studied up to now. You will see pattern games, mapping games, grouping games, linear games, and so on, so this will be a good opportunity for you to practice identifying each game type. Based on your identification, you should know which fact pattern heuristic to use, which logic tools to use, and which diagrams to draw to help you understand the overall placement of the variables. In the meantime, you will begin to recognize the cues that hint that a game can be solved immediately after reading the fact pattern (*minimized variables*) versus the cues that tell you that you will need to wait until you get to the questions to solve it (*maximized variables*).

Part A. Minimized-Variable Games

MINIMIZED-VARIABLE GAME I

As Matt closes his eyes to go to sleep, he visualizes nine sheep jumping over a fence. The sheep's names are Anna, Ben, Chris, Dana, Evan, Frank, Garry, Hillary, and Iris. The sheep are either in the pasture or outside of the pasture based on whether or not they have jumped over the fence. Their presence is governed by the following constraints:

If Garry is in the pasture, then Dana is out.
If Frank is in the pasture, then Anna is out.
Iris is in the pasture if Frank is out.
Dana is in the pasture if Chris is in.
Evan is in the pasture if Ben is out.
Hillary is outside of the pasture.
If Garry is outside of the pasture, then Evan is out.

1. Which of the following could be a complete list of the sheep outside of the pasture?

    (A) Dana, Chris, Anna, Hillary.
    (B) Ben, Dana, Iris, Anna.
    (C) Iris, Garry, Evan.
    (D) Garry, Anna, Iris.
    (E) Chris, Dana, Garry, Anna, Iris.

2. If Garry is in the pasture, then which of the following must be true?

    (A) Iris is in the pasture.
    (B) Ben is outside of the pasture.
    (C) Chris is outside of the pasture.
    (D) Frank is in the pasture.
    (E) Evan is in the pasture.

3. Which of the following pairs can never be in the pasture at the same time?

    (A) Frank, Iris.
    (B) Evan, Ben.
    (C) Dana, Chris.
    (D) Anna, Iris.
    (E) Chris, Evan.

4. You will know the exact position of all the sheep if you know that which two sheep are in the pasture?

    (A) Iris, Ben.
    (B) Dana, Evan.
    (C) Anna, Chris.
    (D) Iris, Anna.
    (E) Chris, Iris.

5. At most, how many sheep could be outside of the pasture at the same time?

    (A) five
    (B) six
    (C) seven
    (D) eight
    (E) nine

6. At most, how many sheep could be in the pasture at the same time?

    (A) four
    (B) five
    (C) six
    (D) seven
    (E) eight

MINIMIZED-VARIABLE GAME 2

The coach of a soccer team divides the players into different positions: forwards, midfielders, and defenders. There are three forwards, three midfielders, and two defenders. The players' names are Anna, Ben, Chris, Dana, Evan, Frank, Garry, and Hillary. The following constraints determine who is placed in which position:

Garry plays the same position that Hillary plays.
Ben does not play the same position as Frank, Anna, or Dana.
If Garry is a midfielder, then Ben is a forward.
Anna does not play the same position as Frank.
If Garry is a forward, then Ben is a forward and Dana is a midfielder.

1. Which of the following could be the group of midfielders?
   (A) Anna, Frank, Dana.
   (B) Dana, Anna, Evan.
   (C) Ben, Evan, Chris.
   (D) Garry, Hillary, Ben.
   (E) None of the above.

2. If Chris is a midfielder, then which of the following must be true?
   (A) Frank is a defender.
   (B) Anna is a defender.
   (C) Hillary is a forward.
   (D) Evan is a forward.
   (E) None of the above.

3. If Chris is a forward, then which of the following must be true?
   (A) Anna is a midfielder.
   (B) Garry is a defender.
   (C) Dana is a midfielder.
   (D) Evan is a midfielder.
   (E) None of the above.

4. Who could potentially play any position?
   (A) Anna
   (B) Garry
   (C) Ben
   (D) Evan
   (E) None of the above

5. Who could play only one position?
   (A) Ben
   (B) Garry
   (C) Dana
   (D) Hillary
   (E) None of the above

6. If Frank is a midfielder, then which of the following must NOT be true?
   (A) Hillary is a midfielder.
   (B) Chris is a defender.
   (C) Chris is a forward.
   (D) Anna is a midfielder.
   (E) None of the above

7. How many different possible configurations are there for the positions of the players?
   (A) four
   (B) six
   (C) eight
   (D) ten
   (E) twelve

MINIMIZED-VARIABLE GAME 3

On the days Monday through Friday, a fortune-teller will tell the fortunes of exactly two people each day. Every day the fortune-teller will tell the fortune of a stockbroker and that of a philosopher. The stockbrokers are named Anna, Ben, Chris, Dana, and Evan. The philosophers are named Frank, Garry, Hillary, Iris, and Julian. Whose fortune is told on which day is determined by the following constraints:

Julian's fortune is told on a day that falls before the day that Anna's is told.
Dana's fortune is told on Tuesday.
Chris's fortune is told on the same day that Garry's fortune is told.
Frank's fortune is told on a day that falls after the day that Garry's fortune is told.
Julian's fortune is told on Thursday.
If Chris's fortune is told on Monday, then Dana's and Frank's fortunes are told on the same day.

1. Which of the following could be the order in which the stockbrokers' fortunes are told, from Monday to Friday?

(A) Chris, Dana, Evan, Anna, Ben.
(B) Anna, Evan, Chris, Dana, Ben.
(C) Evan, Dana, Chris, Ben, Anna.
(D) Anna, Ben, Dana, Evan, Chris.
(E) Evan, Chris, Dana, Ben, Anna.

2. Which of the following could be the order in which the philosophers' fortunes are told, from Monday to Friday?

(A) Garry, Frank, Iris, Julian, Hillary.
(B) Frank, Hillary, Iris, Julian, Garry.
(C) Hillary, Iris, Frank, Julian, Garry.
(D) Iris, Garry, Hillary, Julian, Frank.
(E) Garry, Hillary, Frank, Julian, Iris.

3. How many different people could potentially have their fortune told on the same day as Frank's?

(A) one
(B) two
(C) three
(D) four
(E) five

4. How many different people could potentially have their fortune told on the same day as Iris's?

(A) one
(B) two
(C) three
(D) four
(E) five

5. If Hillary's fortune is told on Wednesday, then which of the following must be true?

(A) Ben's fortune is told on Wednesday.
(B) Frank's fortune is told on Tuesday.
(C) Evan's fortune is told on Thursday.
(D) Chris's fortune is told on Wednesday.
(E) Garry's fortune is told on Tuesday.

6. Which of the following must be true?

(A) Evan's fortune is told on the same day as either Julian's or Hillary's.
(B) Anna's fortune is told on the same day as either Iris's or Hillary's.
(C) Dana's fortune is told on the same day as either Frank's or Iris's.
(D) Garry's fortune is told on the same day as either Anna's or Dana's.
(E) Julian's fortune is told on the same day as either Evan's or Ben's.

MINIMIZED-VARIABLE GAME 4

A master hypnotist will see one student on each day this week—Monday through Sunday. The students' names are Anna, Ben, Chris, Dana, Evan, Frank, and Garry. Who is seen on which day and in what order is determined by the following constraints:

Ben is seen on Tuesday.
Evan is seen on the day before Frank is seen.
Ben is not seen on a day consecutive with the day on which Garry is seen.
Evan is not seen on Saturday.
Two days pass between the days on which Dana and Garry are seen.

1. Which of the following could be the order in which the students are seen, from Monday to Sunday?
   (A) Dana, Ben, Anna, Chris, Garry, Evan, Frank
   (B) Anna, Ben, Chris, Dana, Garry, Evan, Frank
   (C) Dana, Ben, Garry, Evan, Frank, Chris, Anna
   (D) Chris, Ben, Anna, Dana, Evan, Frank, Garry
   (E) None of the above.

2. Which of the following must be true?
   (A) Evan is seen on Friday.
   (B) Chris is seen earlier in the week than Garry.
   (C) Evan is seen later in the week than Dana.
   (D) Dana is seen earlier in the week than Garry.
   (E) None of the above.

3. If Garry is seen on Sunday, then which of the following must be true?
   (A) Chris is seen on Monday.
   (B) Chris is seen later in the week than Ben.
   (C) Dana is seen later in the week than Anna.
   (D) Evan is seen earlier in the week than Dana.
   (E) None of the above.

4. On which day could the hypnotist potentially see the greatest number of different students?
   (A) Monday
   (B) Wednesday
   (C) Thursday
   (D) Saturday
   (E) Sunday

5. Which of the following pairs of students could never be seen on consecutive days?
   (A) Anna, Garry.
   (B) Garry, Frank.
   (C) Evan, Chris.
   (D) Frank, Anna.
   (E) None of the above.

6. Which student could potentially be seen on the most days of the week?
   (A) Garry
   (B) Anna
   (C) Frank
   (D) Dana
   (E) Evan

MINIMIZED-VARIABLE GAME 5

At an airport, there are eight hangars for planes on the outside of building A. There is a north hangar, an east hangar, a south hangar, and a west hangar. There are also hangars at the northeast, southeast, southwest, and northwest corners. This arrangement is shown in the following diagram:

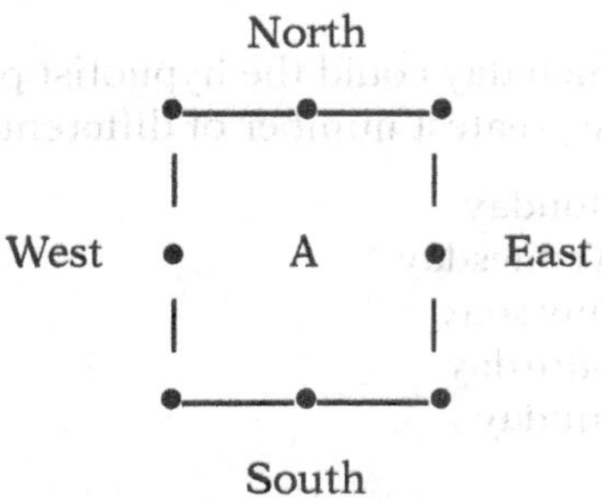

The hangars are either single hangars or double hangars. Whether a specific hangar is a double or a single is determined by the following constraints:

Single hangars are on exactly two corners.
The north hangar is a double.
The southeast hangar is a single.
Each double hangar is next to one double hangar and one single hangar.

1. Which of the following must be a single hangar?
   (A) The south hangar.
   (B) The west hangar.
   (C) The east hangar.
   (D) The northwest hangar.
   (E) The northeast hangar.

2. Which of the following must be a double hangar?
   (A) The south hangar.
   (B) The northwest hangar.
   (C) The northeast hangar.
   (D) The southwest hangar.
   (E) The west hangar.

3. Which of the following must NOT be true if four hangars are doubles?
   (A) The northeast hangar is a single.
   (B) The northwest hangar is a single.
   (C) The north hangar is a single.
   (D) The west hangar is a double.
   (E) The south hangar is a single.

4. Which of the following must NOT be true if the west hangar is a double?
   (A) The northwest hangar is a single.
   (B) The east hangar is a single.
   (C) The northeast hangar is a double.
   (D) The southwest hangar is a double.
   (E) The south hangar is a double.

5. Which of the following could be true?
   (A) The northeast hangar is a double, and the northwest hangar is a double.
   (B) The northeast hangar is a single, and the northwest hangar is a single.
   (C) The northwest hangar is a single, and the south hangar is a single.
   (D) There are five double hangars.
   (E) There are five single hangars.

6. How many different configurations of the hangars are possible?
   (A) two
   (B) three
   (C) four
   (D) five
   (E) six

MINIMIZED-VARIABLE GAME 6

Three groups of people want to be news anchors, but first they have to undergo training. To do this training, the aspiring newscasters—Anna, Ben, Chris, Dana, Evan, and Frank—will be split up into three groups of two people each. Who makes up which training group is determined by the following constraints:

Evan is not in the same group as Dana or Anna.
If Anna is in group 1, then Dana is in group 3.
Chris is in group 3 if Dana is in group 1.
Dana is in a group with Frank or Chris.
Evan is in group 2.

1. Which of the following pairs of people could be in the same group?
   (A) Anna, Evan.
   (B) Chris, Ben.
   (C) Frank, Ben.
   (D) Evan, Dana.
   (E) Ben, Anna.

2. Which of the following people could NOT be in group 3?
   (A) Anna
   (B) Ben
   (C) Chris
   (D) Dana
   (E) Frank

3. Which of the following people could be in any group?
   (A) Anna
   (B) Evan
   (C) Dana
   (D) Chris
   (E) Ben

4. Which of the following is NOT a pair of people who could be trained in group 1?
   (A) Dana, Frank.
   (B) Frank, Anna.
   (C) Anna, Chris.
   (D) Dana, Ben.
   (E) Ben, Anna.

5. If Frank is trained in group 2, then which of the following must be true?
   (A) Dana is trained in group 1.
   (B) Anna is trained in group 3.
   (C) Ben is trained in group 1.
   (D) Evan is not trained in group 2.
   (E) Chris is trained in group 1.

6. How many configurations are possible for the groups?
   (A) five
   (B) six
   (C) seven
   (D) eight
   (E) nine

MINIMIZED-VARIABLE GAME 7

This week, from Monday to Sunday, seven professional piano players will play with the chamber orchestra. One pianist from the following group—Anna, Ben, Chris, Dana, Evan, Frank, and Garry–will play each day. No pianist will play more than once, and the order in which the pianists will play is determined by the following constraints:

If Anna does not play on Wednesday, then Frank plays on the day after Chris plays and Chris plays on the day after Ben plays.
If Anna plays on Wednesday, then Chris plays the day after Frank plays and Ben plays the day after Chris plays.
If Chris does not play on Wednesday, then he plays on Saturday.
Garry plays on Monday.
Evan plays before Dana and Anna.

1. Which of the following could be the order in which the pianists play, from Monday to Sunday?
   (A) Garry, Evan, Anna, Dana, Ben, Chris, Frank.
   (B) Garry, Frank, Chris, Ben, Evan, Dana, Anna.
   (C) Garry, Ben, Chris, Frank, Dana, Evan, Anna.
   (D) Garry, Evan, Dana, Anna, Ben, Chris, Frank.
   (E) None of the above.

2. On which day could four people potentially play?
   (A) Sunday
   (B) Wednesday
   (C) Thursday
   (D) Friday
   (E) None of the above

3. Which of the following people could potentially play on four different days?
   (A) Anna
   (B) Ben
   (C) Evan
   (D) Frank
   (E) None of the above

4. If Dana plays on Wednesday, then which of the following must be true?
   (A) Ben plays on Thursday.
   (B) Evan plays on Tuesday.
   (C) Frank plays on Friday.
   (D) Anna plays on Saturday.
   (E) None of the above.

5. If Anna plays after Dana, then which of the following must be true?
   (A) Evan plays on Tuesday.
   (B) Ben plays on Sunday.
   (C) Chris plays on Wednesday.
   (D) Anna plays on Wednesday.
   (E) None of the above.

6. How many possible orders are there in which the pianists can play?
   (A) two
   (B) four
   (C) six
   (D) eight
   (E) None of the above

MINIMIZED-VARIABLE GAME 8

Four rooms, numbered 1 to 4, will each hold one politician and one lobbyist. The politicians are named Anna, Ben, Chris, and Dana, and the lobbyists are named Evan, Frank, Garry, and Hillary. Who is in which room with whom is determined by the following constraints:

Anna is not in a room numbered consecutively with Chris's or Dana's room.

Garry is not in a room numbered consecutively with Hillary's or Frank's room.

1. Which of the following is NOT a possible order for the lobbyists, from room 1 to room 4?
   (A) Hillary, Frank, Evan, Garry.
   (B) Garry, Evan, Frank, Hillary.
   (C) Frank, Hillary, Garry, Evan.
   (D) Garry, Evan, Hillary, Frank.
   (E) Frank, Hillary, Evan, Garry.

2. If Ben shares room 2 with Hillary, then which of the following must be true?
   (A) Evan shares room 3 with Chris.
   (B) Dana shares room 3 with Chris.
   (C) Garry shares room 4 with Dana.
   (D) Anna shares room 1 with Frank.
   (E) Anna shares room 1 with Garry.

3. If Dana and Hillary are in consecutive rooms, then which of the following must NOT be true?
   (A) Ben is in a room consecutive with Evan's.
   (B) Anna is in room 1 and Garry is in room 4.
   (C) Ben and Evan share room 3.
   (D) Anna is in a lower-numbered room than Garry.
   (E) Chris is in room 1 and Frank is in room 1.

4. Which of the following pairs of people could never share a room?
   (A) Garry, Ben.
   (B) Hillary, Dana.
   (C) Anna, Garry.
   (D) Ben, Frank.
   (E) Frank, Chris.

5. If Anna and Garry share a room, then which of the following must be true?
   (A) Chris is in a lower-numbered room than Frank's.
   (B) Dana and Hillary are not in consecutive rooms.
   (C) Ben and Evan share a room.
   (D) Anna and Garry are in room 4.
   (E) Evan is in a lower-numbered room than Garry's.

6. How many different room configurations are possible?
   (A) 8
   (B) 12
   (C) 16
   (D) 20
   (E) 24

Part B. Maximized-Variable Games

MAXIMIZED-VARIABLE GAME 1

Tara has decided to tutor biology for the summer and is trying to plan her schedule. She can meet with up to two students a day, Monday through Friday, and has three students, Anna, Ben, and Chris. She needs to arrange her schedule according to the following constraints:

Each student meets with Tara twice a week.
No student meets with Tara twice in the same day.
Anna refuses to meet with Tara on Fridays.
Chris will never meet with Tara the day after Ben has a lesson.
Anna and Chris meet with Tara on the same day exactly once a week.
If Anna meets with Tara on Monday, so does Ben.

1. If Anna meets with Tara on Monday and Wednesday, on what day must Chris meet with her?
   (A) Monday
   (B) Tuesday
   (C) Wednesday
   (D) Thursday
   (E) Friday

2. If Ben is the only student to meet with Tara on a Wednesday, on what days must Anna meet with her?
   (A) Monday and Tuesday.
   (B) Monday and Wednesday.
   (C) Monday and Thursday.
   (D) Tuesday and Thursday.
   (E) Tuesday and Friday.

3. If Anna is the only student to meet with Tara on Tuesday and no one meets with her on Friday, who meets with her on Wednesday?
   (A) Chris
   (B) Ben
   (C) Anna and Chris
   (D) Anna and Ben
   (E) Ben and Chris

4. If Ben is allowed to meet with Tara three times one week, on what days could he meet with her?
   (A) Monday, Wednesday, Friday.
   (B) Monday, Thursday, Friday.
   (C) Monday, Tuesday, Wednesday.
   (D) Tuesday, Wednesday, Thursday.
   (E) Monday, Wednesday, Thursday.

5. If Tara adds Dana, a fourth student, what is the maximum number of times Dana could meet with her each week?
   (A) none
   (B) one
   (C) two
   (D) three
   (E) four

6. If Anna cannot meet with Tara on Tuesday or Wednesday, on what day must Chris meet with her?
   (A) Monday
   (B) Tuesday
   (C) Wednesday
   (D) Thursday
   (E) Friday

7. If Ben meets with Tara on Tuesday and Friday, on what day must Chris meet with her?
   (A) Monday
   (B) Tuesday
   (C) Wednesday
   (D) Thursday
   (E) Friday

MAXIMIZED-VARIABLE GAME 2

Seven motorcars are aligned in lanes 1 to 7 in order to race in the Grand Prix. The cars are driven by Anna, Ben, Chris, Dana, Evan, Frank, and Garry. Which racer gets which position is determined by the following constraints:

Ben is in lane 4.
Chris is in the lane that is numbered one less than Frank's lane.
If Anna is in lane 3, then Dana is in lane 6.
Chris is not in lane 2.
Evan is in a lower-numbered lane than Ben.
Chris is in lane 6 if Garry is in lane 1.

1. Which of the following could be the order of the racers, from lane 1 to lane 7?
   (A) Evan, Chris, Frank, Ben, Anna, Garry, Dana.
   (B) Chris, Frank, Anna, Ben, Garry, Dana, Evan.
   (C) Garry, Anna, Evan, Ben, Chris, Frank, Dana.
   (D) Chris, Frank, Evan, Ben, Anna, Dana, Garry.
   (E) Garry, Evan, Anna, Ben, Dana, Chris, Frank.

2. Which of the following could NOT be true?
   (A) Chris is in lane 5.
   (B) Evan is in lane 1.
   (C) Anna is in lane 3.
   (D) Frank is in lane 7.
   (E) Garry is in lane 1.

3. If Garry is in lane 1, then which of the following must be true?
   (A) Dana and Chris are in consecutive lanes.
   (B) Ben and Chris are in consecutive lanes.
   (C) Anna is in a lower-numbered lane than Ben.
   (D) Ben and Evan are in consecutive lanes.
   (E) Anna and Dana are not in consecutive lanes.

4. If Chris is in a lower-numbered lane than Ben, then which of the following must be true?
   (A) Evan is in lane 3.
   (B) Dana is in lane 5.
   (C) Garry and Anna are in consecutive lanes.
   (D) Evan is in a lower-numbered lane than Frank.
   (E) Chris and Evan are in consecutive lanes.

5. If Chris, Frank, and Dana are in higher-numbered lanes than Ben, then which of the following must NOT be true?
   (A) Chris is in a higher-numbered lane than Dana.
   (B) Evan is in a higher-numbered lane than Garry.
   (C) Ben and Anna are in consecutive lanes.
   (D) Anna is in a higher-numbered lane than Garry.
   (E) Dana and Ben are in consecutive lanes.

6. If Evan must not be in a lane consecutive with Ben, then which of the following must be true?
   (A) Garry is in a lower-numbered lane than Frank.
   (B) Frank is in a higher-numbered lane than Ben.
   (C) Dana is in a lower-numbered lane than Ben.
   (D) Anna is in a lower-numbered lane than Ben.
   (E) Evan is in a higher-numbered lane than Chris.

MAXIMIZED-VARIABLE GAME 3

At a local cow-tipping contest, five contestants are paired with five cows in five different fields. There is only one cow per field and only one contestant per cow. The contestants are named Anna, Ben, Chris, Dana, and Evan, and the cows are named Frank, Garry, Hillary, Iris, and Julian. The pairings of contestants and cows in fields are determined by the following constraints:

Hillary is in field 2.
Chris is in the field that is one number higher than Dana's field.
Garry is in a higher-numbered field than Hillary.
Ben is paired with Frank.
Hillary and Frank are not in consecutive fields.

1. Which of the following could be the order of the contestants, in fields 1 through 5?
   (A) Dana, Chris, Ben, Anna, Evan.
   (B) Ben, Anna, Evan, Dana, Chris.
   (C) Chris, Anna, Evan, Ben, Dana.
   (D) Anna, Ben, Dana, Chris, Evan.
   (E) None of the above.

2. If Dana is in field 3, then which of the following must be true?
   (A) Anna is paired with Hillary.
   (B) Evan is not paired with Garry.
   (C) Dana is paired with Julian.
   (D) Anna is in a lower-numbered field than Iris.
   (E) Frank and Garry are in consecutive fields.

3. If Iris is in a higher-numbered field than Hillary, then which of the following must be true?
   (A) Dana is in a higher-numbered field than Hillary.
   (B) Garry or Iris shares a field with Chris.
   (C) Julian is in field 1.
   (D) Ben is in field 5.
   (E) None of the above.

4. If Garry is paired with Chris, then which of the following must NOT be true?
   (A) Iris and Evan share field 4.
   (B) Anna and Evan are in consecutive fields.
   (C) Dana shares field 3 with Hillary.
   (D) Ben and Frank are in field 5.
   (E) None of the above.

5. If Evan and Iris share field 5, then which of the following must NOT be true?
   (A) Chris is paired with Julian.
   (B) Ben and Frank are in field 4.
   (C) Dana is paired with Hillary.
   (D) Anna and Dana are in consecutive fields.
   (E) None of the above.

6. Which of the following could never be paired together?
   (A) Iris, Chris.
   (B) Hillary, Ben.
   (C) Julian, Dana.
   (D) Ben, Frank.
   (E) None of the above.

MAXIMIZED-VARIABLE GAME 4

An office networking team is split into three groups—the leaders, the workers, and the followers. There are three people in the leader group, three people in the worker group, and two people in the follower group. The names of the people on the networking team are Anna, Ben, Chris, Dana, Evan, Frank, Garry, and Hillary. The groups are composed according to the following constraints:

Anna is a follower.
Frank and Dana are not in the same group.
If Ben is a leader, then Chris is a follower.
If Dana is not a follower, then Frank is a worker.
Evan is a leader if Hillary is a worker.

1. Which of the following could be the group of workers?

(A) Dana, Evan, Frank.
(B) Hillary, Ben, Evan.
(C) Anna, Frank, Evan.
(D) Dana, Chris, Hillary.
(E) Hillary, Ben, Frank.

2. Which of the following could never be a worker?

(A) Ben
(B) Chris
(C) Dana
(D) Evan
(E) Frank

3. If Dana and Ben are in the same group, then which of the following must be true?

(A) Hillary is a leader.
(B) Chris is a worker.
(C) Evan is a leader.
(D) Dana is a leader.
(E) Hillary is a worker.

4. Who could never be in the same group as Anna?

(A) Ben
(B) Chris
(C) Evan
(D) Frank
(E) Hillary

5. If Anna is in the same group as Evan, then which of the following must be true?

(A) Ben and Hillary are not in the same group.
(B) Dana and Frank are in the same group.
(C) Garry and Ben are in the same group.
(D) Chris and Hillary are not in the same group.
(E) Frank and Ben are not in the same group.

6. If Hillary and Evan are in the same group, then which of the following must NOT be true?

(A) Frank is a worker.
(B) Chris is a leader.
(C) Frank is a leader.
(D) Evan is a leader.
(E) Ben is a leader.

MAXIMIZED-VARIABLE GAME 5

In an aquarium store, a manager is trying to decide what types of fish to put in eight aquariums. The aquariums are aligned in two rows of four as shown in the following diagram:

```
| 1 | 2 | 3 | 4 |
------------------------
| 5 | 6 | 7 | 8 |
```

Adjacent aquariums are aquariums that are next to each other in the same row. The manager will put only one type of the three types of fish in each aquarium—blennies, cichlids, or darters. The fish are put in the aquariums according to the following constraints:

Darters are in aquarium 7.
Darters cannot be adjacent to darters.
Blennies cannot be across from aquariums with blennies in them.
Blennies must be adjacent to an aquarium with cichlids and an aquarium with darters.

1. Which of the following could be the order of the types of fishes in aquariums 5 through 8?
   (A) Darters, cichlids, darters, cichlids
   (B) Cichlids, blennies, darters, blennies
   (C) Blennies, cichlids, darters, cichlids
   (D) Cichlids, blennies, darters, darters
   (E) None of the above.

2. What is the maximum number of aquariums that could hold blennies?
   (A) one
   (B) two
   (C) three
   (D) four
   (E) five

3. If there are four aquariums with darters, then which of the following must be true?
   (A) There are darters in aquarium 8.
   (B) There are darters in aquarium 2.
   (C) There are darters in aquarium 1.
   (D) There are darters in aquarium 3.
   (E) None of the above.

4. What is the maximum number of aquariums that could hold cichlids?
   (A) three
   (B) four
   (C) five
   (D) six
   (E) seven

5. If there are two aquariums with blennies in them, then which of the following must be true?
   (A) Cichlids are in aquarium 5.
   (B) Darters are in aquarium 4.
   (C) Cichlids are in aquarium 1.
   (D) Darters are in aquarium 2.
   (E) None of the above.

6. If there are darters in aquarium 3, then how many possible configurations of the aquariums are there?
   (A) two
   (B) four
   (C) six
   (D) eight
   (E) ten

MAXIMIZED-VARIABLE GAME 6

A group of nine racers will finish the marathon in a certain order. The racers are named Anna, Ben, Chris, Dana, Evan, Frank, Garry, Hillary, and Iris. They all finish at different times, and their finishing order is determined by the following constraints:

Frank finishes before Anna.
Dana finishes before Ben and Evan.
Iris finishes after Chris.
Garry finishes after Anna.

1. Which of the following could be the order of the finishers, from first to last?
   (A) Frank, Dana, Garry, Ben, Evan, Anna, Chris, Iris, Hillary.
   (B) Frank, Anna, Evan, Chris, Dana, Garry, Ben, Hillary, Iris.
   (C) Chris, Dana, Hillary, Ben, Iris, Frank, Evan, Anna, Garry.
   (D) Hillary, Iris, Chris, Ben, Evan, Dana, Garry, Anna, Frank.
   (E) Dana, Evan, Frank, Hillary, Iris, Ben, Anna, Chris, Garry.

2. What is the earliest position in which Garry could finish?
   (A) first
   (B) second
   (C) third
   (D) fourth
   (E) fifth

3. If Iris finishes third, then which of the following is a pair of people who could finish before her?
   (A) Frank, Dana.
   (B) Hillary, Chris.
   (C) Dana, Hillary.
   (D) Frank, Anna.
   (E) Chris, Ben.

4. If Garry finishes fourth, Hillary fifth, and Ben sixth, then which of the following could be true?
   (A) Anna finishes first.
   (B) Iris finishes seventh.
   (C) Chris finishes ninth.
   (D) Evan finishes eighth.
   (E) Frank finishes ninth.

5. If Dana finishes sixth, then which is the latest position in which Frank could finish?
   (A) third
   (B) fourth
   (C) fifth
   (D) seventh
   (E) ninth

6. If Chris finishes after Evan and Ben and if Frank finishes immediately after Iris, then which of the following must be true?
   (A) Garry finishes ninth.
   (B) Chris and Iris finish consecutively.
   (C) Evan finishes before Anna.
   (D) Dana finishes first.
   (E) Evan finishes before Ben.

MAXIMIZED-VARIABLE GAME 7

Five young romantics named Anna, Ben, Chris, Dana, and Evan live on five different streets numbered from 1 through 5. Five singing valentines are ordered for these young romantics. One singer from the group of singers—Frank, Garry, Hillary, Iris, and Julian—will sing to each of the young romantics. Each singer sings only once, and the person to whom the singer sings and the street where he or she sings are governed by the following constraints:

Dana lives on street 1.
Iris sings to the person living on street 4.
Frank does not sing on a street consecutive with the street that Garry sings on.
If Anna lives on street 2, then Chris lives on street 5 and Julian sings to Chris.
If Ben lives on street 4, then Frank sings to the person living on street 1.
Anna lives on a lower-numbered street than the person Iris sings to.
Ben does not live on street 2.

1. Which of the following could be the order in which the young romantics live, from street 1 to street 5?

   (A) Evan, Chris, Ben, Dana, Anna.
   (B) Dana, Anna, Ben, Chris, Evan.
   (C) Dana, Ben, Anna, Chris, Evan.
   (D) Dana, Chris, Evan, Anna, Ben.
   (E) None of the above.

2. If Chris lives on street 4, then which of the following could be false?

   (A) Garry and Frank do not sing on consecutive streets.
   (B) Evan lives on street 2.
   (C) Frank sings to the person living on street 1.
   (D) Anna lives on street 3.
   (E) None of the above.

3. If Frank sings to the person living on street 2, then which of the following must be true?

   (A) Anna lives on street 3.
   (B) Ben lives on street 4.
   (C) Hillary sings to the person living on street 3.
   (D) Frank sings to Evan.
   (E) None of the above.

4. If Iris sings to Ben, then which of the following must NOT be true?

   (A) Anna lives on street 2.
   (B) Hillary sings to Chris.
   (C) Garry sings to the person living on street 2.
   (D) Julian sings to Anna.
   (E) None of the above.

5. If Anna lives on street 2, then which of the following must be true?

   (A) Iris sings to Evan.
   (B) Frank sings to Ben.
   (C) Garry sings to Dana.
   (D) Hillary sings to Anna.
   (E) None of the above.

6. If Chris lives on street 2 and Frank sings to him, then which of the following could be false?

   (A) Iris sings to Evan.
   (B) Julian sings to Anna.
   (C) Ben lives on street 5.
   (D) Evan and Anna live on consecutive streets.
   (E) None of the above.

MAXIMIZED-VARIABLE GAME 8

Seven students are vying for first place in their high school grade point average. The students study together, so the performance of one person in the group affects the performances of other members of the group. The students' names are Anna, Ben, Chris, Dana, Evan, Frank, and Garry, and their grade point ranks will be determined by the following rules:

Dana finishes sixth overall.

Chris finishes with a lower ranking than Dana.

Exactly one person is ranked between Chris and Evan.

If Anna is ranked second, then Ben is ranked fourth.

Garry is not ranked consecutively with Evan or Chris.

1. Which of the following could be the order of the students from first to last?
   (A) Chris, Evan, Frank, Garry, Ben, Dana, Anna.
   (B) Anna, Ben, Frank, Garry, Chris, Dana, Evan.
   (C) Chris, Anna, Evan, Ben, Frank, Dana, Garry.
   (D) Garry, Anna, Evan, Frank, Chris, Ben, Dana.
   (E) Anna, Garry, Ben, Frank, Evan, Dana, Chris.

2. Which of the following is a complete list of the ranks that Garry could have out of the seven students?
   (A) 1, 2, 5
   (B) 3, 4, 5, 6
   (C) 1, 2, 3, 5, 7
   (D) 1, 2, 3, 4, 6
   (E) 1, 2, 3, 4, 5, 6, 7

3. If Garry is ranked fifth, then which of the following could NOT be true?
   (A) Anna is ranked second.
   (B) Evan is ranked first.
   (C) Chris is ranked fourth.
   (D) Ben is ranked seventh.
   (E) Ben is ranked second.

4. If Garry is ranked first and Anna is ranked second, then which of the following must NOT be true?
   (A) Frank is ranked third.
   (B) Evan is ranked third.
   (C) Chris is not ranked fifth.
   (D) Frank is not ranked third.
   (E) Ben is not ranked fourth.

5. If Chris and Dana are ranked consecutively, then which of the following must be true?
   (A) Chris is ranked fifth.
   (B) Evan is ranked seventh.
   (C) Garry is ranked first.
   (D) Anna is not ranked second.
   (E) Ben and Evan are ranked consecutively.

6. If Garry is ranked third, then which of the following must be true?
   (A) Anna is ranked second.
   (B) Ben is not ranked fourth.
   (C) Frank is ranked first.
   (D) Evan is ranked seventh.
   (E) Chris is ranked fourth.

ANSWERS AND EXPLANATIONS

PART A. MINIMIZED-VARIABLE GAMES

Minimized-Variable Game 1

Initial Setup:

1. H = Out
2. a. C → D → ~~G~~ → ~~E~~ → B ; b. ~~B~~ → E → G → ~~D~~ → ~~C~~
3. a. ~~I~~ → F → ~~A~~ ; b. A → ~~F~~ → I

Question 1: Which of the following could be a complete list of the sheep outside of the pasture?

(A) Hillary must be outside of the pasture.

Question 2: If Garry is in the pasture, then which of the following must be true?

(C) This constraint means that Dana and Chris must also be outside of the pasture.

Question 3: Which of the following pairs can never be in the pasture at the same time?

(E) Chris and Evan cannot be in the pasture together in either logic chain.

Question 4: You will know the exact position of all sheep if you know that which two sheep are in the pasture?

(C) Chris and Anna are sheep that begin the logic chains if they are in the pasture. This means that their being in the pasture ripples through the rest of the game, forcing all the other animals to be either in or out.

Question 5: At the most, how many sheep could be outside of the pasture at the same time?

(C) Hillary must be out. In logic chain 2.a., Chris, Dana, Garry, and Evan can all be out. In either of the logic chains in 3, two variables can be out. Adding these gives you a total of seven sheep.

Question 6: At most, how many sheep could be in the pasture at the same time?

(B) Chris, Dana, and Ben or Ben, Evan, and Garry can be in, and Iris and Frank or Anna and Iris can be in, for a total of five sheep.

Minimized-Variable Game 2

Initial Setup:

F	M	D
G	D	F/A
H	A/F	E/C
B	C/E	

F	M	D
B	G	F/A
C	H	D
E	A/F	

Garry and Hillary cannot be defenders, since Anna and Frank cannot be in the same group, Ben and Frank cannot be in the same group, and Ben and Anna cannot be in the same group. Because this scenario would leave only two groups for these three opposing variables, it would not be workable.

Question 1: Which of the following could be the group of midfielders?

(B) This grouping could occur in the first scenario.

(A) Anna cannot be in the same group with Frank.

(C) Ben, Evan, and Chris can be in the same group only if they are forwards.

(D) Garry, Hillary, and Ben can be in the same group only if they are forwards.

(E) **B** is the correct answer.

Question 2: If Chris is a midfielder, then which of the following must be true?

(C) This constraint is possible only in the first scenario, in which Hillary must be a forward.

Question 3: If Chris is a forward, then which of the following must be true?

(E) This constraint puts you in the first scenario. None of the answer choices works.

Question 4: Who could potentially play any position?

(D) Evan and Chris could both play any position.

Question 5: Who could only play one position?

(A) Ben must be a forward in both scenarios.

Question 6: If Frank plays midfield, then which of the following must NOT be true?

(D) This constraint can happen in either scenario, but, Frank and Anna still cannot play the same position.

Question 7: How many different possible configurations are there for the positions of the players?

(B) Four configurations are possible based on the first scenario, and two configurations are possible based on the second scenario.

Minimized-Variable Game 3

Initial Setup:

	M	T	W	Th	F	M	T	W	Th	F
A–E	C	D	E/B	B/E	A	E/B	D	C	B/E	A
F–J	G	F	H/I	J	I/H	H/I	I/H	G	J	F

Question 1: Which of the following could be the order in which the stockbrokers' fortunes are told, from Monday to Friday?

(C) This order is possible in the second scenario above.

Question 2: Which of the following could be the order in which the philosophers' fortunes are told, from Monday to Friday?

(A) This order is possible in the first scenario above.

Question 3: How many different people could potentially have their fortune told on the same day as Frank's?

(B) Anna could have her fortune told or Dana could have his fortune told on the same day as Frank's.

Question 4: How many different people could potentially have their fortune told on the same day as Iris's?

(D) Evan, Ben, Anna, and Dana could all have their fortunes told on the same day as Iris's.

Question 5: If Hillary's fortune is told on Wednesday, then which of the following must be true?

(B) This constraint is possible only in the first scenario. It requires Iris to have her fortune told on Friday and Frank to have his fortune told on Tuesday.

Question 6: Which of the following must be true?

(E) In both scenarios, Julian's fortune must be told on the same day as Evan's or Ben's.

Minimized-Variable Game 4

Initial Setup:

1. D B A/C G E F C/A
2. A/C B D E F G C/A
3. A/C B C/A D/G E F G/D

Question 1: Which of the following could be the order in which the students are seen, from Monday to Sunday?

(D) This order is possible in scenario 3.

(A) Only two people must be seen between Dana and Garry.

(B) Two people must be seen between Dana and Garry.

(C) Two people must be seen between Dana and Garry.

(D) **D** is the correct answer.

Question 2: Which of the following must be true?

(E) Most of the answer choices can be true, but none of them must be true.

Question 3: If Garry is seen on Sunday, then which of the following must be true?

(C) This constraint is possible only in scenario 3. The earliest that Dana can be seen in this case is on Thursday, and the latest that Anna can be seen is Wednesday.

(A) Chris can be seen on Monday or Wednesday.

(B) Chris could be seen on Monday.

(D) Dana can be seen on Thursday.

(E) **C** is the correct answer.

Question 4: On which day could the hypnotist potentially see the greatest number of different students?

(E) On Sunday, the hypnotist could see Dana, Garry, Chris, or Anna.

(A) Monday:	Chris, Anna, or Dana
(B) Wednesday:	Chris, Anna, or Dana
(C) Thursday:	Garry, Evan, or Dana
(D) Saturday:	Garry or Frank

Question 5: Which of the following pairs of students could never be seen on consecutive days?

(C) Evan and Chris can never be seen consecutively in any of the diagrams.

(A) Anna and Garry could be seen consecutively in scenario 1.

(B) Frank and Garry could be seen consecutively in scenarios 2 and 3.

(D) Frank and Anna could be seen consecutively in scenario 1.

(E) **C** is the correct answer.

Question 6: Which student could potentially be seen on the most days of the week?

(D) Dana can be seen on Monday, Wednesday, Thursday, or Sunday.

(A) Garry can be seen on Thursday, Saturday, or Sunday.

(B) Anna can be seen on Monday, Wednesday, or Sunday.

(C) Frank can be seen on Friday or Saturday.

(E) Evan can be seen on Thursday or Friday.

Minimized-Variable Game 5

Initial Setup:

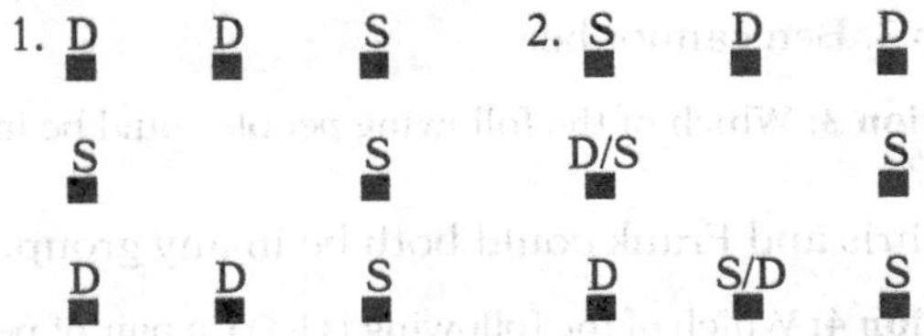

Question 1: Which of the following must be a single hangar?

(C) The east hangar must be a single hangar.

Question 2: Which of the following must be a double hangar?

(D) The southwest hangar must be a double hangar.

Question 3: Which of the following must NOT be true if four hangars are doubles?

(C) There always have to be four hangars that are doubles, so this question is really just asking about what must be true in general. As the initial constraints say, the north hangar must be a double.

Question 4: Which of the following must NOT be true if the west hangar is a double?

(E) This constraint occurs in scenario 2. Since the southwest hangar is always a double and a double must be bordered by a single and a double, either the west or the south hangar must be a single.

Question 5: Which of the following could be true?

(C) In scenario 2, it is possible for both the northwest hangar and the south hangar to be singles.

Question 6: How many different configurations of the hangars are possible?

(B) Due to the double possibility in scenario 2, there are three possibilities for the variables in the game.

Minimized-Variable Game 6

Initial Setup:

1	2	3		1	2	3
A	E	D		D	E	C
B/F/C	C/B/F	F/C		F	B	A

Question 1: Which of the following pairs of people could be in the same group?

(E) Ben and Anna could both be in group 1 in the first scenario.

Question 2: Which of the following people could NOT be in group 3?

(B) Chris, Anna, Dana, and Frank can all be in group 3. Ben cannot be.

Question 3: Which of the following people could be in any group?

(D) Chris and Frank could both be in any group.

Question 4: Which of the following is NOT a pair of people who could be trained in group 1?

(D) Dana and Ben could not be trained together in group 1.

Question 5: If Frank is trained in group 2, then which of the following must be true?

(C) This constraint occurs in the first scenario and means that Chris must be in group 3 and Ben must be in group 1.

Question 6: How many configurations are possible for the groups?

(A) Four configurations can be based on the first scenario and one can be based on the second, making a total of five.

Minimized-Variable Game 7

Initial Setup:

G E A D F C B

G E D A B C F

G B C F E D/A A/D

Question 1: Which of the following could be the order in which the pianists play, from Monday to Sunday?

(D) This order could occur in the middle scenario above.

(A) When Anna plays on Wednesday, there must be an FCB box.

(B) Frank cannot play on Tuesday in any of the scenarios.

(C) Evan has to play before Dana.

(E) **D** is the correct answer.

Question 2: On which day could four people potentially play?

(A) On Sunday, Ben, Frank, Anna, or Dana could play.

(B) Wednesday: Anna, Dana, or Chris

(C) Thursday: Dana, Anna, or Frank

(D) Friday: Frank, Ben, or Evan

(E) **A** is the correct answer.

Question 3: Which of the following people could potentially play on four different days?

(A) Dana and Anna could both play on four different days.

Question 4: If Dana plays on Wednesday, then which of the following must be true?

(B) This constraint occurs in the middle scenario above, in which Evan must play on Tuesday.

Question 5: If Anna plays after Dana, then which of the following must be true?

(E) This constraint is possible in both of the last two scenarios. Many of the answer choices can be true, but none of them must be true.

Question 6: How many possible orders are there in which the pianists can play?

(B) There are four possible configurations because of the double possibility in the last scenario.

Minimized-Variable Game 8

Initial Setup:

A	B	C/D	D/C
G	E	H/F	F/H

A	B	C/D	D/C
H/F	F/H	E	G

C/D	D/C	B	A
G	E	H/F	F/H

C/D	D/C	B	A
H/F	F/H	E	G

Question 1: Which of the following is NOT a possible order for the lobbyists, from room 1 to room 4?

(C) Garry cannot be in a room numbered consecutively with Hillary's room.

Question 2: If Ben shares room 2 with Hillary, then which of the following must be true?

(D) This constraint is possible in the top right scenario, in which Anna must share room 1 with Frank if Ben shares room 2 with Hillary.

Question 3: If Dana and Hillary are in consecutive rooms, then which of the following must NOT be true?

(E) This constraint is possible in any scenario. However, when Chris is in room 1 and Frank is in room 1, Dana and Hillary must both be in room 2.

(A) This choice is possible in the top right scenario.

(B) This choice is possible in the top right scenario.

(C) This choice is possible in the bottom right scenario.

(D) This choice is possible in the top right scenario.

Question 4: Which of the following pairs of people could never share a room?

(A) Garry and Ben cannot share a room in any scenario.

Question 5: If Anna and Garry share a room, then which of the following must be true?

(C) This constraint is possible in the top left and bottom right scenarios. Ben and Evan must share a room in both scenarios.

Question 6: How many different room configurations are possible?

(C) Four possible configurations can arise from each of the four scenarios.

PART B. MAXIMIZED-VARIABLE GAMES

Maximized-Variable Game I

Initial Setup:

M	T	W	Th	F
___	___	___	___	___
*A	___	___	___	A̸

1. Each student meets with Tara twice.
2. No student meets with Tara twice in the same day.
3. [B/C]
4. A = C exactly once.
5. $A_M \rightarrow B_M$

Question 1: If Anna meets with Tara on Monday and Wednesday, on what day must Chris meet with her?

(C) Chris must meet with Tara on Wednesday, because when Anna meets with Tara on Monday, Ben also meets with her on Monday.

Question 2: If Ben is the only student to meet with Tara on a Wednesday, on what days must Anna meet with her?

(D) Anna cannot meet with Tara on Monday, because that would make Ben meet with her on Monday and Wednesday. Chris must meet with Tara the same day as Anna once during the week, and Anna cannot go on Friday. Therefore, Chris would have to meet with Tara the same day as Anna on Tuesday or Thursday, two days that are both the day after a day when Ben meets with her. The box rule disallows this. Therefore, Anna must meet with Tara on Tuesday and Thursday, and Chris must meet with Tara the same day as Anna on Tuesday.

Question 3: If Anna is the only student to meet with Tara on Tuesday and no one meets with her on Friday, who meets with her on Wednesday?

(C) Anna and Chris cannot meet with Tara on Monday, because when Anna goes on Monday, Ben must also go on Monday, so Ben would have to meet with Tara on Monday and on Wednesday or Thursday. But he cannot meet with Tara on Wednesday, because then Chris would have to meet with her on the day after his lesson. Therefore, Anna and Chris meet with Tara on Wednesday, and Ben meets with her on Thursday.

Question 4: If Ben is allowed to meet with Tara three times one week, on what days could he meet with her?

(B) Chris must meet with Tara the same day as Anna on one day, but on another day he could meet with her the same day as Ben and not consecutively. Anna and Chris could meet with Tara on Wednesday if Ben meets with her on Monday, Thursday, and Friday. Chris could meet with Tara on Monday or Thursday since Ben meets with her on—but not the day before—those days.

Question 5: If Tara adds Dana, a fourth student, what is the maximum number of times Dana could meet with her each week?

(E) Dana could meet up to four times with Tara, since Tara has four spaces open (10 – 6).

Question 6: If Anna cannot meet with Tara on Tuesday or Wednesday, on what day must Chris meet with her?

(D) Chris must meet with Tara on Thursday, since he cannot meet with her the same day as Anna on Monday and Anna cannot have her lesson on Friday.

Question 7: If Ben meets with Tara on Tuesday and Friday, on what day must Chris meet with her?

(D) Chris must meet with Tara the same day as Anna on Thursday. He could meet with her the same day as Ben on Tuesday or Friday, so he does not have to meet with her on Monday.

Maximized-Variable Game 2

Initial Setup:

*G	C̸	*A	B	E̸	E̸	E̸
1	2	3	4	5	6	7

1. [C F]
2. $A_3 \rightarrow D_6$
3. $G_1 \rightarrow C_6$

Question 1: Which of the following could be the order of the racers, from lane 1 to lane 7?

(D) This is a possible order of the racers.

(A) Chris cannot be in lane 2 because of the fourth constraint.

(B) Evan must be in a lower-numbered lane than Ben.

(C) If Garry is in lane 1, then Chris is in lane 6.

(E) If Anna is in lane 3, then Dana is in lane 6.

Question 2: Which of the following could NOT be true?

(C) If Anna is in lane 3, then that would force Dana to be in lane 6. This would leave no space for the CF box after Ben. Since Evan must be in a lower-numbered lane than Ben and Chris cannot be in lane 2 because that would force Frank to be in lane 3 where Anna is. The first sufficient-necessary statement becomes a vacancy rule. This is your new diagram:

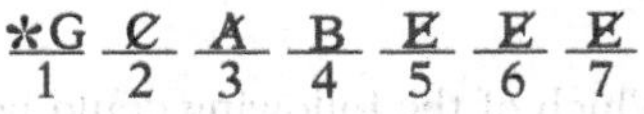

Question 3: If Garry is in lane 1, then which of the following must be true?

(E) This constraint would force Chris to be in lane 6 and Frank in lane 7. Dana and Anna could not be in consecutive lanes, because that would force them to be in lanes 2 and 3, leaving no place for Evan to precede Ben.

Question 4: If Chris is in a lower-numbered lane than Ben, then which of the following must be true?

(A) Chris must be in lane 1, since the fourth initial constraint restricts him from being in lane 2. Then Frank must be in lane 2, and, for Evan to precede Ben, Evan must be in lane 3.

Question 5: If Chris, Frank, and Dana are in higher-numbered lanes than Ben, then which of the following must NOT be true?

(C) If Ben and Anna are in consecutive lanes, then that means that Anna must be in lane 3. This is impossible, as demonstrated in question 2.

Question 6: If Evan must not be in a lane consecutive with Ben, then which of the following must be true?

(B) This constraint means that Evan cannot be in lane 3 but must be in lane 1 or 2. Chris cannot be in lane 2, so Frank cannot be in lane 3. But Chris cannot be in lane 1 either, because that would force Evan to be in lane 3, which is impossible with this question's constraint. Frank and Chris must be after Ben.

Maximized-Variable Game 3

Initial Setup:

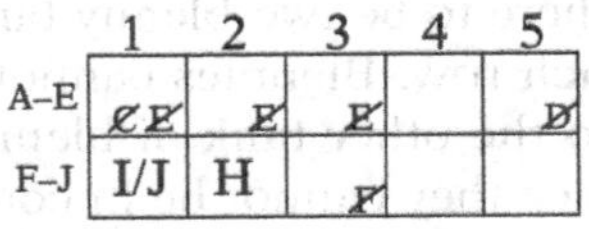

1. 

2. 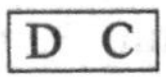

Question 1: Which of the following could be the order of the contestants, in fields 1 through 5?

(E) None of the answer choices could be the order.

(A) Ben cannot be in the first three fields.

(B) Ben cannot be in the first three fields.

(C) Chris must be after Dana.

(D) Ben cannot be in the first three fields.

Question 2: If Dana is in field 3, then which of the following must be true?

(B) This constraint means that Ben must be in field 5, since Chris must already occupy field 4. Since Frank must be paired with Ben, Frank must also be in field 5. Evan and Anna must be in fields 1 and 2. Garry cannot be paired with Evan, since Garry cannot go in field 1 or 2.

Question 3: If Iris is in a higher-numbered field than Hillary, then which of the following must be true?

(C) According to the logic diagram, if Iris is not in field 1, then Julian must be in field 1.

Question 4: If Garry is paired with Chris, then which of the following must NOT be true?

(C) Hillary must always be in field 2.

Question 5: If Evan and Iris share field 5, then which of the following must NOT be true?

(A) This constraint means that the order of the cows, from first to last, would be Julian, Hillary, Garry, Frank, Iris. Ben must be in field 4, and Evan must be in field 5. Since Julian must be in field 1, it would be impossible for him to share a field with Chris, because Dana must be immediately before Chris.

Question 6: Which of the following could never be paired together?

(B) Ben must always be paired with Frank.

Maximized-Variable Game 4

Initial Setup:

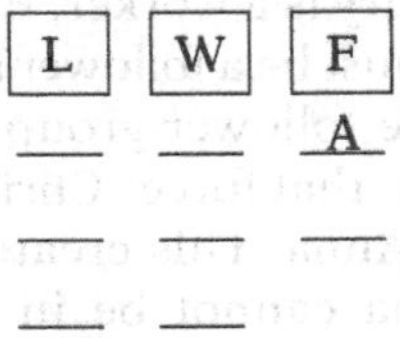

1. $F \neq D$
2. $B_L \rightarrow C_F$; $\not{C}_{\not{F}} \rightarrow \not{B}_{\not{L}}$
3. $H_W \rightarrow E_L$; $\not{E}_{\not{L}} \rightarrow \not{H}_{\not{W}}$
4. $\not{D}_{\not{F}} \rightarrow F_W$; $\not{F}_{\not{W}} \rightarrow D_F$

Question 1: Which of the following could be the group of workers?

(E) Hillary, Ben, and Frank could all be workers.

(A) Dana and Frank cannot be in the same group.

(B) If Hillary is a worker, then Evan is a leader.

(C) Anna is a follower.

(D) If Dana is not a follower, then Frank must be a worker.

Question 2: Which of the following could never be a worker?

(C) Anna could never be a worker. Dana could also never be a worker, because if she is not a follower, then Frank is a worker, and Dana and Frank cannot be in the same group because of the first constraint.

Question 3: If Dana and Ben are in the same group, then which of the following must be true?

(D) Dana cannot be a worker, so she and Ben must both be leaders. When Ben is a leader, Chris must be a follower, so **B** is incorrect. The rest of the answer choices could be true but are not necessarily true.

Question 4: Who could never be in the same group as Anna?

(D) Frank could never be in the same group as Anna, because when Frank is not a worker, Dana must be a follower. If Frank and Anna are both followers, then there is no room for Dana to also be a follower.

Question 5: If Anna is in the same group as Evan, then which of the following must be true?

The following is a diagram for this scenario:

L	W	F
D	F	A
H	B	E
G/C	C/G	

(A) Ben and Hillary cannot be in the same group in this scenario.

Question 6: If Hillary and Evan are in the same group, then which of the following must NOT be true?

(E) This constraint means that Hillary and Evan must both be leaders, since when Hillary is a worker, Evan must be a leader because Anna must be a follower and there is not enough space in the follower group for three variables. If Ben is a leader, that forces Chris to fill up the follower group with Anna. This creates a problem, since Frank and Dana cannot be in the same group, but in this scenario both are forced to be workers.

Maximized-Variable Game 5

Initial Setup:

D/C			D/C
D/C	B/C	D	C

1.

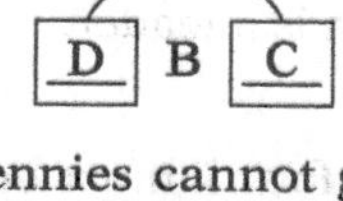

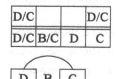

Blennies cannot go at the end of a row, since they need to be bordered by cichlids and darters.

2.

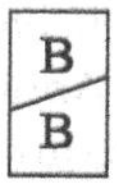

3. D/D

Question 1: Which of the following could be the order of the types of fishes in aquariums 5 through 8?

(A) This is a possible order.

(B) Blennies cannot be at the ends, since they need to be bordered by cichlids and darters.

(C) Blennies cannot be at the ends, since they need to be bordered by cichlids and darters.

(D) Darters cannot go in adjacent tanks.

(E) **A** is the correct answer.

Question 2: What is the maximum number of aquariums that could hold blennies?

(B) Blennies could go in aquariums 6, 2, and 3, but they cannot concurrently go in aquariums 2 and 3 or 6 and 2.

Question 3: If there are four aquariums with darters, then which of the following must be true?

(E) The most darters that could go in either row is two. If there are four darter tanks, then tank 5 must have darters, but darters could be in any of the tanks in the first row.

Question 4: What is the maximum number of aquariums that could hold cichlids?

(E) There are no constraints at all on the presence of cichlids or the absence of the other types of fish. Therefore, the only aquarium that could not hold cichlids is aquarium 7, which holds darters. Cichlids could be in the other seven aquariums.

Question 5: If there are two aquariums with blennies in them, then which of the following must be true?

(A) This constraint means that blennies must be in aquarium 6, since, for there to be two blenny tanks, there must be one in each row. Blennies cannot be across from blennies, so the other tank of blennies must be aquarium 3, since they cannot be in corner tanks or across from other blenny tanks. Cichlids must be in aquarium 5, since the blennies in tank 6 are already next to darters in tank 7.

Question 6: If there are darters in aquarium 3, then how many possible configurations of the aquariums are there?

Here is the basic scenario for this:

D/C	B/C	D	C
D/C	B/C	D	C

This can be broken down into the following three configurations for the aquariums on the left side:

C	B
D/C	C

D/C	C
C	B

D/C	C
D/C	C

(D) Two configurations are possible based on the first and second scenarios. Four configurations are possible from the last scenario. This makes a total of eight possible configurations.

Maximized-Variable Game 6

Initial Setup:

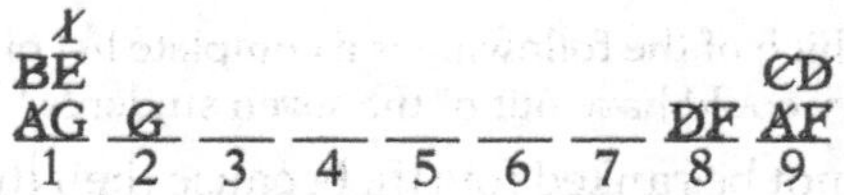

1. F < A < G
2. C < I
3. 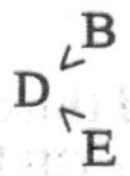

Question 1: Which of the following could be the order of the finishers, from first to last?

(C) This is a possible order.

(A) Anna must finish before Garry.

(B) Dana must finish before Evan.

(D) Frank cannot finish eighth or ninth.

(E) Chris must finish before Iris.

Question 2: What is the earliest position in which Garry could finish?

(C) Since two people must precede Garry, the earliest position in which he could finish is third.

Question 3: If Iris finishes third, then which of the following is a pair of people who could finish before her?

(B) If Iris finishes third, then Chris must finish second or first. Ben could not finish first, and he could not finish second without Dana's finishing before him. Therefore, Chris and Hillary is the correct answer; Hillary could finish anywhere, including first or second.

Question 4: If Garry finishes fourth, Hillary fifth, and Ben sixth, then which of the following could be true?

(D) Evan could finish eighth under this scenario because Chris must finish before Iris. Places 4, 5, and 6 are taken due to this question's constraint. Places 1, 2, and 3 are already taken by Frank, Anna, and Dana since Frank and Anna must be before Garry and Dana because Dana must be before Ben. Therefore, there is no room for Chris to go before Iris when Iris finishes seventh.

Question 5: If Dana finishes sixth, then which is the latest position in which Frank could finish?

(B) The latest that Frank could finish is fourth. This is because Dana must have two people behind her. If she finishes sixth, there is one more spot behind her, and Garry could finish there. This leaves only spots before Dana for Anna to finish in, and then Frank can finish before her in the fourth position.

Question 6: If Chris finishes after Evan and Ben and if Frank finishes immediately after Iris, then which of the following must be true?

This constraint would cause the sequential chain to be as follows:

(C) Keep in mind that Hillary could finish anywhere in this sequence. The only thing that you know for sure is that Evan finishes before Anna.

Maximized-Variable Game 7

Initial Setup:

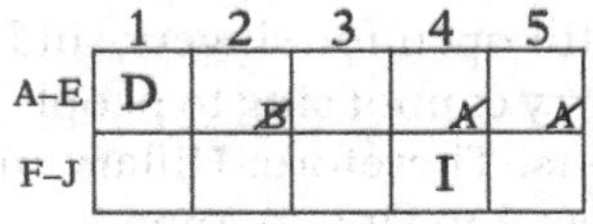

1. 

2. A_2 → 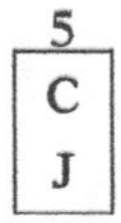

3. $B_4 \rightarrow F_1$

Question 1: Which of the following could be the order in which the young romantics live, from street 1 to street 5?

(E) No answer choice works.

(A) Anna cannot live on the last two streets.

(B) If Anna lives on street 2, then Chris lives on street 5.

(C) Ben cannot live on street 2.

(D) Anna cannot live on the last two streets.

Question 2: If Chris lives on street 4, then which of the following could be false?

This constraint means that Evan has to live on street 2, because there is no one else who can live there. Anna cannot live there, since that would force Chris to live on street 5. Anna lives on street 3 and Ben on street 5:

	1	2	3	4	5
A–E	D	E	A	C	B
F–J				I	

(C) The only thing that could be false is that Frank sings to the person on street 1.

Question 3: If Frank sings to the person living on street 2, then which of the following must be true?

(A) This constraint means that Garry must sing to the person on street 5 so that he is not singing on the street consecutive with the one Frank sings on. Also, Anna cannot be on street 2, because that would force Julian to be on street 5, where Garry is.

Question 4: If Iris sings to Ben, then which of the following must NOT be true?

(C) This constraint means that Frank sings to Dana on street 1. Since Garry cannot sing on a street consecutive with the street Frank sings on, Garry cannot sing to the person on street 2.

Question 5: If Anna lives on street 2, then which of the following must be true?

(D) Hillary must sing to Anna. This is because Anna's living on street 2 forces Julian to sing on street 5. Streets 1, 2, and 3 are still open for singers, and we know that Frank and Garry cannot sing to people living on consecutive streets. Therefore, Hillary must go between them on street 2 to sing to Anna.

Question 6: If Chris lives on street 2 and Frank sings to him, then which of the following could be false?

Here is a diagram for this question:

	1	2	3	4	5
A–E	D	C	A	E	B
F–J	H/J	H	J/H	I	G

(B) The only possibility is for Julian to sing to Dana instead of to Anna.

Maximized-Variable Game 8

Initial Setup:

_ _ _ _ _ D ~~C~~
1 2 3 4 5 6 7

1. G/E

2. G/C

3. C __ E

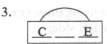

4. $A_2 \rightarrow B_4$

Question 1: Which of the following could be an order of the students, from first to last?

(C) This is a possible order of the variables.

(A) One student must finish between Chris and Evan.

(B) Garry cannot be next to Chris.

(D) If Anna is second, then Ben is fourth.

(E) Chris must have a lower ranking than Dana.

Question 2: Which of the following is a complete list of the ranks that Garry could have out of the seven students?

(C) Garry cannot be ranked fourth, because then there would be nowhere for the CE box to go to avoid having Chris and Garry ranked consecutively with him. Garry cannot be sixth, because Dana is ranked sixth.

Question 3: If Garry finishes ranked fifth, then which of the following could NOT be true?

(C) Chris and Evan must be ranked first and third in this case, because there is nowhere else for the CE box to go.

Question 4: If Garry is ranked first and Anna is ranked second, then which of the following must NOT be true?

(E) This would make Ben rank fourth, because Anna ranks second. There are two places the CE box could go—the third and fifth ranks or the fifth and seventh ranks.

Question 5: If Chris and Dana are ranked consecutively, then which of the following must be true?

(A) There are two possibilities in which this constraint can occur. In the first, Chris is fifth and Evan is seventh. In the second, Chris is fifth and Evan is third. Either way, Chris must go fifth.

Question 6: If Garry is ranked third, then which of the following must be true?

(D) If Garry is ranked third, then the only place for the CE box to go is with Chris fifth and Evan seventh.

CHAPTER 9

PRACTICE TESTS

This chapter contains two practice test sections, each of which is just like the Logic Games section on the real LSAT. Note that each actual LSAT has four sections and that the other three sections of each test cover question types other than Logic Games.

PRACTICE TEST 1

ANSWER SHEET

Directions for Test

- Before beginning the test section, photocopy this Answer Sheet or remove it from the book. Mark your answer to each question in the space provided. If the section has fewer questions than answer spaces, leave the extra spaces blank.
- When you have finished the test, you may check your answers against the Answer Key on page 173. Explanations for each question begin on page 174.

SECTION I
1. Ⓐ Ⓑ Ⓒ Ⓓ Ⓔ
2. Ⓐ Ⓑ Ⓒ Ⓓ Ⓔ
3. Ⓐ Ⓑ Ⓒ Ⓓ Ⓔ
4. Ⓐ Ⓑ Ⓒ Ⓓ Ⓔ
5. Ⓐ Ⓑ Ⓒ Ⓓ Ⓔ
6. Ⓐ Ⓑ Ⓒ Ⓓ Ⓔ
7. Ⓐ Ⓑ Ⓒ Ⓓ Ⓔ
8. Ⓐ Ⓑ Ⓒ Ⓓ Ⓔ
9. Ⓐ Ⓑ Ⓒ Ⓓ Ⓔ
10. Ⓐ Ⓑ Ⓒ Ⓓ Ⓔ
11. Ⓐ Ⓑ Ⓒ Ⓓ Ⓔ
12. Ⓐ Ⓑ Ⓒ Ⓓ Ⓔ
13. Ⓐ Ⓑ Ⓒ Ⓓ Ⓔ
14. Ⓐ Ⓑ Ⓒ Ⓓ Ⓔ
15. Ⓐ Ⓑ Ⓒ Ⓓ Ⓔ
16. Ⓐ Ⓑ Ⓒ Ⓓ Ⓔ
17. Ⓐ Ⓑ Ⓒ Ⓓ Ⓔ
18. Ⓐ Ⓑ Ⓒ Ⓓ Ⓔ
19. Ⓐ Ⓑ Ⓒ Ⓓ Ⓔ
20. Ⓐ Ⓑ Ⓒ Ⓓ Ⓔ
21. Ⓐ Ⓑ Ⓒ Ⓓ Ⓔ
22. Ⓐ Ⓑ Ⓒ Ⓓ Ⓔ
23. Ⓐ Ⓑ Ⓒ Ⓓ Ⓔ
24. Ⓐ Ⓑ Ⓒ Ⓓ Ⓔ
25. Ⓐ Ⓑ Ⓒ Ⓓ Ⓔ
26. Ⓐ Ⓑ Ⓒ Ⓓ Ⓔ
27. Ⓐ Ⓑ Ⓒ Ⓓ Ⓔ
28. Ⓐ Ⓑ Ⓒ Ⓓ Ⓔ
29. Ⓐ Ⓑ Ⓒ Ⓓ Ⓔ
30. Ⓐ Ⓑ Ⓒ Ⓓ Ⓔ

SECTION 1

Time—35 minutes

26 questions

Directions for Logic Games Questions: The questions in these sections are divided into groups. Each group is based on a set of conditions. For each question, choose the answer that is most accurate and complete. For some questions, you may wish to draw a rough diagram to help you select your response. Mark the corresponding space on your Answer Sheet.

Questions 1–6

Six dogs A, B, C, D, E, and F will visit three vets in this next week. Each dog will visit only one vet and each vet will see at least one dog. The vets' names are Julio, Franco, and Marcos. Who the dogs see is determined by the following:

The vet that sees A will only see one dog.
F sees the same vet as C.
If a vet sees B, then that vet does not see E.

1. If Marcos sees A and Julio sees F, then which of the following must be false?

(A) Julio sees E and D.
(B) Marcos sees only one dog.
(C) Franco sees D and C.
(D) Franco sees two dogs.
(E) Julio sees four dogs.

2. Which of the following could NOT be a complete list of the dogs that Julio sees?

(A) F, C, B, D
(B) E, D
(C) A
(D) E, F, C
(E) F, C

3. If A is seen by Marcos and B is seen by Franco, then which of the following dogs does Julio have to see?

(A) A
(B) C
(C) D
(D) E
(E) F

4. If Franco sees only two dogs, then which dog does he have to see?

(A) B
(B) C
(C) D
(D) E
(E) F

5. If Julio sees four dogs, then which dog must he NOT see?

(A) A
(B) C
(C) D
(D) E
(E) F

6. What is the total number of different dogs any of whom Julio could potentially see?

(A) one
(B) two
(C) four
(D) five
(E) six

GO ON TO THE NEXT PAGE

Questions 7–13

At a party, there are a number of people in line for the slip and slide. Certain people like to talk to each other in line and so order themselves accordingly. There are a total of seven people waiting in line: A, B, C, D, E, F, and G. Their order is governed by the following constraints:

A goes immediately before B.
D goes immediately after C.
E goes immediately before F.
G goes before D.
E goes after G.

7. Which of the following is a possible order of the line from first to last?

(A) A, B, C, D, G, E, F.
(B) C, D, G, A, B, E, F.
(C) E, F, C, D, G, A, B.
(D) A, B, G, E, C, D, F.
(E) G, A, B, E, F, C, D.

8. If C goes in slot 4, which slot could the most people potentially go in?

(A) 1
(B) 2
(C) 5
(D) 6
(E) 7

9. If D goes in slot 5, then which of the following must be false?

(A) G goes in slot 1.
(B) G goes before F.
(C) G goes in slot 2.
(D) G goes in a slot numbered lower than 3.
(E) G goes in a lower-numbered slot than C.

10. If A goes after E, then which of the following must be true?

(A) F goes in the last slot.
(B) C goes in slot 4.
(C) D goes in slot 6.
(D) F goes in slot 3.
(E) G goes in slot 1.

11. Which is a complete list of the slots where C can NOT go?

(A) 2, 3, 5.
(B) 1, 4, 5, 6, 7.
(C) 1, 3, 5, 7.
(D) 1, 2, 4, 5.
(E) 1, 3, 5.

12. If D goes last, then we know the exact position of how many variables in all, including D?

(A) one
(B) two
(C) three
(D) four
(E) five

13. If C goes second and E goes before A, then which of the following could not be true?

(A) G goes first.
(B) D goes third.
(C) A goes after F.
(D) E goes fifth.
(E) A and B go consecutively.

GO ON TO THE NEXT PAGE

Questions 14–19

At a motorcycle conference, riders are paired with specific bikes in order to show them off to the crowd. Four riders A, B, C, and D are paired with four bikes R, S, T, and U. Bikes are placed in rooms numbered from 1 to 4; each room has one rider and one bike only. The pairs are governed by the following rules:

Rider A is paired with bike T.
Rider D is not paired with bike S.
Rider C is not paired with bike U.
Rider A is in room 2.
If rider D is in room 1, then rider C is in room 4.
If bike U is in room 3, then rider D is in room 1.

14. If rider C is in room 1, then which of the following must be true?

(A) Rider C is paired with bike R.
(B) Rider D is paired with bike U.
(C) Bike U is in room 4.
(D) Bike T is in a higher-numbered room than bike S.
(E) Rider B is in room 3.

15. If bike U is not in room 3, then which of the following must NOT be true?

(A) Rider D is with bike U.
(B) Bike T is in room 2.
(C) Rider D is in room 1.
(D) Bike U is in room 4.
(E) Rider A is in room 3.

16. If rider C is in room 4 and bike R is in room 1, then which of the following must be true?

(A) Rider B is paired with bike U.
(B) Rider D is in a room after rider A.
(C) Bike S is not paired with rider C or B.
(D) Bike T is in a consecutive room with rider C.
(E) Bike T is in a room that is consecutive with only one other bike.

17. If Bike U is paired with rider D, then which of the following must be false?

(A) Rider B is in room 4.
(B) Bike R is room 3.
(C) Bike U is in room 1.
(D) Rider C is in room 3.
(E) Bike S is in room 1.

18. If bike T is not in a consecutive room with rider C or bike S, then which of the following must be true?

(A) Bike R is in room 1.
(B) Bike S is in room 4.
(C) Bike U is in room 3.
(D) Rider D is in room 1.
(E) Rider B is in room 3.

19. If rider D is not paired with bike U, then each of the following could be false EXCEPT:

(A) Rider A is with bike U.
(B) Rider B is with bike U.
(C) Rider C is with bike U.
(D) Bike U is in a room consecutive with bike T.
(E) Bike U is in a room consecutive with bike S.

GO ON TO THE NEXT PAGE

Questions 20–26

A piece of cheese is sitting on the countertop in a house. The mice realize that the only way that they can get around the cat to get the cheese is by forming teams. Team Distract will have only three rodents. Team Sprint will have only three rodents. Team Capture will have exactly two rodents. The mice are named A, B, C, D, E, F, G, and H. The following rules govern the overall makeup of the teams:

Rodent E is not on a team with rodent D.
Rodent B is on a team with rodent F.
If rodent F is on team Distract, then rodents D and C will be on team Sprint.
If rodent F is on team Sprint, then rodents E and G will also be on team Sprint.
If rodent F is on team Capture, then rodents A and D will be on team Sprint.

20. Which of the following pairs of rodents could NOT be part of team Sprint?

(A) E and A.
(B) C and D.
(C) G and C.
(D) H and E.
(E) A and C.

21. Which of the following is a possible makeup of team Capture?

(A) G, H.
(B) H, D.
(C) E, B.
(D) F, H.
(E) D, C.

22. Which rodent could be assigned to only one team?

(A) A
(B) B
(C) C
(D) D
(E) E

23. Which of the following pairs of rodents always share a team?

(A) A, D.
(B) C, G.
(C) E, A.
(D) H, G.
(E) F, B.

24. Which rodents could never share a team?

(A) C, E.
(B) F, D.
(C) E, B.
(D) G, H.
(E) A, D.

25. Which of the following is a complete list of the rodents that could be on team Sprint?

(A) A, C, D, G, H.
(B) B, C, D, G, H.
(C) A, C, D, E, G, H.
(D) A, D, G, H.
(E) C, D, G, H.

26. If H and A are on team Capture, then which of the following must NOT be true?

(A) F and B are on team Distract.
(B) F and G are on different teams.
(C) C and E share a team.
(D) D and C are on team Sprint.
(E) A and H do not share a team with another rodent.

S T O P

IF YOU FINISH BEFORE TIME RUNS OUT, CHECK YOUR WORK.

ANSWER KEY

Section I
1. C
2. E
3. D
4. C
5. A
6. E
7. E
8. B
9. C
10. E
11. C
12. B
13. D
14. C
15. E
16. A
17. A
18. B
19. B
20. A
21. A
22. D
23. E
24. B
25. A
26. C

ANSWERS AND EXPLANATIONS

Game 1: Grouping

Initial Setup:

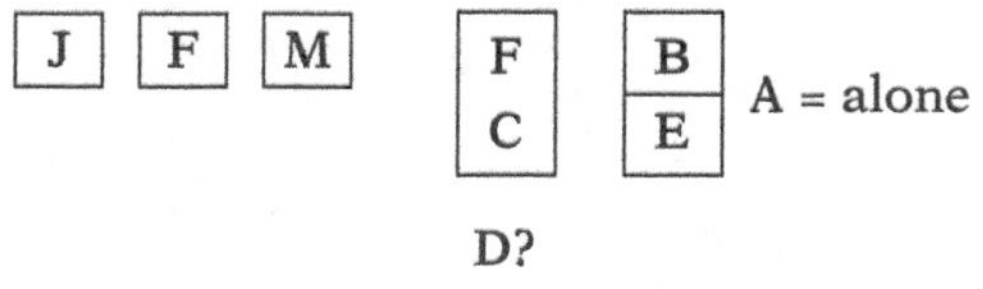

1. Correct Answer: **C.** Thus Franco cannot see D and C because Julio must see C.

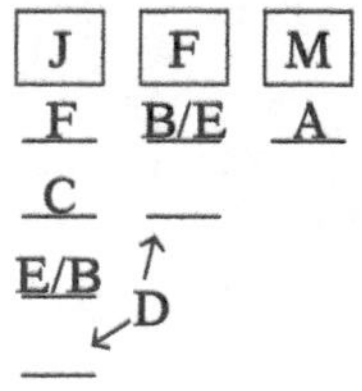

2. Correct Answer: **E.** He could not only see F and C, because A would have to be seen alone and this would cause the third vet to have to see B and E together, which is impossible.

3. Correct Answer: **D.** Julio would have to see E.

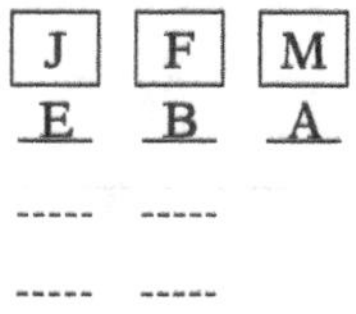

4. Correct Answer: **C.** If any vet sees only two dogs, then that vet is required to see D.

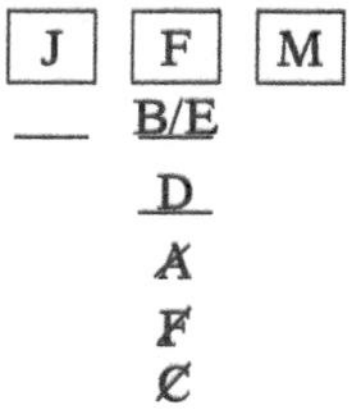

5. Correct Answer: **A.** He cannot see A. He has the option of not seeing either E or B, but not both.

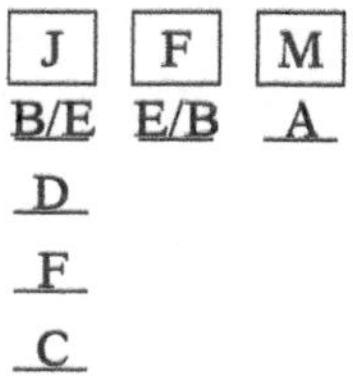

6. Correct Answer: **E.** Any vet can see all of the dogs.

Game 2: Linear

Initial Setup:

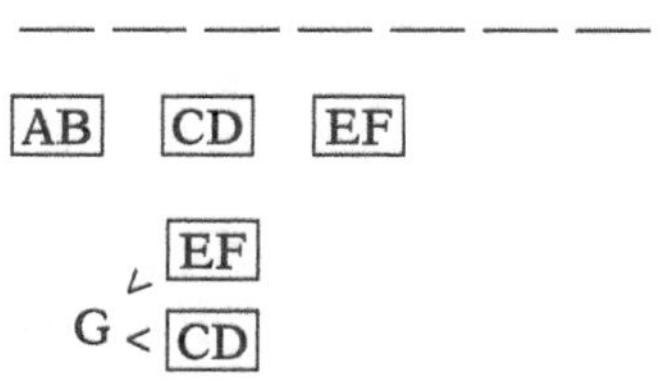

After reviewing this setup, it appears that there are eight configurations for the variables according to the following diagrams.

1.	a.	A	B	G	E	F	C	D
	b.				C	D	E	F
2.	a.	G	A	B	C	D	E	F
	b.				E	F	C	D
3.	a.	G	C	D	A	B	E	F
	b.				E	F	A	B
4.	a.	G	E	F	A	B	C	D
	b.				C	D	A	B

7. Correct Answer: **E.** This is a possible setup. See scenario 2b.

8. Correct Answer: **B.** If C goes in slot 4, then D always goes in slot 5. Slots 6 and 7 could have E, A or F, B respectively. So that is two people each. Slot 1 can have only A or G. Slot 3 is not mentioned, so slot 2 is the answer since it can have B, A, and E.

9. Correct Answer: **C.** D goes in slot 5 in scenarios 1.b., 2.a., and 4.b. This does not matter though, because it is clear from the constraints that G must always go in slot 1 or slot 3.

10. Correct Answer: **E.** This is only possible in scenario 4 and in this scenario G must go in slot 1.

11. Correct Answer: **C.** C can go in slots 2, 4, and 6 so C cannot go in slots 1, 3, 5, and 7.

12. Correct Answer: **B.** D can go last in three scenarios so we only know the position of C.

13. Correct Answer: **D.** This occurs in scenario 3.b. We can see that E must go fourth, not fifth.

Game 3: Complex Linear

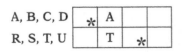

Initial Setup:

A, B, C, D	*	A		
R, S, T, U		T	*	

A	D	C	
ǁ	‡	‡	A = 2
T	S	U	

$U_3 \rightarrow D_1$

$D_1 \rightarrow C_4$

Notice that U3 → D1 → C4.

14. Correct Answer: **C.** This would cause bike U to go in room 4, because it cannot go with rider C and if it goes in room 3, then rider D would have to go in room 1 which is impossible.

C	A		
	T		U

~~U~~

15. Correct Answer: **E.** All of these answer choices are possible.

	A		
	T	~~U~~	

16. Correct Answer: **A.** Rider B has to be paired with bike U in room 3.

D	A	B	C
R	T	U	S

17. Correct Answer: **A.** If bike U is with rider D, then U cannot go in room 3; putting it there would force D into room 1, which would separate it from U. Thus there are two possible ways to place D and U together:

D	A	B	C
U	T	R/S	S/R

B/C	A	C/B	D
R/S	T	S/R	U

In both of these cases, choice (A) is false.

18. Correct Answer: **B.** This would mean that rider C and bike S have to be together in room 4.

	A		C
	T		S

19. Correct Answer: **B.** If rider D is not paired with bike U, then it must be paired with bike R; A is already paired with T, and D cannot be paired with S. Since rider C cannot be paired with bike U, rider B—the only remaining unpaired rider—must be. Thus, choice (B) could never be false.

Game 4: Grouping

Initial Setup:

D	S	C
*	*	___
___	___	___
___	___	

E	B
D	F

$F_D \rightarrow D_S, C_S$

$F_S \rightarrow E_S, G_S$

$F_C \rightarrow A_S, D_S$

Based on this information, we should see how F influences the game based on where he goes. Notice that F can't be on team Sprint, because then there would not be enough room for B to go with him.

D	S	C
F	D	___
B	C	___
___	___	

D	S	C
E	A	F
___	D	B
___	___	

20. Correct Answer: **A.** E could never be on team Sprint with A.

21. Correct Answer: **A.** G and H could be on the team together when F is on team Distract.

22. Correct Answer: **D.** D must always be assigned to team Sprint.

23. Correct Answer: **E.** F and B must share a team in both scenarios.

24. Correct Answer: **B.** F and D can never be on the same team since F is never on team Sprint and D is always on team Sprint.

25. Correct Answer: **A.** The rodents that could be on team Sprint are A, C, D, G, and H. E cannot go there because E cannot be on the same team as D.

26. Correct Answer: **C.** G must be on team Sprint with D and C because E cannot share a team with D.

PRACTICE TEST 2

ANSWER SHEET

Directions for Test

- Before beginning the test, photocopy this Answer Sheet or remove it from the book. Mark your answer to each question in the space provided. If the section has fewer questions than answer spaces, leave the extra spaces blank.
- When you have finished the test, you may check your answers against the Answer Key on page 185. Explanations for each question begin on page 186.

SECTION I
1. (A) (B) (C) (D) (E)
2. (A) (B) (C) (D) (E)
3. (A) (B) (C) (D) (E)
4. (A) (B) (C) (D) (E)
5. (A) (B) (C) (D) (E)
6. (A) (B) (C) (D) (E)
7. (A) (B) (C) (D) (E)
8. (A) (B) (C) (D) (E)
9. (A) (B) (C) (D) (E)
10. (A) (B) (C) (D) (E)
11. (A) (B) (C) (D) (E)
12. (A) (B) (C) (D) (E)
13. (A) (B) (C) (D) (E)
14. (A) (B) (C) (D) (E)
15. (A) (B) (C) (D) (E)
16. (A) (B) (C) (D) (E)
17. (A) (B) (C) (D) (E)
18. (A) (B) (C) (D) (E)
19. (A) (B) (C) (D) (E)
20. (A) (B) (C) (D) (E)
21. (A) (B) (C) (D) (E)
22. (A) (B) (C) (D) (E)
23. (A) (B) (C) (D) (E)
24. (A) (B) (C) (D) (E)
25. (A) (B) (C) (D) (E)
26. (A) (B) (C) (D) (E)
27. (A) (B) (C) (D) (E)
28. (A) (B) (C) (D) (E)
29. (A) (B) (C) (D) (E)
30. (A) (B) (C) (D) (E)

SECTION 1
Time—35 minutes
26 questions

Directions for Logic Games Questions: The questions in this section are divided into groups. Each group is based on a set of conditions. For each question, choose the answer that is most accurate and complete. For some questions, you may wish to draw a rough diagram to help you select your response. Mark the corresponding space on your Answer Sheet.

Questions 1–6

At a dog wash, six people are lined up like an assembly line in order to wash dogs efficiently. The first couple of people are the wetters, then come the soapers, then toward the end are the washers. There are six spaces, one for each person: A, B, C, D, E, and F. The order of these six people is determined by the following constraints:

If E is second, then F is fourth.
If B is fourth, then D is sixth.
If F is fourth, then E is second.
If C is fourth, then B is fifth.
A comes before B, C, and F.

1. Which of the following could be a list of the people participating in the dog wash, in order?

(A) A, F, C, B, D, E.
(B) D, E, A, B, C, F.
(C) A, E, C, F, B, D.
(D) B, E, A, D, C, F.
(E) B, A, C, F, D, E.

2. If A is third, then which of the following must be true?

(A) B is fifth.
(B) C is before F.
(C) D is first.
(D) E is second.
(E) D is before B.

3. If E is second and D is after A, then which of the following can NOT be true?

(A) C is fifth.
(B) A is third.
(C) B is before F.
(D) F is not consecutive with D.
(E) D goes sixth.

4. If F is sixth, then which of the following could be true?

(A) E is second.
(B) B is fourth.
(C) A is fourth.
(D) C is second.
(E) A is fifth.

5. If B is fourth and A is second, then which of the following can NOT be true?

(A) E is third.
(B) F is before C.
(C) C is fifth.
(D) D is after B.
(E) F and B are consecutive in the line.

6. If A is first and C is fourth, then which of the following could be true?

(A) B is before C.
(B) D is third and F is fifth.
(C) E is second.
(D) F is last.
(E) G is fifth.

GO ON TO THE NEXT PAGE

Questions 7–13

A master swordsman promotes a number of students through the Shaolin ranks: A, B, C, D, E, F, G, and H. One person will become Shaolin captain. Three people will become Shaolin elite. Four people will become Shaolin apprentices. Captain is a higher rank than elite. Elite is a higher rank than apprentice. The groups will be determined by the following constraints:

B receives the elite rank.
Neither G nor H can receive an elite ranking.
If A receives the highest rank, then E will receive the lowest.
If A does not receive the highest rank, then E will receive the highest.
A cannot be in the same rank as C.

7. Which of the following is a group of people who could together receive elite ranking?

(A) C, A, B.
(B) A, C, F.
(C) F, C, D.
(D) E, F, C.
(E) B, A, D.

8. Which of the following people could NOT receive the rank of apprentice?

(A) A
(B) B
(C) C
(D) D
(E) E

9. Which of the following people could never be in the same rank?

(A) F, C.
(B) H, D.
(C) E, B.
(D) D, C.
(E) A, F.

10. G can never share a rank with which of the following couples?

(A) D, H.
(B) A, F.
(C) E, C.
(D) F, D.
(E) E, H.

11. We will know the rank of everyone if we know the ranks of which three people?

(A) C, D, B.
(B) A, D, C.
(C) E, C, B.
(D) B, E, G.
(E) G, H, E.

12. If A is an elite, then which of the following could be false?

(A) E is captain.
(B) C is an apprentice.
(C) D is an elite.
(D) G is an apprentice.
(E) B is an elite.

13. If B does not receive the same rank as A or D, then which of the following could be false?

(A) E is captain.
(B) C is an elite.
(C) D is an apprentice.
(D) F is an elite.
(E) A is not an elite.

GO ON TO THE NEXT PAGE

Questions 14–20

In a flower shop, five bouquets are made using two different groups of flowers. One group is the iris group with flowers A, B, C, D, and E. The other group is the rose group with flowers R, S, T, U, and V. These bouquets will all be sold today and in each bouquet one flower from the iris group is paired with one flower from the rose group.

Flower V is sold second.
Flower S is sold fourth.
Flower V is not paired with flowers E or B.
Flower S is not paired with flowers A or C.
Flower T is paired with flower D.
If flower D is sold fifth, then flower B is sold first.

14. Which of the following is a possible order in which the iris flowers are sold?

(A) C, A, E, B, D.
(B) B, A, C, E, D.
(C) D, A, E, C, B.
(D) A, D, C, E, B.
(E) D, E, B, A, C.

15. If C is sold first, then which of the following must be true?

(A) E is sold last.
(B) T is sold third.
(C) B is sold fourth.
(D) A is sold before C.
(E) R is sold first.

16. If A and C are sold later than E, then which of the following could be true?

(A) R is sold later than C and A.
(B) E is sold before R and U.
(C) U is sold before C and A.
(D) D is sold before R and U.
(E) A and C are sold before R and U.

17. If R is sold after S, then which of the following could be true?

(A) A is sold first and E is sold third.
(B) R is sold last with D.
(C) U is sold after S.
(D) R is sold consecutively with two bouquets.
(E) D is sold before E and B.

18. If T is sold fifth, then which of the following must NOT be true?

(A) R and U are sold before C.
(B) A is sold third.
(C) E is sold with S.
(D) B is sold before any other iris.
(E) V is sold consecutively with B.

19. Which of the following is a pair of flowers that could NOT make up a bouquet?

(A) A, V.
(B) C, R.
(C) U, B.
(D) A, S.
(E) D, T.

20. If iris D is sold later than irises B and E, then which of the following must be true?

(A) R is sold first.
(B) U is sold third.
(C) B is sold first.
(D) C is sold third.
(E) E is not sold fourth.

GO ON TO THE NEXT PAGE

Questions 21–26

Two rowing teams are made up from eight people, A, B, C, D, E, F, G, and H. There are two boats and four positions on each boat: front, up-middle, down-middle, and back. Each person has particular preferences regarding boat and sitting position. In order to satisfy the demands of these athletes, the teams and positions must be made according to the following constraints:

A sits farther back than does B, whether or not A and B are in the same boat.
C sits in the same position as B.
If C is in boat 1, then she is in the up-middle position.
If D sits in boat 2, then A sits immediately in front of her in the same boat.
F and H cannot be on the same boat.

21. Which of the following could be the makeup of boat 1 from the front to the back?

(A) H, D, F, A.
(B) G, E, B, A.
(C) C, F, B, A.
(D) F, C, A, D.
(E) A, D, F, B.

22. If D is in the up-middle position, then which of the following must be true?

(A) A is in back position.
(B) C is in boat 2.
(C) F is not in boat 1.
(D) E sits in the down-middle position.
(E) A is in boat 1.

23. If C sits in the down-middle position, then which of the following must be true?

(A) D sits in the back.
(B) A sits in boat 1.
(C) H and C share a boat.
(D) C sits farther forward in the boat than G.
(E) A sits in the back position of a boat.

24. Which of the following could be the order of the people from front to back when D is in boat 2?

(A) C, A, D, E.
(B) A, D, F, C.
(C) C, H, A, D.
(D) B, A, D, H.
(E) D, A, B, F.

25. If C is in boat 1 and D is in boat 2, then which of the following could be true?

(A) H sits in front in boat 2.
(B) A sits in down-middle in boat 1.
(C) E sits in up-middle in boat 1.
(D) C sits ahead of F and H in a boat.
(E) E sits in the same position as B.

26. If E, F, and G sit in boat 2, not necessarily in that order, then which of the following is a complete list of the people who could also sit in boat 2?

(A) C, D.
(B) B, A, C.
(C) H, A, B.
(D) C, A, H, B.
(E) D, H, A, C, B.

STOP

IF YOU FINISH BEFORE TIME RUNS OUT, CHECK YOUR WORK.

ANSWER KEY

Section I
1. C
2. E
3. B
4. D
5. A
6. D
7. E
8. B
9. C
10. D
11. B
12. C
13. A
14. B
15. B
16. C
17. E
18. A
19. D
20. C
21. D
22. B
23. E
24. C
25. A
26. B

ANSWERS AND EXPLANATIONS

Game 1: Linear

Initial Setup:

___ ___ ___ ___ ___ ___

$E_2 \rightarrow F_4$ $F_4 \rightarrow E_2$

$B_4 \rightarrow D_6$ $C_4 \rightarrow B_5$

A < B, C, F

1. Correct answer: **C.** A, E, C, F, B, D could be an order.
   A and B: If B is fourth, then D is sixth.
   D: A goes before B.
   E: This is not true.

2. Correct answer: **E.** If A is third, it means that B, C, and F must go later than third. This means that D and E must go before third. Therefore, D must be before B.

3. Correct answer: **B.** A cannot go third because there would not be room for D, B, and C to follow it.

   A E B/D/C F D/B/C C/B/D

4. Correct answer: **D.** C could go second.

1	2	3	4	5	6
	~~E~~		~~B~~	~~A~~	F
			~~A~~		

5. Correct answer: **A.** E cannot go third.

   E A C/F B F/C D

6. Correct answer: **D.** F could go last.

1	2	3	4	5	6
A	D/F	___	C	B	___
	~~E~~				

Game 2: Grouping

Initial Setup:

Due to the fact that G and H cannot be elite and A or E must be captain, there are only two main configurations for the game:

C	E	A		C	E	A
A	B	E		E	B	G
	___	G			A/C	H
	___	H			D/F	C/A
	~~G~~	___				F/D
	~~H~~					

7. Correct answer: **E.** In scenario 2, B, A, and D could receive elite rankings.

8. Correct answer: **B.** B must always be elite.

9. Correct answer: **C.** B must always be elite and E can only be a captain or apprentice.

10. Correct answer: **D.** G can never be in a group with F and D.

11. Correct answer: **B.** If you know the position of A, D, and C, then you will know the position of everyone else in the game.

12. Correct answer: **C.** This causes C to be an apprentice with G and H. E must be captain, but you cannot be sure of the relative positions of D and F besides the fact that one must be an elite and the other must be an apprentice.

13. Correct answer: **A.** This would force C and F to be elites with B. The only changeable variable in the scenarios would be that A could be captain or E could be captain.

Game 3: Complex Linear

Initial Setup:

	A/C		E/B	*
	V		S	

$D_S \rightarrow B_I$

14. Correct answer: **B.** B, A, C, E, and D is a possible order in which the irises could be sold.
(A) If D is fifth, then B is first.
(C) C cannot be sold fourth.
(D) D has to go with T, so it cannot go second with V.
(E) E cannot go second.

15. Correct answer: **B.** T must be sold third because if it were sold last then B would have to be sold first in the place of C.

C	A	D		
	U	T	S	

16. Correct answer: **C.** This would have to be true for E to be sold first. U could be sold before C and A.

E	A/C	D	B	C/A
R/U	V	T	S	U/R

17. Correct answer: **E.** This would make R be sold last. It would not tell you much else about the game, but D could be sold before E and B.

	A/C		E/B	
	V		S	R

18. Correct answer: **A.** R and U must not be sold before C.

B	A/C	C/A	E	D
R/U	V	U/R	S	T

19. Correct answer: **D.** The constraints of the game require A to not be sold with S. You can look to the diagram above to see that the other pairs are all possible.

20. Correct answer: **C.** This would cause D to be sold last which would invoke the sufficient-necessary condition that requires B to be sold first when D is sold fifth. This is all that we need to know since we can see that answer choice C is correct.

Game 4: Grouping

Initial Setup:

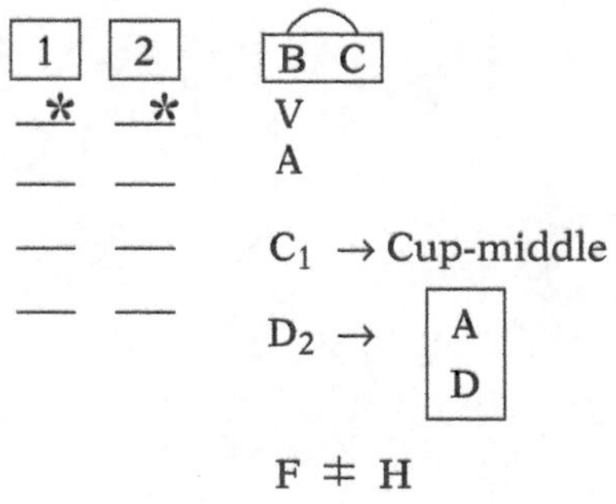

21. Correct answer: **D.** F, C, A, and D could be the order.
(A) B and C cannot be in the same group.
(B) F and H cannot be in the same group.
(C) C and B cannot be in the same group.
(E) This is not correct.

22. Correct answer: **B.** C must be in boat 2 because if C were in boat 1, then C would have to be in the up-middle position and so would B because they sit across from each other.

23. Correct answer: **E.** This question does not really impose any constraints on the game besides forcing A to sit in the back and forcing B to sit in the down-middle position of boat 1.

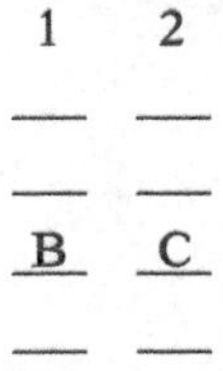

24. Correct answer: **C.** There are two possible scenarios for this:

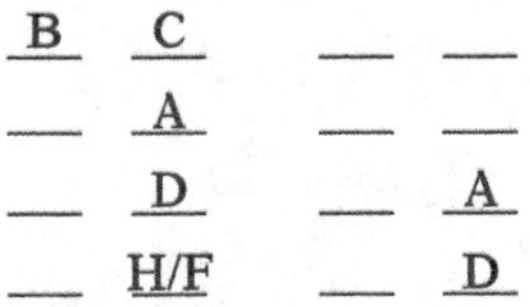

25. Correct answer: **A.** H could sit in the front of boat 2.

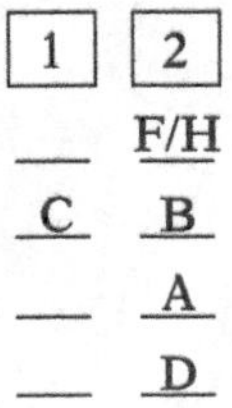

26. Correct answer: **B.** Neither D nor H could sit in boat 2. F cannot be in the same boat with H. If D is in boat 2 then A also has to be in boat 2.

RECAP

Now that you have completed the lessons in this book, you should be able to identify the logic game types:

1. **Formal Logic**
2. **Sequencing**
3. **Linear**
4. **Complex Linear**
5. **Grouping**
6. **Mapping**
7. **Pattern**

You should also be able to determine a logic game's variable type:

1. **Minimized Variables**
2. **Maximized Variables**

Minimized-variable games have a burdensome constraint that allows you to diagram most of the game after reading only the fact pattern. Maximized-variable games require you to diagram most of the game for each specific question.

The logic tools that you learned to solve each of these games are the following:

1. **Sufficient-Necessary**
2. **Contrapositive**
3. **Logic Chain Addition**
4. **Box Rules**
5. **Sequencing Chains**
6. **Direct Placement**
7. **Vacancy Rules**
8. **Occupancy Rules**
9. **Double Possibilities**

For each game type you learned a typical basic diagram:

1. Formal Logic:

D → E
A → B → F → H
C

2. Sequencing:

F G
C < D < H < A < E
B

3. Linear:

			G			
1	2	3	4	5	6	7
	E	B		B		E

4. Complex Linear:

	M	T	W	Th	F
A–E					
F–J					

5. Grouping:

1	2	3
___	___	___
___	___	___
___	___	___

6. Mapping:

a. 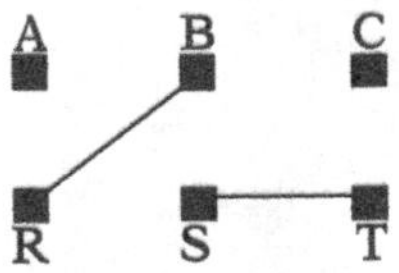

b. 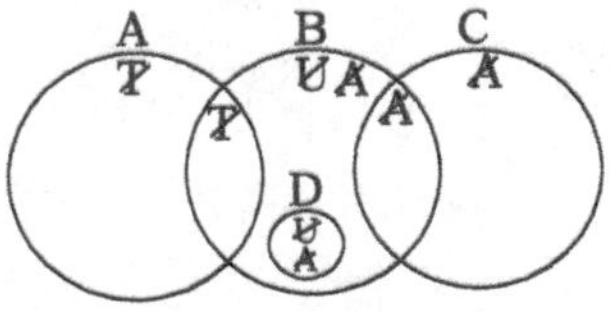

c.

/ (1)	R/ (2)
R/ (3)	G/S (4)
/ (5)	R/ (6)

d.

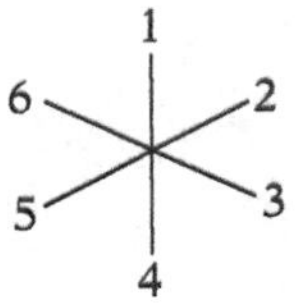

7. Pattern:

a.

RY	Y								
1	2	3	4	5	6	7	8	9	10

b.

					Out	
1	___	___	___	___	___	___
2	___	___	___	___	___	___
3	___	___	___	___	___	___
4	___	___	___	___	___	___
5	___	___	___	___	___	___

c.

			W	B	O	P			B
1	2	3	4	5	6	7	8	9	10

APPENDIX A

ALL ABOUT THE LSAT

In this appendix you will learn when to take the LSAT and how to register for the test; the format of a typical LSAT; how the LSAT is scored; the three main types of LSAT questions; and why it makes sense to guess if you cannot answer a question.

LSAT Basics

The Law School Admission Test (LSAT) is required for admission by the more than 200 law schools in the United States and Canada that are members of the Law School Admission Council (LSAC). Many law schools that are not LSAC members also require applicants to take the LSAT.

According to the LSAC, the LSAT is designed to measure certain skills that are considered vital to success in law school. These include the ability to read and understand complicated text passages, to draw reasonable inferences and conclusions from them, to think critically, and to evaluate logical arguments.

When the LSAT Is Given. The LSAC administers the LSAT four times each year at designated test centers in the United States and Canada and throughout the world. The four test dates are typically on Saturdays in February, June, October, and December. Many law schools require that you take the LSAT by December if you are applying for admission the following fall. However, applicants are often advised to take the test earlier than December, that is, in October or even June of the year before they expect to begin law school.

How to Register. You can register for the LSAT by mail, by telephone, or online. A registration fee is charged. Regular registration takes place until approximately 30 days before the test date. Late registration is allowed until about three weeks before the test date, but a higher fee is charged. You cannot register for the test on the day it is given.

To register, contact the Law School Admission Council at the following address:

Law School Admission Council
662 Penn Street
Box 2000
Newtown, PA 18940-0998
Tel. (215) 968-1001 (service representatives are available on weekdays only)
For online registration: www.LSAC.org

Registration forms are included in the *LSAT and LSDAS Registration/Information Book*, a booklet that is usually available in college and university guidance offices or by mail from the LSAC. If you are registering by mail, fill out the forms in the booklet and mail them in the enclosed, preaddressed return envelope. Faxed registration forms are not accepted.

When you register, you will have the opportunity to select a first-choice and second-choice test center located near you. If both centers you select are full or unavailable, the LSAC will assign you to another center located as near to you as possible.

Alternative Testing Arrangements. If you observe Saturday Sabbaths, you may take the LSAT on the Monday following the regular Saturday testing date. To do so, you must submit to the LSAC a letter from your rabbi or minister on official stationery confirming your religious affiliation.

Special testing accommodations are also available for test-takers with documented disabilities. To request these arrangements, obtain an accommodations request packet by contacting the LSAC either by mail or online. The LSAC urges test-takers who wish to request special testing accommodations to do so well in advance of the registration deadline.

Obtaining Your Score. If you have an online account with the LSAC, you will receive your LSAT score by email about three weeks after taking the test. There is no charge for doing so, and this is the fastest way to obtain your score. You can also obtain your score by telephoning TelScore at (215) 968-1200 approximately three weeks after taking the test. You will be asked to pay a $10 fee by credit card. Approximately four weeks after each test, the LSAC mails score reports to test-takers. If you have an online LSAC account, you will be charged a $25 fee for hardcopy mailings of the score information available to you online.

Taking the Test More Than Once. You may take the LSAT up to three times within any two-year period. However, the LSAC advises test-takers to take the test again only if they believe that their first test score was negatively affected by a circumstance such as anxiety or illness. For most test-takers, taking the test again does not result in a substantially different score, and test-takers should keep in mind that their second or third score might actually be lower than their first. If you do take the test more than once, your score report will show all your scores. In addition, an average score is calculated and reported.

Reporting Scores to Law Schools. Nearly all American Bar Association–approved law schools require test-takers to make use of the Law School Data Assembly Service (LSDAS), a service provided by the LSAC. To take advantage of this service, you must provide the LSDAS with school transcripts and letters of recommendation. The LSDAS combines that information with LSAT scores and copies of your writing sample and creates a complete report that is provided to every law school to which you apply.

What's on the LSAT

The LSAT is one of the most demanding standardized tests in existence. It tests your ability to answer questions that involve difficult logical transitions, syllogisms, and inductive reasoning—and to answer them quickly. The funny thing is that if given enough time, most people would be able to work through the questions and get most of them right. However, the LSAT gives you nowhere near enough time to do this. Instead, you are forced to operate under severe time pressure. Most test sections have between 24 and 27 questions that you are required to answer in a 35-minute time span. This is an average of about 1 minute 25 seconds per question. This is not a lot of time, and it is not surprising that most people do not finish many sections of the test. One main purpose of this book is to teach you how to answer LSAT problems quickly and accurately despite their difficulty.

Format of the Test. The LSAT includes five sections of multiple-choice questions. Of these, only four are graded: two Logical Reasoning sections, one Logic Games section, and one Reading Comprehension section. Another section is what is called "an experimental section." You are not told which section this one will be, but it can be any of one of the three question types and it will not count toward your grade. The experimental section is used only to test questions for future versions of the test.

Another part of the test that is not graded is the writing sample. In this test section, you have 30 minutes in which to write a short essay based on a given scenario. The writing sample is given at the very end of the LSAT, after you have completed all the other sections. It does not contribute to your LSAT score, but it is sometimes read by the admissions committees at the schools to which you apply. The writing sample gives committee members an idea of how well you write and take sides in an argument.

The following chart summarizes the format of a typical LSAT.

Typical LSAT Format

Section*	Number of Questions	Time Allowed, minutes
1 Logic Games	24	35
2 Logical Reasoning	24–26	35
3 Reading Comprehension	27	35
4 Logical Reasoning	24–26	35
5 Writing Sample	—	30
Total	101	170

*Graded sections only.

Note: All sections except the Writing Sample may appear in any order. An ungraded experimental section is also included in each test form.

LSAT Scores

There are typically about 101 questions that are graded on the LSAT. There are usually about 50 in the two logical reasoning sections, 25 in the logic games section, and 27 in the reading comprehension section. If you add up the total number that you get correct on these sections, you will have your **raw score**. No points are deducted for wrong answers, and all questions count the same.

Some LSATs are easier than others, and some are more difficult. To account for this variation, a statistical procedure is used to convert your raw score to a **scaled score**. Scaled scores range from **120 to 180**.

LSAT scores also include a percentile rank. This rank indicates the percentage of test-takers who scored below your reported test score.

LSAT Question Types

The three types of multiple-choice questions on the LSAT are logic games, logical reasoning, and reading comprehension.

Logic Games. The Logic Games section of the LSAT consists of a series of "games," each of which specifies certain relationships among a group of variables. The questions ask you to deduce additional relationships based on the given facts. Generally, math majors and others who are good at analytical reasoning do well on this section.

Here is a sample of a logic game:

> Anna, Bill, Claire, Dale, Emily, and Fanny are flying in an airplane. They sit in six seats that are aligned in two columns of three:
>
> 1 2
> 3 4
> 5 6
>
> Their seating order is determined by the following constraints:
> Anna sits in a lower-numbered seat than Bill.
> Claire sits immediately behind Fanny.
> Dale does not sit in the same row as Fanny or Emily.
> Bill sits in the same column as Emily.

Following this setup there will be five to eight questions, each of which will ask you to make a logical deduction based on the information and the rules ("constraints") of the game. Here is a typical question:

> 1. If Dale sits in seat 2, then which of the following must not be true?
>
> (A) Fanny sits in seat 1.
> (B) Anna does not sit in seat 3.
> (C) Claire sits in seat 5.
> (D) Bill sits in seat 4.
> (E) Emily sits in seat 6.
>
> Correct answer: A

Test-takers who prepare carefully for the Logic Games section can significantly improve their scores. Certain diagramming techniques and ways of setting up the games can greatly increase both speed and accuracy in this test section. This book provides examples and solution techniques for the following nine types of LSAT logic games:

1. Formal logic
2. Sequencing
3. Linear
4. Complex linear
5. Grouping
6. Mapping
7. Pattern
8. Minimized variables
9. Maximized variables

Logical Reasoning. In the Logical Reasoning sections of the LSAT, each question starts with a short passage (the "squib") that discusses a given issue or presents a particular argument. The question then asks you something about the reasoning behind the issue or the argument. Here is a sample:

> Forest Ranger: Bigfoot is an abominable creature that is larger than any bear and certainly larger than any human being. We are pleased to announce that Bigfoot was spotted yesterday in the park's canyon near the waterfall. Several campers were out eating their lunch on a picnic table near the top of the waterfall when they heard growling and strange noises coming from the base of the waterfall. They looked over the edge to the base of the waterfall and saw a big hairy mammal jump into the pool of water about 200 yards away. The campers screamed in surprise and the creature looked up, shook itself dry, and then ran off into the wilderness.
>
> Which of the following, if true, would undermine the Forest Ranger's contention that the creature spotted was Bigfoot?
>
> (A) Bigfoot likes bathing in waterfall pools.
> (B) A camper did not have her glasses with her when looking down to the bottom of the falls.
> (C) Bigfoot roams through northern parklands only during the winter months.
> (D) No hairy mammals were present in the park yesterday besides bears and humans.
> (E) Bigfoot is scared of people, especially when he is spotted and they scream at him.
>
> Correct answer: D

To answer logical reasoning questions correctly, you need to have good critical reading skills and you must be attentive to details. Sometimes small issues present in a long squib can be pivotally important when test-takers are deciding between answer choices. Remembering and being able to understand such details is the key to successfully answering logical reasoning questions. There are seven types of LSAT logical reasoning questions:

1. Conclusion
2. "Resolve"
3. "Strengthen"
4. "Weaken"
5. Reasoning strategy
6. Analogous reasoning
7. Controversy

For each of these seven question types, there are different things to watch for in the squib and different solution strategies. That is why you need to study each type carefully and to practice with sample questions. All that study takes time, but the payoff is higher scores on two of the four graded LSAT sections—fully half of your total LSAT score!

Reading Comprehension. The Reading Comprehension section contains questions of a type that you have most likely seen before on other standardized tests. The SAT has reading comprehension questions, and those on the LSAT are similar in form. A 400- to 500-word passage is presented and followed by six to eight questions that ask about the passage.

Here is an example of part of a reading comprehension passage and a question based on its content:

> As a personification of England, John Bull became a popular caricature during the nineteenth century. John Bull originated as a character in John Arbuthnot's *The History of John Bull* (1712). He became widely known from cartoons by Sir John Tenniel published in the British humor magazine *Punch* during the middle and late nineteenth century. In those cartoons, he was portrayed as an honest, solid, farmer figure, often in a Union Jack waistcoat, and accompanied by a bulldog. He became so familiar that his name frequently appeared in books, plays, periodical titles, and as a brand name or trademark. Although frequently used through World War II, since the 1950s John Bull has been seen less often.

> 1. Which of the following best expresses the main idea of the first paragraph?
>
> (A) Uncle Sam, the personification of America, is used in the same way that John Bull is used in England.
> (B) John Bull is a figure that emerged as a character in a cartoon in a British humor magazine called *Punch*.
> (C) John Bull, a personification of England, was popular during the nineteenth century but has appeared less often since the 1950s.
> (D) John Bull was a farmer figure who wore a Union Jack waistcoat and was commonly accompanied by a bull dog.
> (E) The English people were big fans of John Bull and strongly identified with him as a national figure.
>
> Correct answer: C

To answer reading comprehension questions correctly, you must pay careful attention to details when you read the passages. There are six types of LSAT reading comprehension questions:

1. Main point
2. Author's/character's opinion
3. Claims
4. Syntax
5. Inference
6. Support/undermine

Should You Guess?

On the LSAT, no points are deducted for wrong answers. Therefore, if you really do not know the answer to a question, there is no reason not to guess. In fact, if you are running out of time at the end of a section and there are questions you have not been able to answer, guess an answer for each one and mark your answer sheet accordingly before time is called. You have nothing to lose!

Keep in mind too that you can use the process of elimination to your advantage. Because the LSAT is a multiple-choice test, the correct answer to each question is right in front of you. If you can identify one or more answer choices as obviously wrong and then make your guess, your chances of being correct will be greatly increased.

The Curvebreakers Method

This LSAT logic games guide is based on the test-preparation techniques developed by Curvebreakers, a group of current and former students at Harvard Law School, each of whom scored in the 99th percentile or better on the LSAT. By using this guide, you will benefit from the numerous advantages that the Curvebreakers techniques have over those used in other test-preparation courses.

Most other LSAT guides and courses offer mainly generic test-taking advice applicable to broad categories of LSAT questions. In truth, however, each of these broad categories actually includes a variety of different question types, each with its own individual characteristics and pitfalls. The Curvebreakers techniques focus on each of these specific types in turn, analyzing each one in depth and giving you targeted problem-solving strategies and/or diagramming tools for that specific question type. You also get intensive practice with each question type, so you can familiarize yourself with the kinds of tricks specific to that type.

Curvebreakers Recommendations

1. Work Hard

The LSAT is a test that can be mastered if you are dedicated to improving yourself and getting a good score. Passively reading through lessons is not going to do much good. Instead, be sure to work through the problems in this book when you are wide awake and can give them full attention. If you do this consistently, your score will progressively improve. It is that simple.

2. Make a Study Plan

You should make an LSAT study plan that you can stick to. For example, it is a good idea to take a practice test each weekend on Saturday morning in order to simulate actual LSAT testing conditions. You should also map out consistent times each week when you will be able to work through at least part of each lesson.

3. Read Critically

On the LSAT, the test-writers often bury important points beneath piles of meaningless words and irrelevant sentences. Almost every question contains a pitfall that is intentionally designed to trap unwary test-takers. To prevent those pitfalls from trapping you, train yourself to read critically. Practice this kind of reading every time you sit down to study for the LSAT.

4. Identify Your Weaknesses

After you tackle the "On Your Own" sections in this book, make sure to go back and study the questions that you got wrong. This simple step can make all the difference in your LSAT preparation program. They will enable you to identify your weaknesses and focus your study so that you will not make the same mistakes in the future.

5. Do Not Worry about Time!

Take your time as you work through the lessons in this book. Focus on learning the characteristics of the different question types instead of worrying about how quickly or how slowly you are answering the questions. You can work on improving your test-taking speed when you take the practice tests at the back of this book. If you need further practice, use the materials on the Curvebreakers Web site for speed drills.

APPENDIX B

SOME FINAL ADVICE FOR TEST-TAKERS

Now that you have finished reading the lessons and working your way through the "On Your Own" sections and sample test sections, you might ask, "Where do I go from here?" It all depends on your goals, how satisfied you are with your performance, and how much time you have available to devote to studying for the LSAT.

Your LSAT score is the single most important ingredient in your law school application. Admissions officials call the LSAT "the great equalizer" for good reason: It is the single factor that allows them to compare applicants without regard to their different backgrounds, histories, interests, and the like. It also gives them a very good idea about your potential for success in the legal field.

It thus makes sense to spend whatever time you have left before test day to prepare yourself as well as you possibly can. Go back over the examples, exercises, and practice tests in this book. Refresh your memory regarding the characteristics of each type of LSAT question. Rework logic games that gave you trouble the first time through. Work on improving your pacing and on building up the stamina you'll need to get through all four hours of the test without tiring. If you have time, seek out supplementary materials and use the time you have left to keep practicing and improving your skills.

The Week before the LSAT

1. Get Up at 8:00 A.M. Every Day. For a week before the test, force yourself to get up each day at 8:00 A.M. and go to sleep before midnight. This will get your body accustomed to being awake during the hours of the LSAT. It will also ensure that you get enough sleep to be fully rested in time for the test. You don't want to be even a little sleepy during the LSAT!

2. Scout Out the Testing Center. It is a good idea to scout out your assigned testing center at some point during the week before test day. If you drive or walk past the testing center, you'll know exactly where you need to be, and that's one less thing you'll have to worry about. There's nothing worse that getting lost on the morning when you have to take the LSAT! It's no fun to be late either, so note the traffic patterns and figure out when you need to leave home in order to get to the testing center with time to spare.

3. Relax in the Two Days before the Test. During the two days just before the test, don't study at all. Any improvements that you could make in those two days would be marginal at best, and it's not worth tiring out your brain for test day. Give your brain time to rest and recharge so that it can perform at its peak on LSAT morning.

Do whatever works to minimize your stress level. For example, you might want to take a long break to relax and go out with friends. Make sure, though, to get to sleep before midnight on both nights before the exam.

During the Test

1. Sit Far Away from Others. The LSAT is not a group activity. It is something that you have to do by yourself, and having other people nearby can be distracting. Therefore, if at all possible, you should position yourself near the aisle or in a corner of the room so that people are not moving around you. Every movement is a potential distraction, and every distraction is a second or two that you could have spent improving your score.

2. Pace Yourself. Pay attention to the passage of time during the test so that you know whether or not you need to work faster. You might also want to set some time aside to work on a particularly difficult question. Consider bringing a personal stopwatch to the test to keep track of the time. If you decide to do so, train with the watch beforehand so that it doesn't cause you additional stress on test day.

3. Read Critically. Keep this tip in mind at all times. If you are able to train yourself to read critically and to pay attention to details, then you will have an advantage over other test-takers. Small details are the points of entire passages, so if you pay close attention to each squib and every passage, then you will be better able to recall the information when a question asks for it.

Also, if you read critically, you will be less likely to make careless errors. Test-makers love to use words like *not*, *except*, *only if*, and *and* that you might overlook if you aren't reading carefully but which can change the entire meaning of a question. If you miss one of these words because you aren't reading critically, chances are you'll pick the wrong answer.

4. Cross Out Obviously Wrong Answers. Now that you have practiced with many sample LSAT questions, you should be able to look at each actual test question and recognize the three out of every five answer choices that are typically obviously wrong. Take a moment to cross out those wrong choices. Then you'll be able to focus on the remaining two, of which one is the correct answer and the other is the seemingly plausible "second-best choice." In addition, if you are forced to guess, then narrowing down the choices will improve your chances of picking the correct answer.

5. Answer Every Question. On the LSAT there is no penalty for guessing, so mark an answer to every question even if you have no idea what the correct answer is. If you are able to eliminate a couple of choices before guessing, then all the better—you'll be that much more likely to pick the right answer. Just know that it is never in your best interest to leave a question blank.

6. Diagram Whenever Possible. The diagramming tools that you learned in this book for logic games set you apart from your competition. Don't forget these tools on the day of the test! Use them as often as you can so that you will derive the maximum benefit from them.

7. Don't Get Stressed. Speaking of stress, it is important to maintain a cool head during the test. Staying relaxed and in control will help you devote your full brainpower to answering questions instead of worrying about how you're doing. If you hit some questions that you can't answer, guess and move on. You have to. You can worry all you want when the test if over, but if you start to worry during the test, your concentration could suffer and your score could drop. This is a bad move.

Remember too that the section you're worried about could easily be the so-called experimental section, which doesn't even count toward your grade. Often the questions in that section, which are being field-tested to see if they work as well as they ought to, can seem more difficult than the questions on the rest of the test. So don't let a particularly tough section throw you. Keep a cool head and concentrate on doing well on the rest of the test.